On Core
Mathematics

Middle School Grade 7

HOUGHTON MIFFLIN HARCOURT

Table of Contents Grade 7

33 lessons

Unit 4   Geometry: Modeling Geometric Figures

Unit 5   Geometry: Circumference, Area, and Volume

Learning the Common Core State Standards

Has your state adopted the Common Core standards? If so, then students will be learning both mathematical content standards and the mathematical practice standards that underlie them. The supplementary material found in *On Core Mathematics Grade 7* will help students succeed with both.

> Here are some of the special features you'll find in *On Core Mathematics Grade 7*.

INTERACTIVE LESSONS

Students actively participate in every aspect of a lesson. They carry out an activity in an Explore and complete the solution of an Example. This interactivity promotes a deeper understanding of the mathematics.

Name _____ Class _____ Date _____

2-2

COMMON CORE

Proportional Relationships, Tables, and Equations

Essential question: *How can you use tables and equations to identify and describe proportional relationships?*

1 EXPLORE Discovering Proportional Relationships

A giant tortoise moves at a slow but steady pace. It takes the giant tortoise 3 seconds to travel 10.5 inches.

A Use the bar diagram to help you determine how many inches a tortoise travels in 1 second. What operation did you use to find the answer?

10.5 in.

| 1 sec | 1 sec | 1 sec |

?

3.5 inches; division

B Complete the table.

Time (sec)	1	2	3	4	5
Distance (in.)	3.5	7	10.5	14	17.5

C For each column of the table, find the ratio of the distance to the time. Write each ratio in simplest form.

Distance / Time:
$\frac{3.5}{1} = 3.5$ $\frac{7}{2} = 3.5$ $\frac{10.5}{3} = 3.5$ $\frac{14}{4} = 3.5$ $\frac{17.5}{5} = 3.5$

D What do you notice about the ratios? **The ratios are eq**

E **Conjecture** How do you think the distance a tort
The relationship is constant.

REFLECT

1a. Suppose the tortoise travels for 12 seconds. Ex
distance the tortoise travels.
Multiply 12 seconds times 3.5 inches per

1b. How would you describe the rate or speed at which a
The rate is constant.

Unit 2   39   Lesson 2

A **proportional relationship** is a relationship between two quantities in which the ratio of one quantity to the other quantity is constant. A giant tortoise can live as long as 150 years. One reason these reptiles live so long is their slow heart rate. A giant tortoise's heart beats only 6 times per minute. The giant tortoise's heart rate is an example of a proportional relationship. The ratio of the number of heart beats to the number of minutes is 6.

2 EXAMPLE Identifying Proportional Relationships

Alberto types 45 words per minute. Is the relationship between the number of words and the number of minutes a proportional relationship? Why or why not?

A Complete the table.

Time (min)	1	2	3	4	5
Number of Words	45	90	135	180	225

B Complete the ratios.

$\frac{\text{Number of Words}}{\text{Time}} = \frac{45}{1} = \frac{90}{2} = \frac{135}{3} = \frac{180}{4} = \frac{225}{5} = 45$

The ratios are ____ **constant**

The *common ratio* is ____ **45**

So, the relationship is **proportional**

TRY THIS!

2a. The table shows the distance Allison drove on one day of her vacation. Is the relationship between the distance and the time a proportional relationship? Why or why not?

Time (h)	1	2	3	4	5
Distance (mi)	65	120	195	220	300

No; the ratios are not equal.

REFLECT

2b. Do you think Allison drove at a constant speed for th
Why or why not?
No; the ratio of distance to time is not constan

t 2   40   Lesson 2

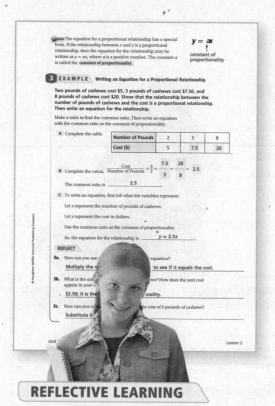

The equation for a proportional relationship has a special form. If the relationship between x and y is a proportional relationship, then the equation for the relationship may be written as $y = ax$, where a is a positive number. The constant a is called the **constant of proportionality**.

$$y = ax$$
constant of proportionality

3 EXAMPLE Writing an Equation for a Proportional Relationship

Two pounds of cashews cost $5, 3 pounds of cashews cost $7.50, and 8 pounds of cashews cost $20. Show that the relationship between the number of pounds of cashews and the cost is a proportional relationship. Then write an equation for the relationship.

Make a table to find the common ratio. Then write an equation with the common ratio as the constant of proportionality.

A Complete the table.

Number of Pounds	2	3	8
Cost ($)	5	7.5	20

B Complete the ratios. $\dfrac{\text{Cost}}{\text{Number of Pounds}} = \dfrac{5}{2} = \dfrac{7.5}{3} = \dfrac{20}{8} = 2.5$

The common ratio is _____ 2.5

C To write an equation, first tell what the variables represent.

Let x represent the number of pounds of cashews.

Let y represent the cost in dollars.

Use the common ratio as the constant of proportionality.

So, the equation for the relationship is _____ $y = 2.5x$

REFLECT

3a. How can you use _____ equation?
Multiply the _____ to see if it equals the cost.

3b. What is the uni_____ ews? How does the unit cost appear in your _____
$2.50; it is the _____ ionality.

3c. How can you u_____ he cost of 6 pounds of cashews?
Substitute 6 _____

Unit _____   Lesson 2

REFLECTIVE LEARNING

Students learn to be reflective thinkers through the follow-up questions after each Explore and Example in a lesson. The Reflect questions challenge students to really think about the mathematics they have just encountered and to share their understanding with the class.

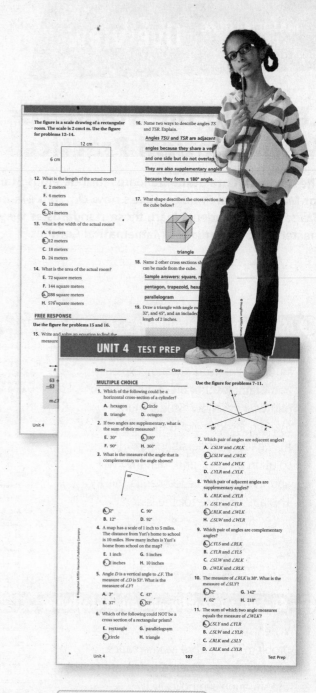

The figure is a scale drawing of a rectangular room. The scale is 2 cm:4 m. Use the figure for problems 12–14.

12 cm

6 cm

12. What is the length of the actual room?
E. 2 meters
F. 6 meters
G. 12 meters
H. 24 meters

13. What is the width of the actual room?
A. 6 meters
B. 12 meters
C. 18 meters
D. 24 meters

14. What is the area of the actual room?
E. 72 square meters
F. 144 square meters
G. 288 square meters
H. 576 square meters

FREE RESPONSE

Use the figure for problems 15 and 16.

15. Write and solve an equation to find the measure _____

16. Name two ways to describe angles TS and TSR. Explain.
Angles TSU and TSR are adjacent angles because they share a ver_____ and one side but do not overlap_____ They are also supplementary angles_____ because they form a 180° angle.

17. What shape describes the cross section in the cube below?

triangle

18. Name 2 other cross sections th_____ can be made from the cube.
Sample answers: square, r_____
pentagon, trapezoid, hexa_____
parallelogram

Draw a triangle with angle m_____ 32°, and 45°, and an included_____ length of 2 inches.

UNIT 4 TEST PREP

Name _____ Class _____ Date _____

MULTIPLE CHOICE

1. Which of the following could be a horizontal cross-section of a cylinder?
A. hexagon   C. circle
B. triangle   D. octagon

2. If two angles are supplementary, what is the sum of their measures?
E. 30°   G. 180°
F. 90°   H. 360°

3. What is the measure of the angle that is complementary to the angle shown?

88°

A. 2°   C. 90°
B. 12°   D. 92°

4. A map has a scale of 1 inch to 5 miles. The distance from Yuri's home to school is 10 miles. How many inches is Yuri's home from school on the map?
E. 1 inch   G. 5 inches
F. 2 inches   H. 10 inches

5. Angle D is a vertical angle to $\angle F$. The measure of $\angle D$ is 53°. What is the measure of $\angle F$?
A. 3°   C. 43°
B. 37°   D. 53°

6. Which of the following could NOT be a cross section of a rectangular prism?
E. rectangle   G. parallelogram
F. circle   H. triangle

Use the figure for problems 7–11.

7. Which pair of angles are adjacent angles?
A. $\angle SLW$ and $\angle RLK$
B. $\angle SLW$ and $\angle WLK$
C. $\angle SLY$ and $\angle WLK$
D. $\angle YLR$ and $\angle YLK$

8. Which pair of adjacent angles are supplementary angles?
E. $\angle RLK$ and $\angle YLR$
F. $\angle SLY$ and $\angle YLR$
G. $\angle RLK$ and $\angle WLK$
H. $\angle SLW$ and $\angle WLR$

9. Which pair of angles are complementary angles?
A. $\angle YLS$ and $\angle RLK$
B. $\angle YLR$ and $\angle YLS$
C. $\angle SLW$ and $\angle RLK$
D. $\angle WLK$ and $\angle RLK$

10. The measure of $\angle RLK$ is 38°. What is the measure of $\angle SLY$?
E. 52°   G. 142°
F. 62°   H. 218°

11. The sum of which two angle measures equals the measure of $\angle WLK$?
A. $\angle SLY$ and $\angle YLR$
B. $\angle SLW$ and $\angle YLR$
C. $\angle RLK$ and $\angle SLY$
D. $\angle RLK$ and $\angle YLR$

Unit 4   107   Test Prep

TEST PREP

At the end of a unit, students have an opportunity to practice the material in multiple choice and free response formats common on standardized tests.

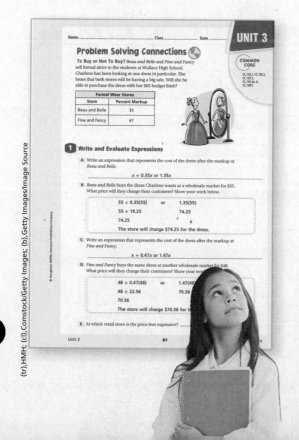

Name _____ Class _____ Date _____

UNIT 3

Problem Solving Connections

To Buy or Not To Buy? *Beau and Belle* and *Fine and Fancy* sell formal attire to the students at Wallace High School. Charlene has been looking at one dress in particular. She hears that both stores will be having a big sale. Will she be able to purchase the dress with her $65 budget limit?

COMMON CORE
CC.7EE.1, CC.7EE.2, CC.7EE.3, CC.7EE.4a, & CC.7RP.3

Formal Wear Stores

Store	Percent Markup
Beau and Belle	35
Fine and Fancy	47

1 Write and Evaluate Expressions

A Write an expression that represents the cost of the dress after the markup at *Beau and Belle*.

$x + 0.35x$ or $1.35x$

B *Beau and Belle* buys the dress Charlene wants at a wholesale market for $55. What price will they charge their customers? Show your work below.

$55 + 0.35(55)$ or $1.35(55)$
$55 + 19.25$ 74.25
74.25

The store will charge $74.25 for the dress.

C Write an expression that represents the cost of the dress after the markup at *Fine and Fancy*.

$x + 0.47x$ or $1.47x$

D *Fine and Fancy* buys the same dress at another wholesale market for $48. What price will they charge their customers? Show your wo_____

$48 + 0.47(48)$ or $1.47(48)$
$48 + 22.56$ 70.56
70.56

The store will charge $70.56 for t_____

E At which retail store is the price less expensive?

Unit 3   81

PROBLEM SOLVING CONNECTIONS

Special features that focus on problem solving occur near the ends of units. These features help students pull together the mathematical concepts and skills taught in a unit and apply them to real-world situations.

Learning the Standards for Mathematical Practice

The Common Core State Standards include eight Standards for Mathematical Practice. Here's how *On Core Mathematics Grade 7* helps students learn those standards as they master the Standards for Mathematical Content.

1 Make sense of problems and persevere in solving them.

In *On Core Mathematics Grade 7*, students will work through Explores and Examples that present a solution pathway to follow. Students are asked questions along the way so they gain an understanding of the solution process, and then they will apply what they've learned in the Try This and Practice for the lesson.

1 EXPLORE   Calculating Markups

To make a profit, a store manager must mark up the prices on the items he sells. A sports store buys skateboards from a supplier for s dollars. The store's manager decides to mark up the price for retail sale by 42%.

A The markup is _42_ % of the price, s.

B Find the amount of the markup. Use a bar model.

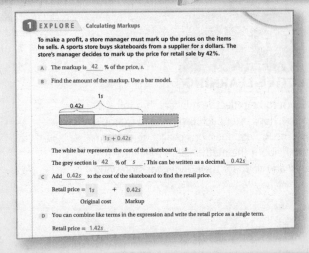

The white bar represents the cost of the skateboard, _s_ .

The grey section is _42_ % of _s_ . This can be written as a decimal, _0.42s_ .

C Add _0.42s_ to the cost of the skateboard to find the retail price.

Retail price = $1s$ + $0.42s$
          Original cost   Markup

D You can combine like terms in the expression and write the retail price as a single term.

Retail price = _1.42s_

2 Reason abstractly and quantitatively.

When students solve a real-world problem in *On Core Mathematics Grade 7*, they will learn to represent the situation symbolically by translating the problem into a mathematical expression or equation. Students will use these mathematical models to solve the problem and then state the answer in terms of the problem context. Students will reflect on the solution process in order to check their answers for reasonableness and to draw conclusions.

1a. How can you tell that the final depth for Tomas will be deeper than −20 feet without doing any calculations?
Sample answer: The two descents have a greater absolute value than the one ascent that Tomas makes. Therefore, he will be deeper than his starting point of −20 ft.

2e. Why do you evaluate the power in the equation before multiplying?
Sample answer: You must follow the order of operations and evaluate the exponents before multiplying.

③ Construct viable arguments and critique the reasoning of others.

Throughout *On Core Mathematics Grade 7*, students will be asked to make conjectures, construct mathematical arguments, explain their reasoning, and justify their conclusions. Reflect questions offer opportunities for cooperative learning and class discussion. Students will have additional opportunities to critique reasoning in Error Analysis problems.

REFLECT

1c. **Conjecture** Work with other students to make a conjecture about the sign of the sum when the addends have the same sign.

Sample answer: When the addends have the same sign, the sum has the sign

of the addends.

12. **Error Analysis** Kate says the radius of the circle is 8 feet. What is Kate's error? Find the correct diameter of the circle.

Kate found the diameter of the circle, she needs

to divide it by 2 to get the radius; 4 ft

C = 25.12 ft

x ft

1. Combine your results with your classmates and calculate the experimental probability. Do you think this value is a better approximation of the theoretical probability than your result from only 10 trials?

Sample answer: I think the experimental probability from the combined

trials is closer to the theoretical probability.

④ Model with mathematics.

On Core Mathematics Grade 7 presents problems in a variety of contexts such as science, business, and everyday life. Students will use mathematical models such as expressions, equations, tables, and graphs to represent the information in the problem and to solve the problem. Then students will interpret their results in the problem context.

1 EXPLORE Finding Total Cost

CC.7.RP.3

The bill at a restaurant for the Smith family came to $40. They want to leave a 15% tip. What is the total cost of the meal?

A Find the amount of the tip. Use a bar model.

Total Cost

$40

Tip = 15%

The white bar represents $40. It is divided into ___10___ equal pieces.

Each section represents ___10___ %, or $ ___4___

The tip is 15% or $1\frac{1}{2}$ sections of the model.

1 section = $ ___4___, so $\frac{1}{2}$ of a section = $ ___2___

$1\frac{1}{2}$ sections = $ ___4___ + $ ___2___ = $ ___6___

The tip is $ ___6___

B Find the total cost of the meal.

To find the total cost of the meal, add together the bill total and the tip.

| $40 | + | $6 | = | $46 |
| Bill total | | Tip | | Total Cost |

C Another way to find the tip is to multiply the bill total by the percent of the tip.

Write 15% as a decimal. ___0.15___

| $40 | × | 0.15 | = | $6 |
| Bill total | | Percent | | Tip |

| $40 | + | $6 | = | $46 |
| Bill total | | Tip | | Total Cost |

⑤ Use appropriate tools strategically.

Students will use a variety of tools in *On Core Mathematics Grade 7*, including manipulatives, paper and pencil, and technology. Students might use manipulatives to develop concepts, paper and pencil to practice skills, and technology (such as graphing calculators, spreadsheets, or geometry software) to investigate more complicated mathematical ideas.

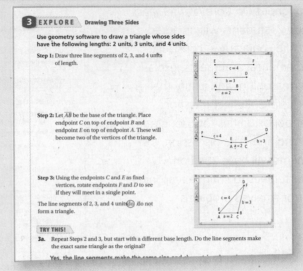

3 EXPLORE Drawing Three Sides

Use geometry software to draw a triangle whose sides have the following lengths: 2 units, 3 units, and 4 units.

Step 1: Draw three line segments of 2, 3, and 4 units of length.

Step 2: Let $\overline{AB}$ be the base of the triangle. Place endpoint C on top of endpoint B and endpoint E on top of endpoint A. These will become two of the vertices of the triangle.

Step 3: Using the endpoints C and E as fixed vertices, rotate endpoints F and D to see if they will meet in a single point.

The line segments of 2, 3, and 4 units do not form a triangle.

TRY THIS!

3a. Repeat Steps 2 and 3, but start with a different base length. Do the line segments make the exact same triangle as the original?

Yes, the line segments make the same size and shape triangle.

1 EXPLORE Generating a Small Sample

A The manager will want to use a random sample to represent the entire shipment. One way to simulate a random sample is to use a graphing calculator to generate random integers.

To simulate picking out random light bulbs between 1 and 1,000:

• Press [MATH], scroll right and select **PRB**, then select **5: randInt(**.
• Enter the smallest value, comma, largest possible value.
• Hit [ENTER] to generate random numbers.

In this specific case, you will enter **randInt(** 1 , 1,000) because there are ___1,000___ light bulbs in the shipment.

The numbers that are generated will each represent bulbs in the shipment.

Let numbers 1 to 200 represent bulbs that are ___defective___.

Numbers 201 to 1,000 will represent bulbs that are ___working___.

Generate four numbers and record your results in the table below.

⑥ Attend to precision.

Precision refers not only to the correctness of arithmetic calculations, algebraic manipulations, and geometric reasoning but also to the proper use of mathematical language, symbols, and units to communicate mathematical ideas. Throughout *On Core Mathematics Grade 7* students will demonstrate their skills in these areas when asked to calculate, describe, show, explain, prove, and predict.

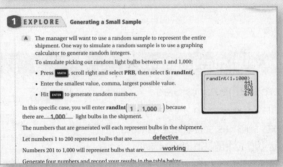

5. A train travels at 72 miles per hour. Will the graph of the train's rate of speed show that the relationship between the number of miles traveled and the number of hours is a proportional relationship? Explain.

Yes, the graph will show a proportional relationship because the data for the number of miles traveled and the number of hours will form a straight line and pass through the origin.

The graph shows the relationship between time and the distance run by two horses.

6. How long does it take each horse to run 1 mile?

Horse Training

6. Reasoning A composite figure is formed by combining a square and a triangle. Its total area is 32.5 ft². The area of the triangle is 7.5 ft². What is the length of each side of the square?

5 ft

1a. *Theoretical probability* is a way to describe how you found the chance of winning a MP3 player in the scenario above. Using the spinner example to help you, explain in your own words how to find the theoretical probability of an event.

Sample answer: The theoretical probability of an event is a ratio comparing the number of ways the event can occur to the total number of outcomes for the experiment.

1b. Suppose you choose Spinner A. What is the probability that you will not win? Show your work below.

⑦ Look for and make use of structure.

⑧ Look for and express regularity in repeated reasoning.

In *On Core Mathematics Grade 7*, students will look for patterns or regularity in mathematical structures such as expressions, equations, operations, geometric figures, and diagrams. Students will use these patterns to generalize beyond a specific case and to make connections between related problems.

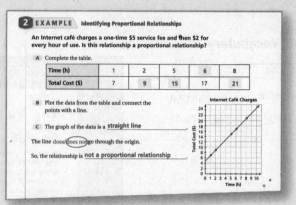

2 EXAMPLE Identifying Proportional Relationships

An Internet café charges a one-time $5 service fee and then $2 for every hour of use. Is this relationship a proportional relationship?

A Complete the table.

Time (h)	1	2	5	6	8
Total Cost ($)	7	9	15	17	21

B Plot the data from the table and connect the points with a line.

C The graph of the data is a ___straight line___

The line does/does not go through the origin.

So, the relationship is ___not a proportional relationship___

1 EXPLORE Measuring Angles

A Using a ruler, draw a pair of intersecting lines. Label each angle from 1 to 4.

Sample answer:

B Use a protractor to help you complete the chart. Sample answers given.

Angle	Measure of Angle
m∠1	150°
m∠2	30°
m∠3	150°
m∠4	30°
m∠1 + m∠2	180°
m∠2 + m∠3	180°
m∠3 + m∠4	180°
m∠4 + m∠1	180°

REFLECT

1a. **Conjecture** Share your results with other students. Make a conjecture about pairs of angles that are opposite of each other. Make a conjecture about pairs of angles that are next to each other.

Sample answer: Opposite pairs of angles have the same measure. Pairs of

angles that are next to each other have measures that add up to 180°.

1 EXPLORE Exploring Circumference

A Use a measuring tape to find the circumference of five circular objects. Then measure the distance across each item to find its diameter. Record the measurements of each object in the table below. **Check students' work.**

Object	Circumference C	Diameter d	$\frac{C}{d}$

B Divide the circumference of each object by its diameter. Round your answer to the nearest hundredth.

C Describe what you notice about the ratio $\frac{C}{d}$ in your table.
Sample answer: $\frac{C}{d}$ is always close to or a little more than three.

REFLECT

1a. **Conjecture** Compare your results with other students. Make

H&S Graphics, Inc

UNIT 1

The Number System

Unit Vocabulary

additive inverse (1-2)

opposite (1-2)

rational number (1-1)

UNIT 1

The Number System

Unit Focus

In this unit, you will learn how to recognize rational numbers. You will convert rational numbers to their equivalent decimal form. You will also learn how to add, subtract, multiply, and divide rational numbers that are positive and negative, and you will solve multi-step problems that involve rational numbers.

Unit at a Glance

COMMON CORE

Lesson		Standards for Mathematical Content
1-1	Rational Numbers and Decimals	CC.7.NS.2d
1-2	Adding Rational Numbers	CC.7.NS.1a, CC.7.NS.1b, CC.7.NS.1d
1-3	Subracting Rational Numbers	CC.7.NS.1c, CC.7.NS.1d
1-4	Multiplying Rational Numbers	CC.7.NS.2a, CC.7.NS.2c
1-5	Dividing Rational Numbers	CC.7.NS.2b, CC.7.NS.2c
1-6	Solving Problems with Rational Numbers	CC.7.NS.3
	Problem Solving Connections	
	Test Prep	

UNIT 1

Unpacking the Common Core State Standards

Use the table to help you understand the Standards for Mathematical Content that are taught in this unit. Refer to the lessons listed after each standard for exploration and practice.

COMMON CORE Standards for Mathematical Content	What It Means For You
7.NS.1 Apply and extend previous understandings of addition and subtraction to … rational numbers…. **7.NS.1a** Describe situations in which opposite quantities combine to make 0. **7.NS.1b** Understand $p + q$ as the number located a distance $|q|$ from p, in the positive or negative direction depending on whether q is positive or negative. Show that a number and its opposite have a sum of 0 (are additive inverses). Interpret sums of rational numbers by describing real-world contexts. **7.NS.1c** Understand subtraction of rational numbers as adding the additive inverse, $p - q = p + (-q)$. Show that the distance between two rational numbers on the number line is the absolute value of their difference, and apply this principle in real-world contexts. **7.NS.1d** Apply properties of operations as strategies to add and subtract rational numbers. Lessons 1-2, 1-3	You will learn how to add and subtract rational numbers with the same sign and with different signs. You will learn that subtracting a rational number is the same as adding its additive inverse.
7.NS.2 Apply and extend previous understandings of multiplication and division …to…rational numbers. **7.NS.2a** Understand that multiplication is extended from fractions to rational numbers by requiring that operations continue to satisfy the properties of operations, particularly the distributive property, leading to products such as $(-1)(-1) = 1$ and the rules for multiplying signed numbers. Interpret products of rational numbers by describing real-world contexts. **7.NS.2b** Understand that integers can be divided, provided that the divisor is not zero, and every quotient of integers (with non-zero divisor) is a rational number. If p and q are integers, then $-\left(\frac{p}{q}\right) = \frac{(-p)}{q} = \frac{p}{(-q)}$. Interpret quotients of rational numbers by describing real-world contexts. **7.NS.2c** Apply properties of operations as strategies to multiply and divide rational numbers. Lessons 1-4, 1-5	You will multiply and divide positive and negative rational numbers. You will solve real-world applications with multiplication and division of rational numbers. You will explore the meaning of division by 0.

Unpacking the Common Core State Standards

This page lists and explains the Standards for Mathematical Content that are addressed in this unit. For information about the Standards for Mathematical Practice, which are integrated throughout the text, see Teacher Edition pages vii–xiii.

Additional Standards in This Unit

7.NS.2d Convert a rational number to a decimal using long division; know that the decimal form of a rational number terminates in 0s or eventually repeats Lesson 1-1

7.NS.3 Solve real-world and mathematical problems involving the four operations with rational numbers. Lesson 1-6

Notes

_____

_____

_____

_____

_____

_____

_____

_____

_____

Rational Numbers and Decimals

Essential question: *How can you convert a rational number to a decimal?*

COMMON CORE Standards for Mathematical Content

CC.7.NS.2d Convert a rational number to a decimal using long division; know that the decimal form of a rational number terminates in 0s or eventually repeats.

Vocabulary
rational number

Prerequisites
Dividing multi-digit numbers

Math Background

A rational number is a number that can be written as a ratio, or fraction, of two integers a and b: $\frac{a}{b}$, where b is not zero. The set of integers is a subset of rational numbers because each integer p can be written as $\frac{p}{1}$. Every rational number can be expressed in decimal form. To convert a rational number from fraction form to decimal form, divide the numerator by the denominator. The decimal form of a rational number may either terminate or repeat a pattern. An example of a rational number with a terminating decimal is $\frac{45}{100} = 0.45$. An example of a rational number with a decimal that repeats a pattern is $\frac{6}{11} = 0.545454\ldots$ or $0.\overline{54}$.

INTRODUCE

Connect to prior learning by writing a common fraction, such as $\frac{1}{2}$, and asking students to give you the decimal form. Students should be able to answer 0.5 quickly without dividing. Ask students how to convert $\frac{1}{2}$ to 0.5 by dividing 1 by 2, and review long division of $1.0 \div 2$. Then review long division with multi-digits by giving an example such as converting $\frac{12}{15}$ to 0.8.

TEACH

1 EXPLORE

Materials
Calculator

Questioning Strategies
- How do you convert $\frac{1}{4}$ to a decimal using a calculator? **Divide 1 by 4.**
- What are two possible decimal forms of a rational number? **They may terminate or repeat a pattern.**

> ⋮ MATHEMATICAL PRACTICE   **Highlighting the Standards**
>
> This Explore is an opportunity to address Standard 5 (Use appropriate tools strategically). Students use a calculator to explore and analyze the decimal forms of rational numbers. Using a calculator to view many conversions from fraction form to decimal form facilitates students' use of inductive logic to make conjectures about all the possible decimal forms.

2 EXAMPLE

Avoid Common Errors
Be sure that students do not stop dividing too soon. Remind them to keep adding zeros after the decimal point in the dividend until they find the correct decimal form of the rational number.

Questioning Strategies
- Why isn't the decimal in 1a a rational number if the decimal continues with a pattern? **The decimal has a pattern but does not repeat a pattern.**
- While performing long division, how do you know when you have a repeating pattern in the quotient? **Divide until you have a number or a pattern of numbers repeating and you can see that the repeating pattern will continue.**

Name_____ Class_____ Date_____

1-1

Rational Numbers and Decimals

COMMON CORE

CC.7NS.2d

Essential question: *How can you convert a rational number to a decimal?*

A **rational number** is a number that can be written as a ratio of two integers a and b, where b is not zero. For example, $\frac{4}{7}$ is a rational number, as is 0.37 because it can be written as the fraction $\frac{37}{100}$.

1 EXPLORE Describing Decimal Forms of Rational Numbers

A Use a calculator to find the equivalent decimal form of each fraction. Remember that numbers that repeat can be written as 0.333... or 0.$\overline{3}$.

Fraction	$\frac{1}{4}$	$\frac{5}{8}$	$\frac{2}{3}$	$\frac{2}{9}$	$\frac{12}{5}$	$\frac{1}{5}$	$\frac{7}{8}$
Decimal Equivalent	0.25	0.625	0.666...	0.222...	2.4	0.2	0.875

B Now find the corresponding fraction of the decimal equivalents given in the last two columns in the table. Write the fractions in simplest form.

C **Conjecture** What do you notice about the digits after the decimal point in the decimal forms of the fractions? Compare notes with your neighbor and refine your conjecture if necessary.

The digits after the decimal point either repeat or terminate.

REFLECT

1a. Consider the decimal 0.101001000100001000001... Do you think this decimal represents a rational number? Why or why not?

Sample answer: No; since the digits after the decimal point do not

terminate or repeat it does not represent a rational number.

1b. Do you think a negative sign affects whether or not a number is a rational number? Use $-\frac{8}{5}$ as an example.

No; $-\frac{8}{5} = -1.6$, which is a rational number since the decimal terminates.

Rational numbers can be negative.

1c. Do you think a mixed number is a rational number? Explain.

A mixed number is a rational number because it can be rewritten as an

improper fraction, which is a ratio of two integers.

© Houghton Mifflin Harcourt Publishing Company

You can convert a rational number to a decimal using long division.

2 EXAMPLE Writing Rational Numbers as Decimals Using Long Division

Write each rational number as a decimal.

A $\frac{5}{16}$

Divide 5 by 16.
Add a zero after the decimal point.
Subtract 48 from 50.
Use the grid to help you complete the long division.

Add zeros in the dividend and continue dividing until the remainder is 0.

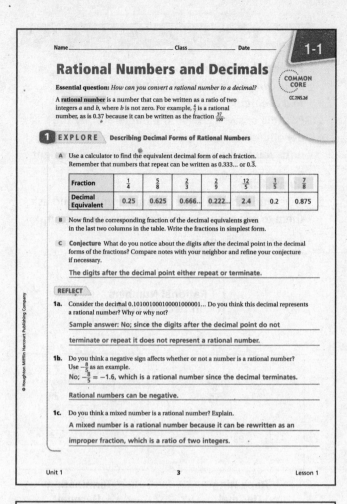

The decimal equivalent of $\frac{5}{16}$ is ____0.3125____.

B $\frac{1}{11}$

Divide 1 by 11.
Add a zero after the decimal point.
10 can be divided by 11 zero times.
Use the grid to help you complete the long division.

You can stop dividing once you discover a repeating pattern in the quotient.

Write the quotient with its repeating pattern and indicate that the repeating numbers continue.

The decimal equivalent of $\frac{1}{11}$ is ____0.0909...____.

REFLECT

2a. Do you think that decimals that have repeating patterns always have the same number of digits in their pattern? Explain.

No, the number of digits in the repeating patterns can be different. $\frac{1}{11}$, or

0.09..., has 2 repeating digits, and $\frac{1}{3}$, or 0.3..., has 1 repeating digit.

© Houghton Mifflin Harcourt Publishing Company

3 EXAMPLE

Cooperative Learning

Suggest that students work together through the example. This will promote student discourse on converting rational numbers to decimals. Also, working together will help students understand when they can end the division process and describe the decimal form of the rational number.

Questioning Strategies

- Why do you add zeros to the dividend? Adding zeros to the dividend after the decimal part does not change the value of the dividend, yet it allows you to continue dividing until it repeats or terminates.

- How do you know when to stop the division process? You stop when the remainder is 0 (the quotient terminates) or you can identify that there is a repeating pattern in the decimal part.

TRY THIS

Students may solve problems 3a and 3b with an alternative method: instead of writing the mixed number as an improper fraction, they may convert only the fraction part of the mixed number. The whole number can be added to the resulting decimal. For example, in part 3b, students may divide 1 by 3 to get 0.333..., and then add the whole number 3 to the resulting decimal to get 3.333....

CLOSE

Essential Question

How can you convert a rational number to a decimal?
Possible answer: Divide the numerator by the denominator. Continue until the remainder is 0 or until you find a repeating pattern in the quotient.

Summarize

Give students the list of rational numbers and ask them to put each number into the correct group.

$\frac{1}{2}$, 5.273, $4\frac{4}{9}$, $\frac{25}{99}$, $\frac{8}{15}$, $\frac{3}{4}$, $\frac{2}{10}$, 2

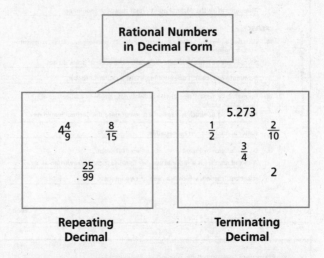

PRACTICE

Where skills are taught	Where skills are practiced
1 EXPLORE	EXS. 1–9, 23
2 EXAMPLE	EXS. 1–9
3 EXAMPLE	EXS. 10–22

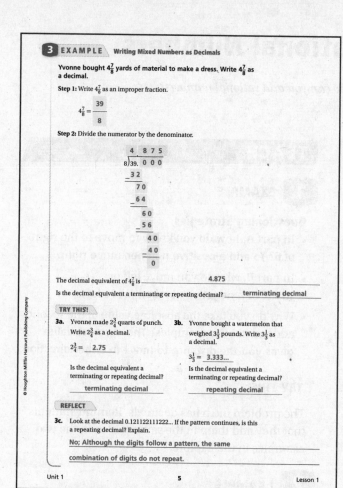

3 EXAMPLE Writing Mixed Numbers as Decimals

Yvonne bought $4\frac{7}{8}$ yards of material to make a dress. Write $4\frac{7}{8}$ as a decimal.

Step 1: Write $4\frac{7}{8}$ as an improper fraction.

$$4\frac{7}{8} = \frac{39}{8}$$

Step 2: Divide the numerator by the denominator.

```
        4 . 8 7 5
  8 )39 . 0 0 0
     3 2
     ──
       7 0
       6 4
       ──
         6 0
         5 6
         ──
           4 0
           4 0
           ──
             0
```

The decimal equivalent of $4\frac{7}{8}$ is _____4.875_____

Is the decimal equivalent a terminating or repeating decimal? ___terminating decimal___

TRY THIS!

3a. Yvonne made $2\frac{3}{4}$ quarts of punch. Write $2\frac{3}{4}$ as a decimal.

$$2\frac{3}{4} = \underline{\ 2.75\ }$$

Is the decimal equivalent a terminating or repeating decimal?

___terminating decimal___

3b. Yvonne bought a watermelon that weighed $3\frac{1}{3}$ pounds. Write $3\frac{1}{3}$ as a decimal.

$$3\frac{1}{3} = \underline{\ 3.333...\ }$$

Is the decimal equivalent a terminating or repeating decimal?

___repeating decimal___

REFLECT

3c. Look at the decimal 0.121122111222... If the pattern continues, is this a repeating decimal? Explain.

No; Although the digits follow a pattern, the same

combination of digits do not repeat.

Unit 1   5   Lesson 1

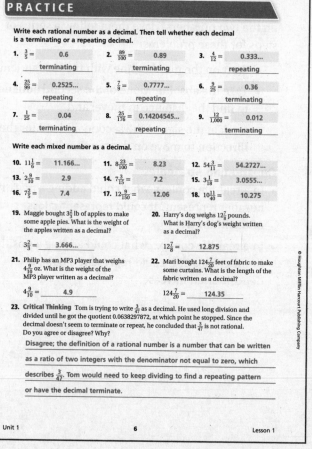

PRACTICE

Write each rational number as a decimal. Then tell whether each decimal is a terminating or a repeating decimal.

1. $\frac{3}{5} = \underline{\ 0.6\ }$ terminating

2. $\frac{89}{100} = \underline{\ 0.89\ }$ terminating

3. $\frac{4}{12} = \underline{\ 0.333...\ }$ repeating

4. $\frac{25}{99} = \underline{\ 0.2525...\ }$ repeating

5. $\frac{7}{9} = \underline{\ 0.7777...\ }$ repeating

6. $\frac{9}{25} = \underline{\ 0.36\ }$ terminating

7. $\frac{1}{25} = \underline{\ 0.04\ }$ terminating

8. $\frac{25}{176} = \underline{\ 0.14204545...\ }$ repeating

9. $\frac{12}{1,000} = \underline{\ 0.012\ }$ terminating

Write each mixed number as a decimal.

10. $11\frac{1}{6} = \underline{\ 11.166...\ }$

11. $8\frac{23}{100} = \underline{\ 8.23\ }$

12. $54\frac{3}{11} = \underline{\ 54.2727...\ }$

13. $2\frac{9}{10} = \underline{\ 2.9\ }$

14. $7\frac{3}{15} = \underline{\ 7.2\ }$

15. $3\frac{1}{18} = \underline{\ 3.0555...\ }$

16. $7\frac{2}{5} = \underline{\ 7.4\ }$

17. $12\frac{9}{150} = \underline{\ 12.06\ }$

18. $10\frac{11}{40} = \underline{\ 10.275\ }$

19. Maggie bought $3\frac{2}{3}$ lb of apples to make some apple pies. What is the weight of the apples written as a decimal?

$$3\frac{2}{3} = \underline{\ 3.666...\ }$$

20. Harry's dog weighs $12\frac{7}{8}$ pounds. What is Harry's dog's weight written as a decimal?

$$12\frac{7}{8} = \underline{\ 12.875\ }$$

21. Philip has an MP3 player that weighs $4\frac{9}{10}$ oz. What is the weight of the MP3 player written as a decimal?

$$4\frac{9}{10} = \underline{\ 4.9\ }$$

22. Mari bought $124\frac{7}{20}$ feet of fabric to make some curtains. What is the length of the fabric written as a decimal?

$$124\frac{7}{20} = \underline{\ 124.35\ }$$

23. Critical Thinking Tom is trying to write $\frac{3}{47}$ as a decimal. He used long division and divided until he got the quotient 0.0638297872, at which point he stopped. Since the decimal doesn't seem to terminate or repeat, he concluded that $\frac{3}{47}$ is not rational. Do you agree or disagree? Why?

Disagree; the definition of a rational number is a number that can be written

as a ratio of two integers with the denominator not equal to zero, which

describes $\frac{3}{47}$. Tom would need to keep dividing to find a repeating pattern

or have the decimal terminate.

Unit 1   6   Lesson 1

Unit 1   6   Lesson 1

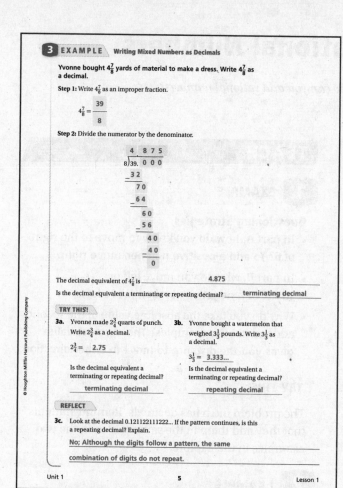 (sidebar) © Houghton Mifflin Harcourt Publishing Company

Notes

Adding Rational Numbers

Essential question: *How can you add rational numbers?*

© Houghton Mifflin Harcourt Publishing Company

COMMON CORE Standards for Mathematical Content

CC.7.NS.1a Describe situations in which opposite quantities combine to make 0...

CC.7.NS.1b Understand $p + q$ as the number located a distance $|q|$ from p, in the positive or negative direction depending on whether q is positive or negative. Show that a number and its opposite have a sum or 0 (are additive inverses). Interpret sums of rational numbers by describing real-world contexts.

CC.7.NS.1d Apply properties of operations as strategies to add and subtract rational numbers.

Vocabulary

additive inverse

Prerequisites

Positive and negative numbers
Absolute value

Math Background

When adding positive integers, move to the right on the number line. When adding negative integers, move to the left on the number line. These same movements apply to adding positive and negative rational numbers. The absolute value of a number is its distance from 0. For example, $|-3| = 3$ because -3 is 3 units from 0. Literally, additive inverse means two numbers that "undo" each other when added. The additive inverse of any number is its opposite. For example, the additive inverse of $-\frac{2}{5}$ is $\frac{2}{5}$ because $-\frac{2}{5} + \frac{2}{5} = 0$.

INTRODUCE

Connect to prior learning by having students solve the following integer problems using a number line:

$-3 + 6 \quad$ **3**
$-3 - 6 \quad$ **−9**
$-3 + 3 \quad$ **0**

Explain that they will solve problems with rational numbers in a similar fashion. Adding a *positive* rational number means to *move right* on the number line while adding a *negative* rational number means to *move left* on the number line. The amount moved may or may not be an integer quantity.

TEACH

1 EXAMPLE

Questioning Strategies

- In part A, how do you know to move to the right of 6? To add a positive number, move right.
- In part B, why do you move left of $-\frac{3}{4}$? To move a negative number, move left.
- Why do you take the absolute value of the second addend in both examples? The absolute value gives you the distance to move in either direction.

TRY THIS

The problem in 1b has decimals. Remind students that they add them in the same way as in the two examples in the Explore.

2 EXAMPLE

Avoid Common Errors

Students may be confused with the different signs on the two numbers. Have them follow a series of steps for these problems:

- Start on the number line with the first addend;
- Take the absolute value of the second addend to find the distance to move; and
- Look at the sign of the second addend for the direction to move on the number line.

Questioning Strategies

- In a real-life context, what could adding a negative number represent? It could represent a loss or a withdrawal.
- In a real-life context, what could adding a positive number mean? It could represent a gain, a deposit or an increase.

Name_____ Class_____ Date_____

1-2

COMMON CORE

CC.7NS.1a,
CC.7NS.1b,
CC.7NS.1d

Adding Rational Numbers

Essential question: *How can you add rational numbers?*

1 EXAMPLE Adding Rational Numbers with the Same Sign

A Andrea has 6 cups of fruit punch in a bowl. She adds 3 cups of fruit punch to the bowl. How many cups of punch are there altogether?

Find $6 + 3$.

Start at 6.

Move $|3| = 3$ units to the *right* because the second addend is *positive*.

The result is ___9___.

There are ___9___ cups of punch.

B Kyle pours out $\frac{3}{4}$ cup of milk from a pitcher. Then he pours out another $\frac{1}{2}$ cup from the pitcher. How many cups of milk does he pour out altogether?

Use negative numbers to represent amounts that are poured out of the pitcher.

Find $-\frac{3}{4} + \left(-\frac{1}{2}\right)$. Start at $-\frac{3}{4}$.

Move $\left|-\frac{1}{2}\right| = \frac{1}{2}$ unit to the *left* because the second addend is *negative*.

The result is ___$-1\frac{1}{4}$___.

Kyle pours out ___$1\frac{1}{4}$___ cups.

TRY THIS!

Use a number line to find each sum.

1a. $3 + 1\frac{1}{2} =$ ___$4\frac{1}{2}$___

1b. $-2.5 + (-4.5) =$ ___-7___

REFLECT

1c. Conjecture Work with other students to make a conjecture about the sign of the sum when the addends have the same sign.

Sample answer: When the addends have the same sign, the sum has the sign of the addends.

To add two rational numbers with the same sign, find the sum of their absolute values. Then use the same sign as the sign of the two rational numbers.

2 EXAMPLE Adding Rational Numbers with Different Signs

A A football team gains 4 yards on their first play. Then they lose 7 yards on their next play. What is the team's overall gain or loss on the two plays?

Use a positive number to represent a gain and a negative number to represent a loss.

Find $4 + (-7)$.

Start at 4.

Move $|-7| = 7$ units to the ___left___ because the second addend is ___negative___.

The result is ___-3___.

The team gains /(loses) ___3___ yards.

B Ernesto writes a check for $2.50. Then he deposits $6 in his checking account. What is the overall increase or decrease in the account's balance?

Use a positive number to represent a deposit and a negative number to represent a withdrawal or a check.

Find $-2.5 + 6$.

Start at -2.5.

Move $|6| = 6$ units to the ___right___ because the second addend is ___positive___.

The result is ___3.5___.

The account balance (increases)/decreases by $___3.50___.

TRY THIS!

Use a number line to find each sum.

2a. $-8 + 5 =$ ___-3___

2b. $\frac{1}{2} + \left(-\frac{3}{4}\right) =$ ___$-\frac{1}{4}$___

REFLECT

2c. Conjecture Work with other students to make a conjecture about the sign of the sum when the addends have different signs.

Sample answer: When the addends have different signs, the sign of the sum will be the same as the addend with the greater absolute value.

This Example is an opportunity to address Standard 4 (Model with mathematics). Students model real-life situations with rational number expressions, and then model the rational number expressions on a number line to simplify the expression. Students then interpret their numerical answers back into the context of the original situations.

3 EXAMPLE

Teaching Strategies

To help students understand the concept of additive inverse, write positive and negative rational numbers on the board. Then have student volunteers come up to the board and write the additive inverse underneath each number. Then have other students check that each pair gives additive inverses by adding the two numbers.

Questioning Strategies

- What kind of change do you get when you add a pair of additive inverses? **You get a change of 0, meaning no change.**
- What is the additive inverse of a negative number? **The additive inverse is the same number except with a positive sign.**
- What is the additive inverse of a positive number? **The additive inverse is the same number except with a negative sign.**
- What is the additive inverse of zero? **The additive inverse is zero.**

CLOSE

Essential Question

How can you add rational numbers?
Possible answer: If the two numbers have the same sign, you add them together and give the sum the same sign as the two numbers. If the two numbers have different signs, add their absolute values and use the sign of the larger rational number. If the two numbers are additive inverses, their sum is 0.

Summarize

Have students write one problem for each of the following situations.

1. The sum of two negative numbers
2. The sum of one negative and one positive number
3. The sum of two additive inverses

Have each student exchange papers with a partner and solve each other's problems. Then have them review together the rules for adding rational numbers.

PRACTICE

Where skills are taught	Where skills are practiced
1 EXAMPLE	EXS. 2, 10
2 EXAMPLE	EXS. 1, 3–7, 9, 11–16
3 EXAMPLE	EX. 8

To add two rational numbers with different signs, find the difference of their absolute values. Then use the sign of the rational number with the greater absolute value.

3 EXAMPLE Finding the Additive Inverse

A Abby takes 5 gallons of water out of an aquarium. Later, she adds 5 gallons of water to the aquarium. What is the overall increase or decrease in the amount of water in the aquarium?

Use a positive number to represent water added to the aquarium and a negative number to represent water taken out of the aquarium.

Find $-5 + 5$. Start at ___−5___.

Move $|5| = 5$ units to the ___right___

because the second addend is ___positive___.

The result is ___0___.

This means ___the overall change is 0 gallons___.

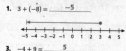

B Kendrick adds $\frac{3}{4}$ cup of chicken stock to a pot. Then he takes $\frac{3}{4}$ cup of stock out of the pot. What is the overall increase or decrease in the amount of chicken stock in the pot?

Use a positive number to represent chicken stock added to the pot and a negative number to represent chicken stock taken out of the pot.

Find $\frac{3}{4} + \left(-\frac{3}{4}\right)$. Start at ___$\frac{3}{4}$___.

Move $\left|-\frac{3}{4}\right| = \frac{3}{4}$ units to the ___left___

because the second addend is ___negative___.

The result is ___0___.

This means ___the overall change is 0 cups___.

REFLECT

3a. **Conjecture** Work with other students to make a conjecture about the sum of a number and its opposite.

The sum of a number and its opposite is 0.

3b. What is the opposite of 50? What is the opposite of -75?

−50; 75

The **opposite**, or **additive inverse**, of a number is the same distance from 0 on a number line as the original number, but on the other side of 0. The sum of a number and its additive inverse is 0. Zero is its own additive inverse.

PRACTICE

Use a number line to find each sum.

1. $3 + (-8) = $ ___−5___

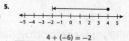

2. $-1\frac{1}{2} + \left(-2\frac{1}{2}\right) = $ ___−4___

3. $-4 + 9 = $ ___5___

4. $\frac{1}{4} + \left(-\frac{3}{4}\right) = $ ___$-\frac{1}{2}$___

Tell what sum is modeled on each number line. Then find the sum.

5.

$4 + (-6) = -2$

6.

$-3 + 4 = 1$

7.

$1\frac{1}{4} + (-1) = \frac{1}{4}$

8.

$-1\frac{3}{4} + 1\frac{3}{4} = 0$

Find each sum without using a number line.

9. $-31 + 16 = $ ___−15___   **10.** $-15.3 + (-12.1) = $ ___−27.4___   **11.** $24\frac{1}{3} + \left(-54\frac{1}{3}\right) = $ ___−30___

12. $-40 + (-18) + 40 = $ ___−18___   **13.** $15 + (-22) + 9 = $ ___2___   **14.** $-1 + 1 + (-25) = $ ___−25___

15. Describe a real-world situation that can be represented by the expression $-10 + (-2)$. Then find the sum and explain what it represents in terms of the situation.

Sample answer: A football team lost 10 yards on a play. On the next play they lost another 2 yards. −12; total number of yards lost in 2 plays.

16. A contestant on a game show has 30 points. She answers a question correctly to win 15 points. Then she answers a question incorrectly and loses 25 points. What is the contestant's final score?

$30 + 15 + (-25) = 20$; the final score is 20 points.

17. **Error Analysis** A student evaluated $-4 + x$ for $x = -9$ and got an answer of 5. What might the student have done wrong?

Sample answer: The student might have substituted 9 instead of −9 into the expression.

Subtracting Rational Numbers

Essential question: *How do you subtract rational numbers?*

COMMON CORE **Standards for Mathematical Content**

CC.7.NS.1c Understand subtraction of rational numbers as adding the additive inverse, $p - q = p + (-q)$. Show that the distance between two rational numbers on the number line is the absolute value of their difference, and apply this principle in real-world contexts.

CC.7.NS.1d Apply properties of operations as strategies to add and subtract rational numbers.

Prerequisites
Adding integers

Math Background
When subtracting a rational number, you move in the direction opposite of that when adding the rational number. For example, subtracting 5 is the opposite of adding 5, so you move to the left. Likewise, subtracting −5 is the opposite of adding −5, so you move to the right.

INTRODUCE

Connect to prior learning by reviewing adding positive and negative integers and rational numbers. Give students some examples to calculate using a number line. Explain that they will subtract integers and rational numbers by finding absolute value and moving that amount in the appropriate direction.

TEACH

1 EXPLORE

Questioning Strategies
- In part A, how do you know to move to the left? You are subtracting 7, which is the same as adding a negative integer. When you add a negative integer, you move to the left.
- In part B, why do you move to the right? You are subtracting a negative number, which you can think of as the opposite of adding a negative number, so move to the right.

> **MATHEMATICAL PRACTICE** **Highlighting the Standards**
>
> This Explore is an opportunity to address Standard 2 (Reason abstractly and quantitatively). Students reason through subtraction of rational numbers using previous knowledge of adding rational numbers. This knowledge helps them make correct conclusions about the subtraction of rational numbers.

2 EXPLORE

Differentiated Instruction
Explanations from their peers may help struggling students understand subtraction of negative rational numbers. Have students pair up and work on Try This together. Sometimes a classmate's explanation is better than a teacher's explanation in helping a student grasp a concept.

Questioning Strategies
- Why is $-2 - 7$ the same as $-2 + (-7)$? With both expressions, you start at −2 and you move 7 units to the left.
- How can you change a subtraction problem into an addition problem? Subtraction is the opposite of adding, or adding the opposite, so change subtraction to adding the opposite.

Name_____ Class_____ Date_____

1-3

COMMON
CORE

CC.7NS.1c
CC.7NS.1d

Subtracting Rational Numbers

Essential question: *How do you subtract rational numbers?*

1 EXPLORE   Subtracting Rational Numbers

A The temperature on Monday was 5 °C. The temperature on Thursday was 7 degrees less than the temperature on Monday. What was the temperature on Thursday?

Subtract to find Thursday's temperature.
Find $5 - 7$. Start at 5.
Move $|7| = 7$ units to the *left* because you are subtracting a *positive* number.

The result is ___−2___.
The temperature on Thursday was ___−2___ °C.

−5 −4 −3 −2 −1 0 1 2 3 4 5

B The temperature on Friday was −7 °C. The temperature on Sunday was −4 °C. How many degrees did the temperature change from Friday to Sunday?

Subtract to find the difference in temperature.
Find $-4 - (-7)$. Start at −4.
Move $|7| = 7$ units to the *right* because you are subtracting a *negative* number.

The result is ___3___.

The temperature change from Friday to Sunday was ___3___ °C.

−5 −4 −3 −2 −1 0 1 2 3 4 5

TRY THIS!

Use a number line to find each difference.

1a. $-6 - 2 = $ ___−8___

−10 −9 −8 −7 −6 −5 −4 −3 −2 −1 0

1b. $1\frac{1}{2} - (-2) = $ ___$3\frac{1}{2}$___

−1   0   1   2   3   4

REFLECT

1c. Work with other students to compare addition of negative numbers on a number line to subtraction of negative numbers on a number line.

Sample answer: When adding a negative number, move to the left. When
subtracting a negative number, move to the right.

© Houghton Mifflin Harcourt Publishing Company

2 EXPLORE   Adding the Opposite

A Joe is diving 2 feet below sea level. He decides to descend 7 more feet. How many feet below sea level is he?

Use negative numbers to represent the number of feet below sea level.

Find $-2 - 7$.
Start at −2.
Move $|7| = 7$ units to the ___left___
because you are subtracting a ___positive___ number.
The result is ___−9___. Joe is ___9___ feet below sea level.

−10 −9 −8 −7 −6 −5 −4 −3 −2 −1 0

B Marianne wrote a check for $2. She then withdrew $7 from her checking account at the bank. How much did Marianne take out of her checking account?

Use negative numbers to represent amounts of money Marianne took out of her checking account.

Find $-2 + (-7)$.
Start at −2.
Move $|-7| = 7$ units to the ___left___
because you are adding a ___negative___ number.
The result is ___−9___. Marianne withdrew ___$9___.

−10 −9 −8 −7 −6 −5 −4 −3 −2 −1 0

TRY THIS!

Use a number line to find each difference or sum.

2a. $-3 - 3 = $ ___−6___

−8 −7 −6 −5 −4 −3 −2 −1 0 1 2

2b. $-3 + (-3) = $ ___−6___

−8 −7 −6 −5 −4 −3 −2 −1 0 1 2

REFLECT

2c. Compare the results from **2a** and **2b**.

They have the same result, −6.

2d. Work with other students to make a conjecture about how to change a subtraction problem into an addition problem.

Sample answer: Change the minus sign to a plus, and change the
second number to its opposite.

To subtract a number, add its opposite. This can also be written as $p - q = p + (-q)$.

© Houghton Mifflin Harcourt Publishing Company

Avoid Common Errors

Students may try to solve the example by just subtracting −5 from −11. Remind students that they need to read the question carefully. Since the question asks for vertical distance, the number should be either positive or 0. Distance is never represented by a negative number.

Questioning Strategies

- Define *distance between two numbers* in your own words. **The distance between two numbers is the number of units between the two numbers.**

- Does order of numbers matter in subtracting? **Yes, you usually get opposite answers when you change the order.**

- Does order of numbers matter when subtracting in absolute value? **No, you subtract and then take absolute value. You get the same value.**

CLOSE

Essential Question

How do you subtract rational numbers?
Possible answer: If subtracting a positive number, you move to the left on the number line. It is the same as adding the opposite of the number. If subtracting a negative number, you move to the right on the number line. It is the same as adding the opposite of the negative number.

Summarize

Have students write a journal entry that answers the question: *How is subtracting rational numbers different from adding rational numbers?* Encourage them to share their answers with a classmate.

PRACTICE

Where skills are taught	Where skills are practiced
1 EXPLORE	EXS. 1–4
2 EXPLORE	EXS. 5–16
3 EXPLORE	EX. 17

3 EXPLORE Finding the Distance between Two Numbers

A cave explorer climbed from an elevation of −11 meters to an elevation of −5 meters. What vertical distance did the explorer climb?

There are two ways to find the vertical distance.

A Start at __−11__ .

Count the number of units on the vertical number line up to −5.

The explorer climbed __6__ meters.

This means that the vertical distance between

−11 meters and −5 meters is __6__ meters.

B Find the difference between the two elevations and use absolute value to find the distance.

−11 − (−5) = __−6__ .

Take the absolute value of the difference because distance traveled is always a nonnegative number.

|−11 − (−5)| = __6__

The vertical distance is __6__ meters.

REFLECT

3a. Does it matter which way you subtract the values when finding distance? Explain.

__No, it does not matter since you take the absolute value of the difference.__

3b. Would the same methods work if both the numbers were positive? What if one of the numbers were positive and the other negative?

__Sample answer: Yes, the method still works when both numbers are positive__

__and when one is positive and one is negative because you take the absolute__

__value of the difference.__

The distance between two values a and b on a number line is represented by the absolute value of the difference of a and b.

Distance between a and b = $|a−b|$ or $|b−a|$.

PRACTICE

Use a number line to find each difference.

1. 5 − (−8) = __13__

2. $-3\frac{1}{2} - 4\frac{1}{2}$ = __−8__

3. −7 − 4 = __−11__

4. −0.5 − 3.5 = __−4__

Find each difference.

5. −14 − 22 = __−36__

6. −12.5 − (−4.8) = __−7.7__

7. $\frac{1}{3} - \left(-\frac{2}{3}\right)$ = __1__

8. 65 − (−14) = __79__

9. $-\frac{2}{9} - (-3)$ = __$2\frac{7}{9}$__

10. $24\frac{3}{8} - \left(-54\frac{1}{8}\right)$ = __$78\frac{1}{2}$__

11. A girl is snorkeling 1 meter below sea level and then dives down another 0.5 meter. How far below sea level is the girl?

__−1 − 0.5 = −1.5; 1.5 meters below sea level__

12. The first play of a football game resulted in a loss of 12 yards. Then a penalty resulted in another loss of 5 yards. What is the total loss or gain?

__−12 − 5 = −17; total loss 17 yards__

13. A climber starts descending from 533 feet above sea level and keeps going until she reaches 10 feet below sea level. How many feet did she descend?

__533 − (−10) = 543; 543 feet__

14. The temperature on Sunday was −15 °C. The temperature on Monday was 12 degrees less than the temperature on Sunday. What was the temperature on Monday?

__−15 − 12 = −27; −27 °C__

15. The lowest temperature on Thursday was −20 °C. The lowest temperature on Saturday was −12 °C. What was the difference between the lowest temperatures?

__−20 − (−12) = −8; 8 °C__

16. Eleni withdrew $45.00 from her savings account. She then used her debit card to buy groceries for $30.15. What was the total amount Eleni took out of her account?

__−45.00 − 30.15 = −75.15; $75.15__

17. On a number line, what is the distance between −61.5 and −23.4?

__|−61.5 − (−23.4)| = |−38.1| = 38.1; 38.1 units__

Multiplying Rational Numbers

Essential question: *How do you multiply rational numbers?*

© Houghton Mifflin Harcourt Publishing Company

COMMON CORE Standards for Mathematical Content

CC.7.NS.2a Understand that multiplication is extended from fractions to rational numbers by requiring that operations continue to satisfy the properties of operations, particularly the distributive property, leading to products such as $(-1)(-1) = 1$ and the rules for multiplying signed numbers. Interpret products of rational numbers by describing real-world contexts.

CC.7.NS.2c Apply properties of operations as strategies to multiply and divide rational numbers.

Prerequisites
Multiplying fractions

Math Background
Multiplying rational numbers is an extension of multiplication of fractions. In this lesson, students will multiply rational numbers. If the rational numbers have the same sign, their product is positive. If they have different signs, their product is negative. Multiplying by 0 still gives a product of 0. Multiplying a rational number by 1 still gives that number back as the product.

INTRODUCE

Connect to prior learning by reviewing multiplication of two fractions. Have students solve the problem $\left(\frac{2}{5}\right)\left(\frac{3}{8}\right)$. Explain that they will work similar problems but with numbers that could have negative signs.

TEACH

Differentiated Instruction
Explanations from their peers may help struggling students understand multiplication of rational numbers. Have students work together on Try This. Sometimes a classmate's explanation is better than a teacher's explanation in helping a student grasp a concept.

1 EXPLORE

Questioning Strategies

- How is the multiplication problem in part A modeled? **It is shown on the number line as repeated addition of the same number.**

- How does the Commutative Property help you to solve part B? **You change the order so that you can move 1/2 unit 4 times to the left.**

- How does rewriting $(-4)(-3)$ help you solve part C? **You write the product as the opposite of (4)(−3) so that you can model 4 groups of −3, and then find the opposite of that product.**

- What is the purpose of finding the pattern in part D? **To describe the products of signed numbers.**

1-4

Name_____ Class_____ Date_____

Multiplying Rational Numbers

Essential question: *How do you multiply rational numbers?*

1 EXPLORE Multiplying Rational Numbers

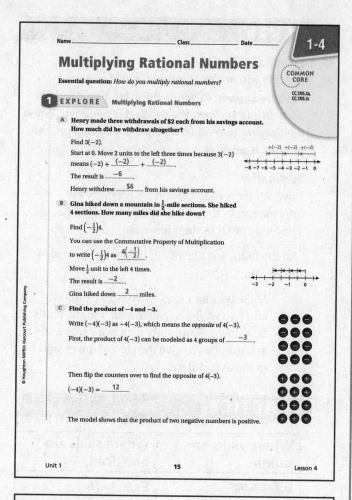

A Henry made three withdrawals of $2 each from his savings account. How much did he withdraw altogether?

Find $3(-2)$.

Start at 0. Move 2 units to the left three times because $3(-2)$

means $(-2) + \underline{(-2)} + \underline{(-2)}$

The result is $\underline{-6}$.

Henry withdrew $\underline{\$6}$ from his savings account.

B Gina hiked down a mountain in $\frac{1}{2}$-mile sections. She hiked 4 sections. How many miles did she hike down?

Find $\left(-\frac{1}{2}\right)4$.

You can use the Commutative Property of Multiplication

to write $\left(-\frac{1}{2}\right)4$ as $\underline{4\left(-\frac{1}{2}\right)}$.

Move $\frac{1}{2}$ unit to the left 4 times.

The result is $\underline{-2}$.

Gina hiked down $\underline{2}$ miles.

C Find the product of -4 and -3.

Write $(-4)(-3)$ as $-4(-3)$, which means the *opposite* of $4(-3)$.

First, the product of $4(-3)$ can be modeled as 4 groups of $\underline{-3}$.

Then flip the counters over to find the opposite of $4(-3)$.

$(-4)(-3) = \underline{12}$

The model shows that the product of two negative numbers is positive.

Unit 1   15   Lesson 4

D Identify a possible pattern. Use the pattern to find the next three products.

$-5(3) = -15$
$-5(2) = -10$
$-5(1) = -5$
$-5(0) = 0$
$-5(-1) = 5$
$-5(-2) = \underline{10}$
$-5(-3) = \underline{15}$
$-5(-4) = \underline{20}$

Find the pattern in the products. Make your observations starting from the top of the list of equations and going down.

The factor of $\underline{-5}$ is always the same.

The second factor that is being multiplied by –5 increases / (decreases) in each equation. By how much? $\underline{1}$

The product of the factors (increases) / decreases in each equation.

By how much? $\underline{5}$

Does this pattern hold true for the first 5 equations? $\underline{yes}$

A pattern for these equations is: If you increases / (decreases) the second

factor by $\underline{1}$ the product (increases) / decreases by $\underline{5}$

Complete the pattern.

REFLECT

1a. What do you notice about the product of two rational numbers with different signs? What do you notice about the product of two rational numbers with the same sign?

The product of two numbers with different signs is a negative number.

The product of two numbers with the same sign is a positive number.

1b. In **D** would the products change if you made your observations starting at the bottom of the list of equations and went up? Would the pattern change?

No, the final products would stay the same. Yes, the second factor

would increase by 1, and the products would decrease by 5.

TRY THIS!

Find each product.

1c. $2(-12) = \underline{-24}$ **1d.** $\left(-\frac{2}{3}\right)\left(-\frac{5}{6}\right) = \underline{\frac{5}{9}}$ **1e.** $(-7)(7.8) = \underline{-54.6}$

Unit 1   16   Lesson 4

Questioning Strategies

Before the charts at the end of the lesson, which number properties and facts are used to show that the product of two negative numbers is positive? **(1) Distributive Property, (2) additive inverse, multiplicative identity, and substitution, (3) Addition Property of Equality, and (4) substitution**

> ◺ **MATHEMATICAL PRACTICE** Highlighting the Standards
>
> This Explore is an opportunity to address Standard 3 (Construct viable arguments and critique the reasoning of others). Students use their knowledge of the definition of multiplication, opposites, and properties to solve parts A to C. They find a pattern in part D to help them make a conclusion about the product of two numbers with different signs and the product of two negative numbers.

Essential Question

How do you multiply rational numbers?
Possible answer: When multiplying two numbers with different signs, the product is negative. When multiplying two numbers with the same sign, the product is positive.

Summarize

Have students reproduce from memory the information in the charts at the end of the lesson. They may put it in their journals.

Use the following activity to help students review the lesson.

> Make up four cards – two with a plus sign and two with a negative sign. Put the cards face down. Randomly pick two cards and ask students to give the sign of the product of those two signs.

PRACTICE

Where skills are taught	Where skills are practiced
1 EXPLORE	EXS. 1–16

The numerical properties that work for positive rational numbers (such as the Distributive Property) must also be true for negative rational numbers. For the properties to work with all rational numbers, the product of two negative numbers must be positive. You can see that this is true using algebra.

Start with something you know about positive and negative numbers:

$$1 + (-1) = 0$$

Use this to write an equation using the Distributive Property:

$$-1[1 + (-1)] = -1(1) + (-1)(-1) \quad \text{Distribute.}$$

You know that $1 + (-1) = 0$.	You know that $(-1)(1) = -1$.	You don't know the value of $(-1)(-1)$, so call it x for now.

$$
\begin{aligned}
-1(0) &= -1 + x \\
0 &= -1 + x \\
1 &= x \\
1 &= (-1)(-1)
\end{aligned}
$$

Simplify.
Addition Property of Equality
Substitute.

So, $(-1)(-1) = 1$. The product of two negative numbers is positive.

The rules for the signs of products of rational numbers can be summarized. Let p and q be rational numbers.

Products of Rational Numbers

Sign of Factor p	Sign of Factor q	Sign of Product pq
+	−	−
−	+	−
+	+	+
−	−	+

Properties of Zero

p	q	Product pq
0	+/−	0
+/−	0	0

PRACTICE

Find each product.

1. $-1(9) =$ __−9__

2. $\left(-\frac{2}{5}\right)\left(-\frac{12}{7}\right) =$ __$\frac{24}{35}$__

3. $(-9)(-6) =$ __54__

4. $-2(50) =$ __−100__

5. $(-4)(15) =$ __−60__

6. $(3)(-52.4) =$ __−157.2__

7. $(6)\left(-\frac{7}{15}\right) =$ __$-2\frac{4}{5}$__

8. $\left(-\frac{19}{9}\right)(0) =$ __0__

9. $(8)(-12) =$ __−96__

10. Flora made 7 withdrawals of $75 each from her bank account. How much did she withdraw in total?

    $7(-75) = -525; \$525$

11. Each of a football team's 3 plays resulted in a loss of 5 yards. How many yards in total did they lose in the 3 plays?

    $3(-5) = -15; 15$ yards

12. The temperature dropped 2 °F every hour for 6 hours. What was the total number of degrees the temperature dropped in the 6 hours?

    $6(-2) = -12; 12$ °F

13. A mountain climber climbed down a cliff $\frac{1}{4}$ mile at a time. He did this 5 times in one day. How many miles did he climb down?

    $\left(-\frac{1}{4}\right)(5) = -1\frac{1}{4}; 1\frac{1}{4}$ miles

14. The price of one share of Acme Company declined $3.50 per day for 4 days in a row. How much did the price of one share decline in total after the 4 days?

    $4(-3.50) = -14; \$14$

15. In one day, 18 people each withdrew $100 from an ATM machine. How much money was withdrawn from the ATM machine?

    $18(-100) = -1,800; \$1,800$

16. Describe a real-world situation that can be represented by the product $(-34)(3)$. Then find the product and explain what the product means in terms of the real-world situation.

    Sample answer: A stock dropped 34 points each day for 3 days. How many

    points did the stock drop over the 3 days? $-34(3) = -102$; the stock dropped

    102 points.

Dividing Rational Numbers

Essential question: *How do you divide rational numbers?*

© Houghton Mifflin Harcourt Publishing Company

COMMON CORE Standards for Mathematical Content

CC.7.NS.2b Understand that integers can be divided, provided that the divisor is not zero, and every quotient of integers (with non-zero divisor) is a rational number. If p and q are integers, then $(-p/q) = (-p)/q = p/(-q)$. Interpret quotients of rational numbers by describing real-world contexts.

CC.7.NS.2c Apply properties of operations as strategies to multiply and divide rational numbers.

Prerequisites

Dividing fractions

Multiplying rational numbers

Math Background

Dividing rational numbers is an extension of dividing fractions and multiplying rational numbers. In this lesson, students will divide rational numbers. If the rational numbers have the same sign, their quotient is positive. If they have different signs, their quotient is negative. Where the negative sign is placed in a division problem does not affect the quotient. Division by 0 is undefined, just as with any number divided by 0. Zero divided by a nonzero rational number is 0.

INTRODUCE

Connect to prior learning by reviewing division problems. Have students solve the problems:

1. $\frac{45}{9}$ 5
2. $63 \div 7$ 9
3. $\frac{\frac{2}{5}}{\frac{8}{5}}$ $\frac{1}{4}$

Students should understand the different notations for division (including the fraction bar) and recall how to divide a fraction by a fraction. Explain that they will work similar problems but with numbers that could have negative signs.

TEACH

1 EXPLORE

Questioning Strategies

- In the context of the problem, why do you set up the division problem with -100? **The diver wants to dive down 100 feet.**
- Why does the answer of -20 make sense in the context of the problem? **100 divided by 5 is 20 and she is diving down 20 feet at a time.**

MATHEMATICAL PRACTICE **Highlighting the Standards**

This Explore is an opportunity to address Standard 2 (Reason abstractly and quantitatively). Students analyze the problem and represent the quantities with the appropriate signs so that they make sense within the context of the problem. They reason that -20 makes a reasonable answer because the diver is descending down. To solve the problem, they use previous knowledge of division of integers.

2 EXPLORE

Questioning Strategies

- What do you notice about the answer to the problem in each of the three parts? **The answer is the same.**
- Why is the answer the same in each of the three parts? **12 divided by 4 is 3. The division does not cancel out the negative sign no matter where the sign is located and so it carries over into the answer each time.**

Name_____ Class_____ Date_____

1-5

COMMON
CORE

CC.7.NS.2b,
CC.7.NS.2c

Dividing Rational Numbers

Essential question: *How do you divide rational numbers?*

1 EXPLORE   Dividing Integers

A diver needs to descend to a depth of 100 feet. She wants to do it in 5 equal descents. How far should she travel in each descent?

A. To solve this problem, you can set up a division problem: $\frac{-100}{5} = ?$

B. Rewrite the division problem as a multiplication problem.
Think: Some number multiplied by 5 equals −100.

$$\underline{5} \times ? = -100$$

C. Remember the rules for integer multiplication. If the product is negative, one of the factors must be negative. Since __5__ is positive, the unknown factor must be positive / (negative).

D. You know that $5 \times \underline{20} = 100$. So, using the rules for integer multiplication you can say that $5 \times \underline{-20} = -100$.

The diver should descend __20__ feet in each descent.

TRY THIS!

Find each quotient.

1a. $\frac{14}{-7} = \underline{-2}$ 1b. $\frac{-36}{-9} = \underline{4}$ 1c. $\frac{-55}{11} = \underline{-5}$ 1d. $\frac{-45}{-5} = \underline{9}$

REFLECT

1e. What do you notice about the quotient of two rational numbers with different signs?

The quotient of two rational numbers with different signs is negative.

1f. What do you notice about the quotient of two rational numbers with the same sign? Does it matter if both signs are positive or both are negative?

The quotient of two rational numbers with the same sign is positive; it does

not matter if they are both positive or both negative.

© Houghton Mifflin Harcourt Publishing Company

Quotients can have negative signs in different places.

2 EXPLORE   Quotients and Placement of Negative Signs

Are the rational numbers $\frac{12}{-4}$, $\frac{-12}{4}$, and $-\left(\frac{12}{4}\right)$ equivalent?

A. Find each quotient. Then use the rules you found in **1** to make sure the sign of the quotient is correct.

$\frac{12}{-4} = \underline{-3}$ $\frac{-12}{4} = \underline{-3}$ $-\left(\frac{12}{4}\right) = \underline{-3}$

B. What do you notice about each quotient?

The quotients are all the same.

C. The rational numbers (are) / are not equivalent.

D. **Conjecture** Explain how the placement of the negative sign in the rational number affects the sign of the quotients.

The sign of the quotient is not affected by the placement of the negative sign.

TRY THIS!

Write equivalent expressions for each quotient.

2a. $\frac{14}{-7}$, $\frac{-14}{7}$, $-\frac{14}{7}$ 2b. $\frac{-32}{-8}$, $\frac{32}{8}$, $-\left(\frac{-32}{8}\right)$ 2c. $\frac{-99}{9}$, $\frac{99}{-9}$, $-\left(\frac{99}{9}\right)$

3 EXAMPLE   Quotients of Rational Numbers

Find each quotient.

A. $\dfrac{\frac{3}{8}}{-\frac{1}{4}}$

The quotient will be (negative) / positive because the signs are ___different___ .

To find the quotient, rewrite as $\frac{3}{8} \times \underline{-\frac{4}{1}}$

$$\frac{3}{8} \times -\frac{4}{1} = -\frac{12}{8}$$

$$= -\frac{3}{2}$$

$$\frac{\frac{3}{8}}{-\frac{1}{4}} = -\frac{3}{2}$$

© Houghton Mifflin Harcourt Publishing Company

© Houghton Mifflin Harcourt Publishing Company

Avoid Common Errors

Students may forget to multiply the numerator by the *reciprocal* of the denominator in part A or in 3b. Suggest that students first write the fraction. When dividing a fraction by a fraction, you multiply the fraction in the numerator by the reciprocal of the fraction in the denominator.

Teaching Strategies

For the Key Concept at the end of the lesson, have students write one example for each line of the chart. Have them also write one example for each of the three rules after the chart.

Questioning Strategies

- Why is the answer to part A negative? **A positive number divided by a negative number is negative.**

- Why is the answer to part B positive? **A negative number divided by a negative number is positive.**

CLOSE

Essential Question

How do you divide rational numbers?
Possible answer: When dividing two numbers with different signs, the quotient is negative. When dividing two numbers with the same signs, the quotient is positive. The placement of the negative sign—whether in the numerator, denominator, or in front of the fraction—does not affect the quotient's value.

Summarize

Have students answer the following questions in their journals: *How is dividing rational numbers similar to dividing positive fractions? How is dividing rational numbers different from dividing positive fractions?*

PRACTICE

Where skills are taught	Where skills are practiced
1 EXPLORE	EXS. 3, 6, 12–17
2 EXPLORE	EXS. 3, 6, 12–17
3 EXAMPLE	EXS. 1–15

Find each quotient.

B $\frac{-5.6}{-1.4}$

The quotient will be negative / ~~positive~~ because the signs are ___the same___ .

Divide.

$\frac{-5.6}{-1.4}$ = ___4___

TRY THIS!

Find each quotient.

3a. $\frac{2.8}{-4}$ = ___−0.7___   3b. $\frac{-\frac{5}{8}}{-\frac{6}{7}}$ = ___$\frac{35}{48}$___   3c. $\frac{-5.5}{0.5}$ = ___−11___

You used the relationship between multiplication and division to find the sign of quotients. You can use multiplication to understand why division by zero is not possible.

Consider the division problem $5 \div 0 = ?$. Write a related multiplication problem: $0 \times ? = 5$. This multiplication sentence says that there is some number times 0 that equals 5. You already know that 0 times any number equals 0. This means division by 0 is not possible, so we say that division by 0 is undefined.

The rules for the signs of quotients of rational numbers can be summarized. Let p and q be rational numbers.

Quotients of Rational Numbers		
Sign of Factor p	Sign of Factor q	Sign of Quotient $\frac{p}{q}$
+	−	−
−	+	−
+	+	+
−	−	+

Properties of Zero		
p	q	Quotient $\frac{p}{q}$
0	+/−	0
+/−	0	Undefined

Also, $-\left(\frac{p}{q}\right) = \frac{-p}{q} = \frac{p}{-q}$, for q not zero.

PRACTICE

Find each quotient.

1. $\frac{0.72}{-0.9}$ = ___−0.8___   2. $\left(-\frac{1\frac{1}{5}}{\frac{7}{5}}\right)$ = ___$-\frac{1}{7}$___   3. $\frac{56}{-7}$ = ___−8___

4. $\frac{251}{4} \div \left(-\frac{3}{8}\right)$ = ___$-\frac{502}{3}$___   5. $\frac{75}{-\frac{1}{5}}$ = ___−375___   6. $\frac{-91}{-13}$ = ___7___

7. $\frac{-\frac{3}{7}}{9}$ = ___$-\frac{4}{21}$___   8. $-\frac{12}{0.03}$ = ___−400___   9. $\frac{0.65}{-0.5}$ = ___−1.3___

10. $\frac{5}{-\frac{2}{8}}$ = ___−20___   11. $5\frac{1}{3} \div \left(-1\frac{1}{2}\right)$ = ___$-\frac{32}{9}$___   12. $\frac{-120}{-6}$ = ___20___

13. The price of one share of ABC Company declined a total of $45 in 5 days. How much did the price of one share decline, on average, per day?

    −45 ÷ 5 = −9; $9 per day, on average

14. A mountain climber explored a cliff that is 225 yards high in 5 equal descents. How many yards was one descent?

    −225 ÷ 5 = −45; 45 yards

15. Describe a real-world situation that can be represented by the quotient −85 ÷ 15. Then find the quotient and explain what the quotient means in terms of the real-world situation.

    Sample answer: The temperature dropped 85° over 15 days. Find the average

    change in temperature per day. −85 ÷ 15 = −5.67; the average change in

    temperature was −5.67 degrees per day.

16. Divide 5 by 4. Is your answer a rational number? Explain.

    Yes, it is a rational number because $1\frac{1}{4}$ can be written as $\frac{5}{4}$, which is a

    ratio of two integers and the denominator is not zero.

17. **Critical Thinking** Should the quotient of an integer divided by a non-zero integer always be a rational number? Why or why not?

    Yes, since an integer divided by an integer is a ratio of two integers and the

    denominator is not zero, the number is rational by definition.

1-6 Solving Problems with Rational Numbers

Essential question: *How do you solve multi-step problems with rational numbers?*

 COMMON CORE Standards for Mathematical Content

CC.7.NS.3 Solve real-world and mathematical problems involving the four operations with rational numbers.

Prerequisites

Rational number operations

Order of operations

Math Background

Students will solve problems that use rational numbers and have more than one operation. These problems will use the order of operations. Operations should be performed in the following order: parentheses, exponents, multiplication, division, addition, and subtraction (or PEMDAS). One way to remember the order is to use a mnemonic: Please Excuse My Dear Aunt Sally.

INTRODUCE

Connect to prior learning by reviewing the order of operations. Share the mnemonic of Please Excuse My Dear Aunt Sally with students to help them remember the order of operations. Give students several examples of expressions with integers and fractions where they will have to use order of operations to simplify.

TEACH

1 EXPLORE

Questioning Strategies
* How do you know when to use a plus or minus sign in the expression? Use a plus sign for the amount the diver ascends and a minus sign for the amount the diver descends.

Avoid Common Errors
Students may represent the amount of descent as a negative number and then incorrectly subtract that amount. Remind students that the descent can be represented by adding a negative number or by subtracting the distance (absolute value).

2 EXAMPLE

Questioning Strategies
* How do you find an average? You add up all the temperatures and divide by the number of temperatures.
* Do you include the negative signs of the negative numbers in the average? Yes, the signs are parts of the numbers.

Avoid Common Errors
In 2c, students may not count the temperature of 0 degrees and divide by 6 instead of 7. Remind them that 0 is a valid number and that the number of data is 7 regardless of the value of those temperatures.

Name_____ Class_____ Date_____

1-6

Solving Problems with Rational Numbers

COMMON CORE
CC.7.NS.3

Essential question: *How do you solve multi-step problems with rational numbers?*

1 EXPLORE Adding and Subtracting Rational Numbers

Tomas works as an underwater photographer. He starts at a depth of 20 feet, ascends 9 feet, descends 12 feet, and then descends 15 feet more. Write and simplify an expression to find his final depth.

A Write an expression to solve this problem.
Tomas starts at (−20) 20 feet
When the diver ascends, you (add)/ subtract that distance.
When the diver descends, you add /(subtract) that distance.

B Write an expression.

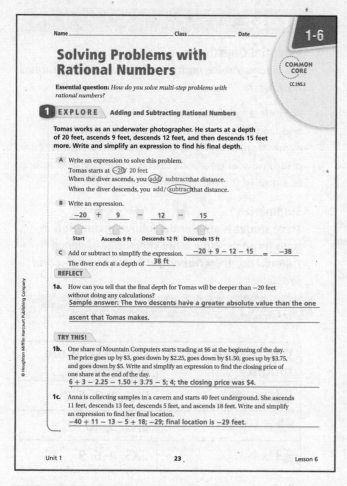

−20 + 9 − 12 − 15

Start Ascends 9 ft Descends 12 ft Descends 15 ft

C Add or subtract to simplify the expression. $-20 + 9 - 12 - 15 = -38$
The diver ends at a depth of ____38 ft____

REFLECT

1a. How can you tell that the final depth for Tomas will be deeper than −20 feet without doing any calculations?
Sample answer: The two descents have a greater absolute value than the one

ascent that Tomas makes.

TRY THIS!

1b. One share of Mountain Computers starts trading at $6 at the beginning of the day. The price goes up by $3, goes down by $2.25, goes down by $1.50, goes up by $3.75, and goes down by $5. Write and simplify an expression to find the closing price of one share at the end of the day.
$6 + 3 - 2.25 - 1.50 + 3.75 - 5$; 4; the closing price was $4.

1c. Anna is collecting samples in a cavern and starts 40 feet underground. She ascends 11 feet, descends 13 feet, descends 5 feet, and ascends 18 feet. Write and simplify an expression to find her final location.
$-40 + 11 - 13 - 5 + 18$; −29; final location is −29 feet.

Unit 1   23   Lesson 6

---

2 EXAMPLE Multiplying and Dividing Rational Numbers

The table gives the daily high temperatures for one week during the winter. Find the average daily high temperature for the week. Round your answer to the nearest tenth.

Day	Mon	Tues	Wed	Thurs	Fri	Sat	Sun
Temperature (°F)	−4.5	−3	2	−1.5	−2	3	−5

$$\text{Average} = \frac{-4.5 + -3 + 2 + -1.5 + -2 + 3 + -5}{7}$$

You use the order of operations to simplify.

The first step is to add the numbers in the ____numerator____

The second step is to ____divide____ by the number in the ____denominator____

$$\text{Average} = \frac{-11}{7} = -1.6$$

The average daily high temperature is approximately ____−1.6 °F____

TRY THIS!

2a. Marcy is digging a hole to plant a tree. She digs 1 foot below ground each day for 5 days. Write and simplify an expression to show the total number of feet that she dug below ground.

$5(-1)$; −5; 5 feet

2b. The table gives the daily high temperatures for one week during the winter. Find the average daily high temperature for the week. Round your answer to the nearest tenth.

Day	Mon	Tues	Wed	Thurs	Fri	Sat	Sun
Temperature (°F)	6	2	0	−6	−2	5	−5

$$\frac{6 + 2 + 0 + (-6) + (-2) + 5 + (-5)}{7} = \frac{0}{7} = 0$$
The average daily high temperature was 0 °F.

Unit 1   24   Lesson 6

© Houghton Mifflin Harcourt Publishing Company

Questioning Strategies

- How could you use a plus sign to write the expression that solves the problem? You could write the amount removed each time as $-\frac{3}{4}$ and then use a plus sign between the two sets of expressions.

- Which operation do you do first? Multiplication before addition

Avoid Common Errors

Students may try to subtract the first number in the expression following the minus sign in the algebraic expression instead of multiplying both pairs of numbers. Have them circle each product to remind themselves to multiply first and then subtract.

MATHEMATICAL PRACTICE **Highlighting the Standards**

This Example is an opportunity to address Standard 1 (Make sense of problems and persevere in solving them). Students must analyze the problems and translate the words into algebraic expressions. These expressions are complicated and they must use their knowledge of rational number operations along with order of operations to solve the problems.

CLOSE

Essential Question

How do you solve multi-step problems with rational numbers?

Possible answer: You read the problem carefully and translate the phrases into mathematical expressions. Then you use order of operations and prior knowledge about rational number operations to simplify the expressions.

Summarize

Have students answer the following question in their journals: *How is my knowledge of signed rational numbers important in solving real-world problems?*

PRACTICE

Where skills are taught	Where skills are practiced
1 EXPLORE	EXS. 1–2, 7–8
2 EXAMPLE	EXS. 3, 10
3 EXAMPLE	EXS. 4–6, 9

REFLECT

2c. In **2b**, how could you use logical reasoning to find the average without having to use the formula for an average?

Sample answer: There are three pairs of additive inverses in the table. Each

pair adds up to 0. When you add the pairs and the seventh zero, the sum of

the temperatures is 0, so the average is 0.

3 EXAMPLE Solving Multi-Step Problems

A chef adds $\frac{1}{2}$ cup of stock to a stew 5 times while it is cooking. During this time, he also removes $\frac{3}{4}$ cup of stew 4 times to serve to guests. Write and simplify an expression to find by how much the overall amount of stew increased or decreased.

Write an expression for the situation.

$$5\left(\frac{1}{2}\right) \qquad - \qquad 4\left(\frac{3}{4}\right)$$

Number of | Amount | Removal of | Number of | Amount
times stock | added | stew | times stew | removed
added | | | removed |

Use the order of operations to simplify the expression.

$$5\left(\frac{1}{2}\right) - 4\left(\frac{3}{4}\right) = 2\frac{1}{2} \quad - \quad 3 \qquad \text{Multiply.}$$

$$= -\frac{1}{2} \qquad \text{Subtract.}$$

The expression simplifies to $-\frac{1}{2}$.

The overall amount of stew increased / (decreased) by $\frac{1}{2}$ cup.

TRY THIS!

3a. A chef adds $\frac{1}{4}$ cup of stock to a soup 7 times while it is cooking. During this time, he removes $\frac{1}{8}$ cup of soup 3 times to taste it. Write and simplify an expression to find how much the overall amount of soup increased or decreased.

$$7\left(\frac{1}{4}\right) - 3\left(\frac{1}{8}\right) = \frac{7}{4} - \frac{3}{8} = \frac{11}{8} = 1\frac{3}{8}; \text{ the soup increases by } 1\frac{3}{8} \text{ cups.}$$

REFLECT

3b. How could you solve problem **3a** without using multiplication?

Sample answer: Add $\frac{1}{4}$ seven times and subtract $\frac{1}{8}$ three times.

PRACTICE

Simplify each expression.

1. $-2 + 4 + 7 - 5$
4

2. $-0.25 + 1.78 - 5.9 + 4.1$
-0.27

3. $5(-2) - 3(4)$
-22

4. $6\left(\frac{7}{8}\right) - 10\left(\frac{4}{5}\right)$
$-2\frac{3}{4}$

5. $-4\left(\frac{1}{8}\right) - 3\left(\frac{2}{5}\right)$
$-1\frac{7}{10}$

6. $\frac{1}{2}(6) + 12\left(\frac{1}{6}\right)$
5

7. Lily and Rose are playing a game. In the game, each player starts with 0 points, and the player with the most points at the end wins. Lily gains 5 points, loses 3, loses 2, and then gains 3. Rose loses 3, loses 4, gains 2, and then gains 3. Write and simplify an expression for each player's points. Then tell who wins the game and by how much.

Lily: $5 - 3 - 2 + 3 = 3$; Rose: $-3 - 4 + 2 + 3 = -2$; Lily wins by 5 points

8. The graph shows the number of inches above or below the average snowfall of a city. What is the total amount of snowfall above or below the average for the given months?

$-1 - 2 + 3 + 4 - 2 + 2$; 4; the total

amount of snowfall is 4 inches

above average.

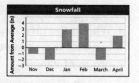

Snowfall

9. Susan uses 15 rolls of ribbon to decorate 10 wedding baskets. Each roll of ribbon is $5\frac{3}{8}$ yards long. After she decorates the baskets, she decides to cut off another $\frac{3}{4}$ yard from the ribbons of each basket. Write and simplify an expression to find out how much ribbon was used on the baskets.

$15\left(5\frac{3}{8}\right) - 10\left(\frac{3}{4}\right) = 15\left(\frac{43}{8}\right) - \frac{30}{4}$; $73\frac{1}{8}$; $73\frac{1}{8}$ yards of ribbon

10. The table gives the daily high temperatures for one week during the summer. Find the average daily high temperature for the week. Round your answer to the nearest tenth.

Day	Mon	Tues	Wed	Thurs	Fri	Sat	Sun
Temperature (°F)	98	90	100	95	88	90	97

$\frac{98 + 90 + 100 + 95 + 88 + 90 + 97}{7} = \frac{658}{7} = 94$

The average daily high temperature was 94 °F.

UNIT 1

Problem Solving Connections
Summer Camp

© Houghton Mifflin Harcourt Publishing Company

 COMMON CORE **Standards for Mathematical Content**

CC.7.NS.1a Describe situations in which opposite quantities combine to make 0....

CC.7.NS.1b Understand $p + q$ as the number located a distance.... Interpret sums of rational numbers by describing real-world contexts.

CC.7.NS.1c Understand subtraction of rational numbers....

CC.7.NS.1d Apply properties of operations to ... add and subtract rational numbers.

CC.7.NS.2a Understand that multiplication is extended from fractions to rational numbers ...

CC.7.NS.2b Understand that integers can be divided.... Interpret quotients of rational numbers by describing real-world contexts.

CC.7.NS.2c Apply properties of operations ... to multiply and divide rational numbers.

CC.7.NS.2d Convert a rational number to a decimal using long division....

CC.7.NS.3 Solve real-world and mathematical problems involving the four operations with rational numbers.

INTRODUCE

Explain to students that this project will help them use rational numbers and rational number operations to solve problems about life at summer camp.

TEACH

1 Cooking

Avoid Common Errors

Students might just multiply the whole-number part of each mixed number measurement when converting to servings for 66 people. Remind them to convert each mixed number to an improper fraction before multiplying.

Questioning Strategies

- How do you convert each measurement to a recipe for 66? **You change each measurement to an improper fraction and multiply by 11. Then convert the product back so that it is a whole number or a mixed number.**

- Why do you multiply by 11? **You need 11 times the recipes because 11 times 6 is 66.**

2 Weather

Teaching Strategies

Students may have difficulty finding the average involving negative numbers. Remind students that subtraction of a number is the same as adding the opposite of the number.

Questioning Strategies

- When finding an average, by what number do you divide the sum? **You divide the sum by the number of temperatures that were totaled.**

- What is the meaning of *average* in a real-world context? **It represents the *typical* value of a group of values.**

Name_____ Class_____ Date_____

Problem Solving Connections

Camp Fun! Waterfall Summer Camp has opened up for the season! Several boys and girls are going this week. You will use addition, subtraction, multiplication, and division of rational numbers to learn about life at camp.

COMMON CORE
CC.7.NS.1
CC.7.NS.2
CC.7.NS.3

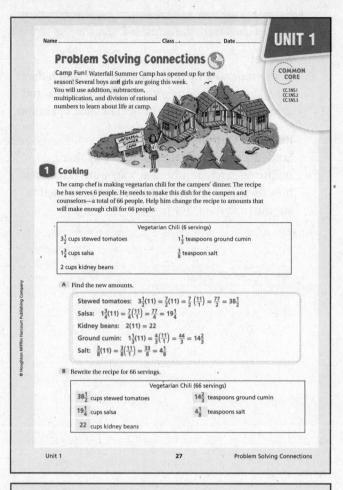

1 Cooking

The camp chef is making vegetarian chili for the campers' dinner. The recipe he has serves 6 people. He needs to make this dish for the campers and counselors—a total of 66 people. Help him change the recipe to amounts that will make enough chili for 66 people.

Vegetarian Chili (6 servings)	
$3\frac{1}{2}$ cups stewed tomatoes	$1\frac{1}{3}$ teaspoons ground cumin
$1\frac{3}{4}$ cups salsa	$\frac{3}{8}$ teaspoon salt
2 cups kidney beans	

A Find the new amounts.

Stewed tomatoes: $3\frac{1}{2}(11) = \frac{7}{2}(11) = \frac{7}{2}\left(\frac{11}{1}\right) = \frac{77}{2} = 38\frac{1}{2}$

Salsa: $1\frac{3}{4}(11) = \frac{7}{4}\left(\frac{11}{1}\right) = \frac{77}{4} = 19\frac{1}{4}$

Kidney beans: $2(11) = 22$

Ground cumin: $1\frac{1}{3}(11) = \frac{4}{3}\left(\frac{11}{1}\right) = \frac{44}{3} = 14\frac{2}{3}$

Salt: $\frac{3}{8}(11) = \frac{3}{8}\left(\frac{11}{1}\right) = \frac{33}{8} = 4\frac{1}{8}$

B Rewrite the recipe for 66 servings.

Vegetarian Chili (66 servings)	
$38\frac{1}{2}$ cups stewed tomatoes	$14\frac{2}{3}$ teaspoons ground cumin
$19\frac{1}{4}$ cups salsa	$4\frac{1}{8}$ teaspoons salt
22 cups kidney beans	

2 Weather

Waterfall Summer Camp is located in the mountains and is open from April to October. The table shows average monthly temperatures at the campsite.

Month	Apr	May	Jun	Jul	Aug	Sept	Oct
Temperature (°F)	25	70	65	85	92	82	71

A What is the average monthly temperature for the period of April through September? Round your answer to the nearest tenth. Show your work.

$\frac{25 + 70 + 65 + 85 + 92 + 82}{6} = \frac{419}{6} = 69.8$

The average temperature is 69.8 °F.

B The local newspaper reported that the average monthly temperature for April through September was not typical of the temperatures at the campsite. What do you think is the reason for this? How could you find a more typical representation of the average monthly temperature for the campsite?

Sample answer: The average temperature for April was probably too low. You can find a better representation by removing the temperature for April and finding the average for May through September.

C Find a more typical average for the monthly temperature.

Sample answer: $\frac{70 + 65 + 85 + 92 + 82}{5} = \frac{394}{5} = 78.8$

A more typical average temperature is 78.8 °F.

D The average monthly temperature from April to October was 70 °F. Find the average temperature for October and write it in the table.

$\frac{25 + 70 + 65 + 85 + 92 + 82 + Oct}{7} = 70$

$\frac{419 + Oct}{7} = 70$

$419 + Oct = 490$

$Oct = 490 - 419$

$Oct = 71 °F$

Notes

Golf

Teaching Strategies
To help students write expressions for the problems, have them discuss how to solve each problem before they focus on the number operations.

Questioning Strategies
- How do you represent a score below par? **A negative number represents a score below par.**
- How do you know to use parentheses when writing the expression for part E? **You are finding twice the sum. The sum will be in parentheses.**

 Hiking

Questioning Strategies
- What is the order of operations that you use to simplify the expression for part B? **Add the numbers in parentheses first and then multiply by the outer number.**
- What is the order of operations that you use to simplify the expression for part C? **Multiply each mixed number by 2 first. Then add those products together. Then multiply by the outer number.**

CLOSE

Journal
Have students write a journal entry in which they list all four operations with rational numbers and show examples from the project of each operation.

Research Options
Students can extend their learning by doing online research on where averages are calculated, how they are reported, and how they are used to support a certain viewpoint.

© Houghton Mifflin Harcourt Publishing Company

3 Golf

Some of the campers play 9 holes of golf one day. Par, or the expected number of strokes, for the 9-hole course is 32. Every hole has a par value. A golfer's score is the number of strokes above or below par. A golfer's score is above par if he or she takes more strokes than the par value of the hole. A golfer's score is below par if he or she takes fewer strokes than the par value of the hole. A score below par is indicated by a negative number.

Round of 9-Hole Golf							
Golfer	Jan	Sergei	Sue	Yanni	Raz	Leon	Felicity
Score	−6	6	3	−4	2	−3	−5

A Which golfer had the best score? Explain. Now order the players from best score to worst score.

Jan had the best score because she was 6 strokes below par. She took the least

number of strokes on the course. Jan, Felicity, Yanni, Leon, Raz, Sue, Sergei

B Which of the golfers have scores that are additive inverses? Explain.

Additive inverses have a sum of 0; the sum of Sue's and Leon's scores

is 0: 3 + (−3) = 0; the sum of Sergei's and Jan's scores is 0: 6 + (−6) = 0.

C What is the average score of all the golfers?

$$\frac{-6 + 6 + 3 - 4 + 2 - 3 - 5}{7} = \frac{-7}{7} = -1;$$

The average score is 1 below par.

D Troy's score is 2 times Leon's score. What is Troy's score?

(−3)2 = −6. Troy's score is 6 below par.

E Twice the sum of 4 and Yanni's score is Counselor Trina's score. What is Counselor Trina's score?

2(4 + (−4)) = 2(0); 0; Counselor Trina's score is 0, or par.

© Houghton Mifflin Harcourt Publishing Company

---

4 Hiking

The campers go for a hike using the map shown below.

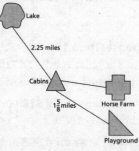

Lake

2.25 miles

Cabins

$1\frac{5}{8}$ miles

Horse Farm

Playground

A The distance from the cabins to the horse farm is one-third of the distance from the lake to the playground. How would you find the distance from the cabins to the horse farm?

Add the distance from the lake to the cabins and the distance from

the cabins to the playground. Then multiply by one-third.

B How far is it from the cabins to the horse farm?

$\frac{1}{3}\left(2.25 + 1\frac{5}{8}\right) = \frac{1}{3}\left(2\frac{2}{8} + 1\frac{5}{8}\right) = \frac{1}{3}\left(3\frac{7}{8}\right) = \frac{1}{3}\left(\frac{31}{8}\right) = \frac{31}{24} = 1\frac{7}{24};$

The cabins are $1\frac{7}{24}$ miles from the horse farm.

C Junie walks from the cabins to the lake and back. She then walks to the playground and back. She does each trip twice a week. How much does she walk in total in one week?

$2\left(2\left(2\frac{1}{4}\right) + 2\left(1\frac{5}{8}\right)\right) = 2\left(\frac{9}{2} + \frac{13}{4}\right) = 2\left(\frac{31}{4}\right) = \frac{31}{2} = 15\frac{1}{2};$

Junie walks $15\frac{1}{2}$ miles in one week.

© Houghton Mifflin Harcourt Publishing Company

© Houghton Mifflin Harcourt Publishing Company

COMMON CORE CORRELATION

Standard	Items
CC.7.NS.1a	8, 13
CC.7.NS.1b	8, 13
CC.7.NS.1c	3, 7, 12
CC.7.NS.1d	3, 7, 12
CC.7.NS.2a	5, 14
CC.7.NS.2b	1, 6
CC.7.NS.2c	1, 5, 6, 14
CC.7.NS.2d	2, 11, 16
CC.7.NS.3	4, 9, 10, 15, 17, 18, 19

TEST PREP DOCTOR ✛

Multiple Choice: Item 3

- Students who answered **A** may have chosen 5 meters because it is used in the statement of the question.
- Students who answered **B** may have subtracted 5 from 30.
- Students who answered **D** may have come up with 10 by adding 5 meters above sea level twice. Then they added 30 to the number.

Multiple Choice: Item 11

- Students who answered **A** may have rounded their quotient to the nearest tenth.
- Students who answered **B** may have rounded their quotient to the nearest hundredth.
- Students who answered **D** may have rounded their quotient up to 0.90.

Free Response: Item 14

- Students who answered **32** may have multiplied 128 by $\frac{1}{4}$ instead of $\frac{3}{4}$.
- Students who answered **384** may have multiplied 128 by 3 but did not divide by 4.
- Students who answered **512** may have multiplied 128 by 4.

Free Response: Item 19

- Students who answered **−$47** did not subtract the bank charge for covering overdraft.
- Students who answered **$163** only subtracted one withdrawal of $70.
- Students who answered **$93** only subtracted two withdrawals of $70.

Name _____ Class _____ Date _____

MULTIPLE CHOICE

1. Misha has a board that is $17\frac{1}{2}$ inches long that he has to cut into 3 equal pieces. How long should each piece be?

   A. $5\frac{2}{3}$ inches

   B. $5\frac{5}{6}$ inches

   C. $8\frac{3}{4}$ inches

   D. $14\frac{1}{2}$ inches

2. Jenni buys a piece of fabric that is $4\frac{7}{8}$ yards long. What is the decimal equivalent of $4\frac{7}{8}$?

   F. 0.875

   H. 4.875

   G. 4.8

   J. 4.95

3. A diver is working 30 meters below sea level. Another diver is taking a break on a platform directly above him that is 5 meters above sea level. How far apart are the two divers?

   A. 5 meters

   C. 35 meters

   B. 25 meters

   D. 40 meters

4. Thuy has $625 in her checking account. She writes two checks for $23 each and then makes one deposit of $146. What is Thuy's final checking account balance?

   F. $433

   H. $771

   G. $725

   J. $817

5. Uma's salad dressing recipe calls for $\frac{1}{2}$ cup of yogurt. She wants to triple the recipe. How much yogurt does she need?

   A. $1\frac{1}{2}$ cups

   C. 3 cups

   B. 2 cups

   D. $3\frac{1}{2}$ cups

6. Sally's baked bean recipe calls for 5 pounds of sugar and 20 pounds of dried beans. How many pounds of sugar are needed for a recipe using just 1 pound of dried beans?

   F. $\frac{1}{5}$ pound

   H. 1 pound

   G. $\frac{1}{4}$ pound

   J. 4 pounds

7. The temperature in Franklin City is –5 °C. The temperature in Silver City is four degrees less. What is the temperature in Silver City?

   A. –9 °C

   C. –4 °C

   B. –5 °C

   D. 9 °C

8. Jim raised $43.64 for the community food bank. Rina raised $165.23 for the food bank, and Everett raised $23.09 for the food bank. How much did they all raise together?

   F. $66.73

   H. $208.87

   G. $165.23

   J. $231.96

9. Michel's checking account balance was $345. Michel withdrew $160 three times. What is his current balance?

   A. –$480

   C. $135

   B. –$135

   D. $185

10. The table below shows Giorgio's scores at a state golf tournament. What is Giorgio's average score for the five rounds?

Round	1	2	3	4	5
Score	3	1	–3	–2	–4

   F. –4

   H. –2

   G. –3

   J. –1

11. A new poll shows that $\frac{9}{11}$ of all students like to eat pizza. Jan wants to write $\frac{9}{11}$ as a decimal. What is $\frac{9}{11}$ in decimal form?

   A. 0.8

   C. 0.8181...

   B. 0.81

   D. 0.90

12. A treasure chest sits 1,256 feet below sea level. A captain looking for the treasure is in a house 769 feet above sea level. What is the vertical distance between the treasure chest and the house?

   F. –496 feet

   G. 496 feet

   H. 1,256 feet

   J. 2,025 feet

13. The ABC Corporation had a profit of $3,476 in February. It had a loss of $4,509 in March. What was its net gain for February and March?

   A. –$7,985

   C. $1,033

   B. –$1,033

   D. $7,985

FREE RESPONSE

14. Sheila has to pack 128 baskets of apples. She has packed $\frac{1}{4}$ of the baskets. How many baskets are left for her to pack?

   $\frac{3}{4}$ of the baskets are left; $\frac{3}{4} \times \frac{128}{1} = \frac{96}{1}$; she has 96 baskets left to pack.

15. Marley gets on an elevator on the 30th floor of a building. She goes up 6 floors to pick up a package then goes down 14 floors for a meeting. Write and simplify an expression to show what floor Marley is now on.

   $30 + 6 - 14$; 22; Marley is now on the 22nd floor.

16. Leanne was asked on a math test if the number 0.58 is a rational number. She says it is not a rational number. Is she correct? Why or why not?

   Leanne is not correct. 0.58 is rational because it can be written as $\frac{58}{100}$.

17. Mr. Frommer's original loan balance was $4,376. He made three monthly payments of $129. He also made an extra payment of $98. Write and simplify an expression that finds Mr. Frommer's new balance.

   $4,376 - 3(129) - 98$; 3,891; his new balance is $3,891.

18. The drop in temperature from 6:00 A.M. to 12:00 P.M. was 14 °F. What is the average hourly drop in temperature for that time frame?

   There are 6 hours from 6:00 A.M. to 12 P.M.

   $\frac{-14}{6} = \frac{-7}{3} = -2\frac{1}{3}$. The average hourly drop in temperature was $-2\frac{1}{3}$ °F.

19. Herbert's checking account balance was $233. His account has overdraft protection if he withdraws more than his balance, but the bank charges $12 for covering the overdraft. Herbert made 4 withdrawals of $70 each. Does Herbert's account require overdraft protection? Why or why not? What is his final balance?

   $233 - 4(70) = 233 - 280 = -47$; Herbert needs overdraft protection because his balance is below 0. His final balance is $-$47 - $12 = -$59.

Notes

Ratios and Proportional Relationships

Unit Vocabulary

complex fraction   (2-1)

constant of
proportionality   (2-2)

percent
increase/decrease   (2-4)

proportional
relationship   (2-2)

simple interest   (2-4)

UNIT 2

Ratios and Proportional Relationships

Unit Focus

You will continue to refine your computation skills as you learn to simplify complex fractions. You'll find unit rates by dividing rational numbers. Proportional relationships are a relationship in which the ratio of one quantity to another is constant. This constant plays an important role in mathematics. You will learn to identify the constant of proportion in tables, graphs, and equations. You'll also be able to recognize when a relationship is not proportional. Finally, you will learn to apply percents to a variety of contexts, including sales tax, commissions, and simple interest.

Unit at a Glance

COMMON CORE

Lesson		Standards for Mathematical Content
2-1	Unit Rates	CC.7.RP.1, CC.7.NS.3
2-2	Proportional Relationships, Tables, and Equations	CC.7.RP.2a, CC.7.RP.2b, CC.7.RP.2c, CC.7.RP.3
2-3	Proportional Relationships and Graphs	CC.7.RP.2a, CC.7.RP.2b, CC.7.RP.2d, CC.7.RP.3
2-4	Applying Percents	CC.7.RP.3
	Problem Solving Connections	
	Test Prep	

Unit 2   33   Ratios and Proportional Relationships

© Houghton Mifflin Harcourt Publishing Company

Unpacking the Common Core State Standards

Use the table to help you understand the Standards for Mathematical Content that are taught in this unit. Refer to the lessons listed after each standard for exploration and practice.

COMMON CORE Standard for Mathematical Content	What It Means For You
CC.7.RP.1 Compute unit rates associated with ratios of fractions, including ratios of lengths, areas and other quantities measured in like or different units. Lesson 2-1	Given two quantities, you will express their relationship as a unit rate. Given a specific quantity, you will use unit rates to find a related quantity. You will simplify complex fractions by dividing.
CC.7.RP.2a Decide whether two quantities are in a proportional relationship, e.g., by testing for equivalent ratios in a table or graphing on a coordinate plane and observing whether the graph is a straight line through the origin. Lesson 2-2, 2-3	You will use the definition of a proportional relationship to determine whether a relationship presented in a table or graph is proportional.
CC.7.RP.2b Identify the constant of proportionality (unit rate) in tables, graphs, equations, diagrams, and verbal descriptions of proportional relationships. Lesson 2-2, 2-3	You will determine the constant of proportionality for proportional relationships. These relationships may be shown in a table, graph, or equation.
CC.7.RP.2c Represent proportional relationships by equations. Lessons 2-2, 2-3	Using the constant of proportionality, you will be able to write an equation that represents a specific proportional relationship.
CC.7.RP.2d Explain what a point (x, y) on the graph of a proportional relationship means in terms of the situation, with special attention to the points $(0, 0)$ and $(1, r)$ where r is the unit rate. Lesson 2-3	Using your understanding of proportional relationships, you will explain how the point $(1, r)$ is related to the unit rate. You'll also explain the meaning of specific points on the graph, such as $(0, 0)$.
CC.7.RP.3 Use proportional relationships to solve multistep ratio and percent problems. Lessons 2-2, 2-3, 2-4	Your understanding of proportional relationships will help you solve problems. You will use your percent skills to solve real-world problems involving simple interest, tax, tips, commissions, fee, percent increase and decrease, and percent error.
CC.7.NS.3 Solve real-world and mathematical problems involving the four operations with rational numbers. Lesson 2-1	You will continue to add, subtract, multiply, and divide with rational numbers, with a specific focus on complex fractions.

Unpacking the Common Core State Standards

This page lists and explains the Standards for Mathematical Content that are addressed in this unit. For information about the Standards for Mathematical Practice, which are integrated throughout the text, see Teacher Edition pages vii–xiii.

Notes

_____

_____

_____

_____

_____

_____

_____

_____

_____

Unit Rates

Essential question: *How do you find and compare unit rates?*

COMMON CORE Standards for Mathematical Content

CC.7.RP.1 Compute unit rates associated with ratios of fractions, including ratios of lengths, areas and other quantities measured in like or different units.

CC.7.NS.3 Solve real-world and mathematical problems involving the four operations with rational numbers.

Vocabulary
complex fraction

unit rates

Prerequisites
Ratios

Math Background
Ratios describe a relationship between two quantities. A *rate* is a ratio of two quantities with different units. A *unit rate* is a rate with the value of 1 unit in the denominator. Usually the word "per" can be used to describe a unit rate. For example, $3 per book is the unit rate $3/1 book. While students have previously calculated unit rates, they will now use unit rates to solve problems, including problems involving complex fractions. A complex fraction is a fraction composed of one or more fractions in the numerator and/or denominator. To simplify a complex fraction, divide the numerator by the denominator.

INTRODUCE

Connect to prior learning by asking students to find a unit rate if you pay $4 for 2 pounds of apples. Students should be able to tell you $2 per pound. Then, propose that you pay $4.50 for $1\frac{1}{2}$ pounds of apples. Have students use red paper semi-circles to represent the half-pounds of apples and divide $4.50 evenly among the semi-circles to find the unit rate of $3/lb.

TEACH

1 EXPLORE

Questioning Strategies
- How do you know how many parts to use in the bar diagram? **The amount of time tells you how many parts of an hour to use.**
- For Jeff's hike, how can you calculate the distance from one-half hour to one hour without the other fraction $\left(\frac{3}{4}\right)$ between them? **Since the rate is constant, you can double the distance from one-half hour to one hour.**

MATHEMATICAL PRACTICE   Highlighting the Standards

This Example is an opportunity to address Standard 2 (Reason abstractly and quantitatively.). Students use the bar diagrams and tables to help them calculate the distance each person hiked. Students use proportional thinking to complete each table, considering the information contained in the table and how to use it to fill in the empty cells. They have to realize that they can double the distance for half an hour to determine the distance for one hour. The fractional units require proportional reasoning and the fraction bars assist with abstract reasoning.

2 EXAMPLE

Questioning Strategies
- How do you simplify the rate? **Divide the numerator by the denominator.**
- How do you write 30 as a fraction? $\frac{30}{1}$

Avoid Common Errors
When simplifying complex fractions, students may forget to multiply the numerator by the reciprocal of the denominator. Have students write both steps: (1) express the complex fraction as division of fractions, and (2) express division as multiplication of the reciprocal.

2-1

Unit Rates

Essential question: *How do you find and compare unit rates?*

COMMON
CORE
CC.7.RP.1
CC.7.NS.3

1 EXPLORE Finding Rates

Jeff hikes $\frac{1}{2}$ mile every $\frac{1}{4}$ hour. Lisa hikes $\frac{1}{3}$ mile every $\frac{1}{6}$ hour.
How far do they each hike in 1 hour? 2 hours?

A Use the bar diagram to help you
determine how many miles Jeff hikes.
How many $\frac{1}{4}$ hours are in 1 hour?
How far does Jeff hike in 1 hour?

? miles

| $\frac{1}{4}$ hour | $\frac{1}{4}$ hour | $\frac{1}{4}$ hour | $\frac{1}{4}$ hour |

$\frac{1}{2}$ mile

<u>4; 2 miles</u>

B Complete the table for Jeff's hike.

Distance (mi)	$\frac{1}{2}$	1	$1\frac{1}{2}$	2	4
Time (h)	$\frac{1}{4}$	$\frac{1}{2}$	$\frac{3}{4}$	1	2

C Complete the bar diagram to help you
determine how far Lisa hikes. How
many miles does she hike in one hour?

2 miles

| $\frac{1}{6}$ hour | $\frac{1}{6}$ hour | $\frac{1}{6}$ hour | $\frac{1}{6}$ hour | $\frac{1}{6}$ hour | $\frac{1}{6}$ hour |

2 miles

$\frac{1}{3}$ mile

D Complete the table for Lisa's hike.

Distance (mi)	$\frac{1}{3}$	$\frac{2}{3}$	1	2	4
Time (h)	$\frac{1}{6}$	$\frac{1}{3}$	$\frac{1}{2}$	1	2

REFLECT

1a. How did you find Jeff's distance for $\frac{3}{4}$ hour?

Sample answer: Multiply $\frac{1}{2}$ mile by 3.

1b. Which hiker walks farther in one hour? What does this tell you about the
speeds at which they each hike?

Both hikers walk 2 miles in 1 hour, so they are hiking at the same speed.

© Houghton Mifflin Harcourt Publishing Company

A ratio is used to compare two quantities. When these quantities have different
units, the ratio is called a rate. Ratios and rates can be expressed as fractions.
When a rate has a denominator of 1, it is called a **unit rate**. To find a unit rate,
divide the numerator by the denominator.

Sometimes rates are expressed as complex fractions. A **complex fraction** is a
fraction that has a fraction as its numerator, denominator, or both. To simplify a
complex fraction, use what you know about dividing rational numbers and divide
the fraction in the numerator by the fraction in the denominator.

$$\frac{\frac{a}{b}}{\frac{c}{d}} = \frac{a}{b} \div \frac{c}{d} = \frac{a}{b} \times \frac{d}{c}$$

2 EXAMPLE Finding Unit Rates

While remodeling his kitchen, Arthur paints the cabinets. He estimates
that he paints 30 square feet every half-hour. How many square feet
does Arthur paint per hour?

Step 1: Find Arthur's rate for painting the cabinets.

$$\frac{30 \text{ square feet}}{\frac{1}{2} \text{ hour}}$$

Step 2: Find the unit rate.

$\frac{30}{\frac{1}{2}} = 30 \div \frac{1}{2}$ *Rewrite the fraction.*

$= \frac{30}{1} \times \frac{2}{1}$ *To divide, multiply by the reciprocal.*

$= \underline{\quad 60 \quad}$ *Multiply to find the unit rate.*

Arthur paints <u>60</u> square feet per hour

TRY THIS!

2a. Paige mows $\frac{1}{6}$ acre in $\frac{1}{4}$ hour. How many acres does Paige mow per hour?

$\frac{1}{6} \div \frac{1}{4} = \frac{1}{6} \times \frac{4}{1} = \frac{4}{6} = \frac{2}{3}$; $\frac{2}{3}$ acre per hour

REFLECT

2b. How could you find the unit rate
for **2a** by using a table? Complete
the table.

Acres	$\frac{1}{6}$	$\frac{1}{3}$	$\frac{1}{2}$	$\frac{2}{3}$
Time (h)	$\frac{1}{4}$	$\frac{1}{2}$	$\frac{3}{4}$	1

Continue the pattern in the table to find the number of acres that Paige

mows in 1 hour.

© Houghton Mifflin Harcourt Publishing Company

Notes

Questioning Strategies

- Which container seems to be leaking faster? Answers will vary, but it should be noted that it is difficult to determine the answer by only using the fractions.

- How can you determine for sure which container is leaking faster? Find and compare the unit rates.

Teaching Strategies

Encourage students to determine what the label on the unit rate will be (gallons per hour) before setting up the complex fraction. The label will help students know to use gallons for the numerator and hours for the denominator.

CLOSE

Essential Question

How do you find and compare unit rates?

Possible answer: To find a unit rate, divide the numerator of the rate by its denominator. To compare rates with the same units, find the unit rates, and compare the numerators.

Summarize

Have students write a complex fraction in their journals, and explain how to simplify it. Encourage students to describe both of the following steps separately: (1) express the complex fraction as division of fractions, and (2) express division as multiplication of the reciprocal.

PRACTICE

Where skills are taught	Where skills are practiced
1 EXPLORE	EX. 1
2 EXAMPLE	EXS. 2–11
3 EXAMPLE	EXS. 12–13

3 EXAMPLE Comparing Unit Rates

Two containers filled with water are leaking. Container A leaks at a rate of $\frac{2}{3}$ gallon every $\frac{1}{4}$ hour. Container B leaks at a rate of $\frac{3}{4}$ gallon every $\frac{1}{3}$ hour. Determine which container is leaking water more rapidly.

Find the unit rate for container A.

$$\frac{\frac{2}{3}}{\frac{1}{4}} = \frac{2}{3} \div \frac{1}{4} = \frac{2}{3} \times \frac{4}{1} = \frac{8}{3} = 2\frac{2}{3} \text{ gallons per hour}$$

Find the unit rate for container B.

$$\frac{\frac{3}{4}}{\frac{1}{3}} = \frac{3}{4} \div \frac{1}{3} = \frac{3}{4} \times \frac{3}{1} = \frac{9}{4} = 2\frac{1}{4} \text{ gallons per hour}$$

Compare the unit rates.

Compare the whole-number parts of the numbers.

$$\underline{\ \ 2\ \ } = \underline{\ \ 2\ \ } \quad \text{The whole number parts are equal.}$$

Compare the fractional parts.

Find a common denominator by multiplying the denominators.

$$\underline{\ 3\ } \times \underline{\ 4\ } = \underline{\ 12\ }$$

$$\frac{2}{3} = \frac{8}{12} \qquad \frac{1}{4} = \frac{3}{12}$$

$$\frac{8}{12} \text{ is } \boxed{\text{greater than}}/\text{less than } \frac{3}{12}$$

Therefore, $2\frac{2}{3}$ is $\boxed{\text{greater than}}$/less than $2\frac{1}{4}$.

Container ___**A**___ is leaking more rapidly.

TRY THIS!

3a. Two liquid storage containers are being filled. Liquid enters the first container at a rate of $\frac{2}{3}$ gallon per $\frac{1}{4}$ minute. Liquid pours into the second storage container at a rate of $\frac{3}{5}$ gallon per $\frac{1}{6}$ minute. Determine which container is being filled faster.

First container: $\frac{2}{3} \div \frac{1}{4} = \frac{2}{3} \times \frac{4}{1} = \frac{8}{3} = 2\frac{2}{3}$; **$2\frac{2}{3}$ gallons per minute; Second**

container: $\frac{3}{5} \div \frac{1}{6} = \frac{3}{5} \times \frac{6}{1} = \frac{18}{5} = 3\frac{3}{5}$; **$3\frac{3}{5}$ gallons per minute; the second**

container is being filled faster.

REFLECT

3b. How do you know which units to use as the numerator in 3a?

The rate is gallons per minute, so "gallons" is the numerator.

PRACTICE

1. Brandon enters bike races. He bikes $8\frac{1}{2}$ miles every $\frac{1}{2}$ hour. Complete the table to find how far Brandon bikes for each time interval.

Distance (mi)	$8\frac{1}{2}$	17	$25\frac{1}{2}$	34	$42\frac{1}{2}$
Time (h)	$\frac{1}{2}$	1	$1\frac{1}{2}$	2	$2\frac{1}{2}$

Simplify each complex fraction.

2. $\frac{\frac{3}{4}}{\frac{2}{3}} = \ \underline{1\frac{1}{8}}$ **3.** $\frac{\frac{1}{2}}{\frac{5}{8}} = \ \underline{\frac{4}{5}}$ **4.** $\frac{\frac{4}{5}}{\frac{2}{3}} = \ \underline{1\frac{1}{5}}$ **5.** $\frac{\frac{6}{7}}{\frac{1}{7}} = \ \underline{6}$

Find each unit rate.

6. Julio walks $3\frac{1}{2}$ miles in $1\frac{1}{4}$ hours.

   $2\frac{4}{5}$ miles per hour

7. Kenny reads $\frac{5}{8}$ page in $\frac{2}{3}$ minute.

   $\frac{15}{16}$ page per minute

8. Marcia uses $\frac{3}{4}$ cup sugar when she halves the recipe.

   $1\frac{1}{2}$ cups per recipe

9. Sandra tiles $\frac{5}{8}$ square yards in $\frac{1}{3}$ hour.

   $3\frac{3}{4}$ square yards per hour

The information for two cell phone companies is given.

On Call	Talk Time
3.5 hours: $10	$\frac{1}{2}$ hour: $1.25

10. What is the unit rate for On Call?

   about $2.86 per hour

11. What is the unit rate for Talk Time?

   $2.50 per hour

12. Determine which of the companies offers the best deal. Explain your answer.

   Talk Time; their rate per hour is lower.

13. What if? Another company offers a rate of $0.05 per minute.

   a. How would you find the unit rate per hour?

     Multiply 0.05 times 60 because there are 60 minutes in 1 hour.

   b. Is this a better deal than On Call or Talk Time?

     The unit rate is $3 per hour, so it is not a better deal.

Proportional Relationships, Tables, and Equations

Essential question: *How can you use tables and equations to identify and describe proportional relationships?*

© Houghton Mifflin Harcourt Publishing Company

COMMON CORE Standards for Mathematical Content

CC.7.RP.2a Decide whether two quantities are in a proportional relationship, e.g., by testing for equivalent ratios in a table or graphing on a coordinate plane and observing whether the graph is a straight line through the origin.

CC.7.RP.2b Identify the constant of proportionality (unit rate) in tables, graphs, equations, diagrams, and verbal descriptions of proportional relationships.

CC.7.RP.2c Represent proportional relationships by equations.

CC.7.RP.3 Use proportional relationships to solve multistep ratio and percent problems.

Vocabulary

proportional relationship

constant of proportionality

Prerequisites

Writing equations

Math Background

Proportionality implies a constant relationship between two quantities. The increase or decrease in the value of one of the quantities leads to a corresponding change in the other. The relationship can be seen in a table, where the ratio of the corresponding quantities is equivalent for all pairs of numbers. The relationship between the two quantities can be written in an equation as a variable equal to a constant multiple of another variable, or $y = ax$, where a is the constant of proportionality.

INTRODUCE

Have students use a given table of values that represents a unit rate such as $4 per hour. For each corresponding pair of values, have students find the unit rate of dollars per hour. Ask students how they found their ratio. They will probably say they multiplied or divided. Tell students that they will learn about these types of proportional relationships and how to represent them.

TEACH

1 EXPLORE

Questioning Strategies

- Why did you choose division? **The total time given is 3 seconds. To find how far the tortoise travels in 1 second, you need to divide the total into 3 equal parts.**

- Why are all of the ratios equal in simplest terms? **They are equal because the relationship is proportional.**

Technology

Have students use spreadsheets to find the ratio of distance to time for each column in the spreadsheet. Have students explain how they could use this ratio and the spreadsheet to continue the table.

2 EXAMPLE

Questioning Strategies

- How is the ratio related to the unit rate? **The ratio is the unit rate.**

- What do you know about the common ratio if the relationship is proportional? **The common ratio is constant.**

MATHEMATICAL PRACTICE **Highlighting the Standards**

This Example is an opportunity to address Standard 7 (Look for and make use of structure.). Students use this table to draw conclusions about a proportional relationship. They conclude that a relationship between two quantities is proportional if the ratio between the two quantities remains constant.

Name _____ Class _____ Date _____

2-2

Proportional Relationships, Tables, and Equations

COMMON CORE

CC.7RP.2a
CC.7RP.2b
CC.7RP.2c
CC.7RP.3

Essential question: *How can you use tables and equations to identify and describe proportional relationships?*

1 EXPLORE   Discovering Proportional Relationships

A giant tortoise moves at a slow but steady pace. It takes the giant tortoise 3 seconds to travel 10.5 inches.

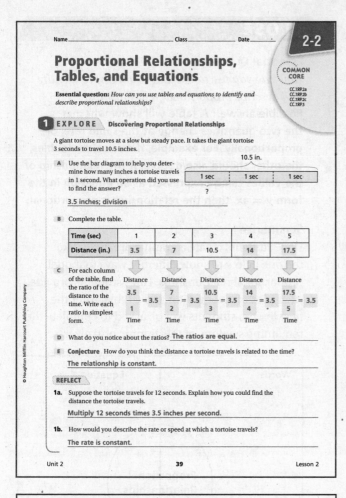

A Use the bar diagram to help you determine how many inches a tortoise travels in 1 second. What operation did you use to find the answer?

10.5 in.

1 sec	1 sec	1 sec
?		

3.5 inches; division

B Complete the table.

Time (sec)	1	2	3	4	5
Distance (in.)	3.5	7	10.5	14	17.5

C For each column of the table, find the ratio of the distance to the time. Write each ratio in simplest form.

$\dfrac{\text{Distance}}{\text{Time}} = \dfrac{3.5}{1} = 3.5$ $\dfrac{\text{Distance}}{\text{Time}} = \dfrac{7}{2} = 3.5$ $\dfrac{\text{Distance}}{\text{Time}} = \dfrac{10.5}{3} = 3.5$ $\dfrac{\text{Distance}}{\text{Time}} = \dfrac{14}{4} = 3.5$ $\dfrac{\text{Distance}}{\text{Time}} = \dfrac{17.5}{5} = 3.5$

D What do you notice about the ratios? The ratios are equal.

E **Conjecture** How do you think the distance a tortoise travels is related to the time?

The relationship is constant.

REFLECT

1a. Suppose the tortoise travels for 12 seconds. Explain how you could find the distance the tortoise travels.

Multiply 12 seconds times 3.5 inches per second.

1b. How would you describe the rate or speed at which a tortoise travels?

The rate is constant.

A **proportional relationship** is a relationship between two quantities in which the ratio of one quantity to the other quantity is constant. A giant tortoise can live as long as 150 years. One reason these reptiles live so long is their slow heart rate. A giant tortoise's heart beats only 6 times per minute. The giant tortoise's heart rate is an example of a proportional relationship. The ratio of the number of heart beats to the number of minutes is 6.

2 EXAMPLE   Identifying Proportional Relationships

Alberto types 45 words per minute. Is the relationship between the number of words and the number of minutes a proportional relationship? Why or why not?

A Complete the table.

Time (min)	1	2	3	4	5
Number of Words	45	90	135	180	225

B Complete the ratios.

$\dfrac{\text{Number of Words}}{\text{Time}} = \dfrac{45}{1} = \dfrac{90}{2} = \dfrac{135}{3} = \dfrac{180}{4} = \dfrac{225}{5} = 45$

The ratios are _____constant_____.

The *common ratio* is _____45_____.

So, the relationship is _____proportional_____.

TRY THIS!

2a. The table shows the distance Allison drove on one day of her vacation. Is the relationship between the distance and the time a proportional relationship? Why or why not?

Time (h)	1	2	3	4	5
Distance (mi)	65	120	195	220	300

No; the ratios are not equal.

REFLECT

2b. Do you think Allison drove at a constant speed for the entire trip? Why or why not?

No; the ratio of distance to time is not constant.

Questioning Strategies

- How does the common ratio relate to the equation? **The common ratio is the coefficient of x, or a.**

- How do you assign what each variable represents? **Assuming the constant is greater than 1, the smaller value will be x and the other value will be y.**

Avoid Common Errors

Students may confuse what the variables in the equation represent. Have students substitute one of the values from the table into the equation to see if the answer is the corresponding value in the table. If so, the students correctly selected the variables representing the values.

CLOSE

Essential Question

How can you use tables and equations to identify and describe proportional relationships?
Possible answer: A table will show whether the two quantities change at the same rate, or proportionally. For example, if one value doubles, the other should also double. If the relationship of the values can be expressed as an equation in the form $y = ax$, then the relationship is proportional.

Summarize

Have students create a graphic organizer like the one below to show different ways to model proportional relationships. Have students provide examples of an equation and a table. After the next lesson, students will be asked to complete the remaining sections of the graphic organizer.

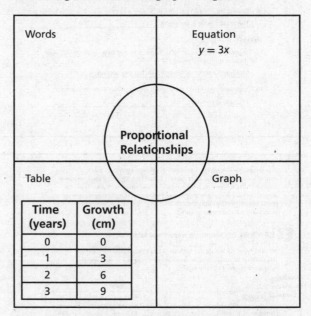

Words	Equation $y = 3x$

Proportional Relationships

Table	Graph

Time (years)	Growth (cm)
0	0
1	3
2	6
3	9

PRACTICE

Where skills are taught	Where skills are practiced
1 EXPLORE	EXS. 1–4
2 EXAMPLE	EXS. 1–4, 10
3 EXAMPLE	EXS. 5–11

The equation for a proportional relationship has a special form. If the relationship between x and y is a proportional relationship, then the equation for the relationship may be written as $y = ax$, where a is a positive number. The constant a is called the **constant of proportionality**.

$$y = ax$$
constant of proportionality

3 EXAMPLE Writing an Equation for a Proportional Relationship

Two pounds of cashews cost $5, 3 pounds of cashews cost $7.50, and 8 pounds of cashews cost $20. Show that the relationship between the number of pounds of cashews and the cost is a proportional relationship. Then write an equation for the relationship.

Make a table to find the common ratio. Then write an equation with the common ratio as the constant of proportionality.

A Complete the table.

Number of Pounds	2	3	8
Cost ($)	5	7.5	20

B Complete the ratios. $\dfrac{\text{Cost}}{\text{Number of Pounds}} = \dfrac{5}{2} = \dfrac{7.5}{3} = \dfrac{20}{8} = 2.5$

The common ratio is _____2.5_____

C To write an equation, first tell what the variables represent.

Let x represent the number of pounds of cashews.

Let y represent the cost in dollars.

Use the common ratio as the constant of proportionality.

So, the equation for the relationship is _____$y = 2.5x$_____

REFLECT

3a. How can you use substitution to check your equation?

Multiply the number of pounds by 2.5 to see if it equals the cost.

3b. What is the unit cost (unit rate) for the cashews? How does the unit cost appear in your equation?

$2.50; it is the constant of proportionality.

3c. How can you use your equation to find the cost of 6 pounds of cashews?

Substitute 6 for x and solve for y.

PRACTICE

Tell whether the relationship is a proportional relationship. If so, give the constant of proportionality.

1.

Number of Minutes	3	4	5	6	7
Number of Seconds	180	240	300	360	420

proportional; 60

2.

Time (h)	1	2	3	4	5
Biking Distance (mi)	12	26	36	44	50

not proportional

3. Naomi reads 9 pages in 27 minutes, 12 pages in 36 minutes, 15 pages in 45 minutes, and 50 pages in 150 minutes.

proportional; 3

4. A scuba diver descends at a constant rate of 8 feet per minute.

proportional; 8

Write an equation for the relationship. Tell what the variables represent.

5. It takes Li 1 hour to drive 65 miles, 2 hours to drive 130 miles, and 3 hours to drive 195 miles.

x is number of hours; y is miles

driven; $y = 65x$

6. There are 3.9 milligrams of calcium in each ounce of cooked chicken.

x is number of ounces; y is

milligrams of calcium; $y = 3.9x$

7.

Gallons of Gasoline	3	4	5	6
Total Cost ($)	9.45	12.60	15.75	18.90

x is gallons of gasoline; y is total

cost; $y = 3.15x$

8.

Cups of Batter	2	6	8	12
Number of Muffins	5	15	20	30

x is cups of batter; y is number of

muffins; $y = 2.5x$

Information on three car rental companies is given.

9. Write an equation that gives the cost y of renting a car for x days from Rent-All.

$y = 18.5x$

Rent-All				
Days	3	4	5	6
Total Cost ($)	55.50	74.00	92.50	111.00

A-1 Rentals	Car Town
The cost y of renting a car for x days is given by $y = 22.5x$.	The cost of renting a car from us is just $19.25 per day!

10. What is the cost per day of renting a car from A-1?

$22.50

11. Which company offers the best deal? Why?

Rent-All has the best deal because it has the lowest rate per day ($18.50).

Proportional Relationships and Graphs

Essential question: *How can you use graphs to represent and analyze proportional relationships?*

Standards for Mathematical Content

CC.7.RP.2a Decide whether two quantities are in a proportional relationship, e.g., by testing for equivalent ratios in a table or graphing on a coordinate plane and observing whether the graph is a straight line through the origin.

CC.7.RP.2b Identify the constant of proportionality (unit rate) in tables, graphs, equations, diagrams, and verbal descriptions of proportional relationships.

CC.7.RP.2d Explain what a point (x, y) on the graph of a proportional relationship means in terms of the situation, with special attention to the points $(0, 0)$ and $(1, r)$ where r is the unit rate.

CC.7.RP.3 Use proportional relationships to solve multistep ratio and percent problems.

Prerequisites

Patterns in tables

Proportions

Graphing in coordinate plane

Math Background

Students graph points in the coordinate plane to represent data. The position along the x-axis represents a quantity and the position along the y-axis represents a corresponding quantity. When the quantities relate in such a way that they form a constant ratio, they are proportional. The proportional points form a line that go through the origin.

INTRODUCE

Have students work in groups. Give each group a different proportional relationship such as 30 pages per minute. Have them graph the relationships on a coordinate plane. Then display the graphs. Have students compare the graphs, verifying that all the points form a line through the origin.

TEACH

 EXPLORE

Questioning Strategies

- What do the x-coordinates represent? **the number of minutes**

- How does the value of the constant of proportionality affect the graph? **It affects the direction (upward or downward) and the steepness of the graph.**

Avoid Common Errors

Students may forget that the graph of a proportional relationship must go through the origin. They may think that any straight line represents a proportional relationship. Have students highlight the origin on the coordinate plane to remind them of this definitive characteristic.

2 EXAMPLE

Questioning Strategies

- What does the y-coordinate represent? **It represents the total charge.**

- How is the $5 entrance fee represented on the graph? **It is the y-intercept.**

MATHEMATICAL PRACTICE | **Highlighting the Standards**

This Example is an opportunity to address Standard 4 (Model with mathematics.). Students use tables to model a relationship between corresponding real-world proportional values. Then students use equations to generally model the proportional relationship. Finally, students use graphs to visually model the proportional relationship. In this way, students are able to use mathematical modeling to represent real-world situations.

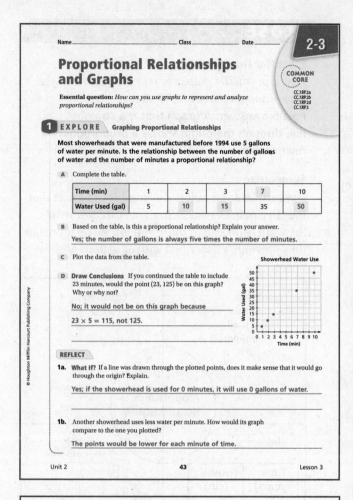

Name_____ Class_____ Date_____

2-3

Proportional Relationships and Graphs

COMMON CORE

CC.7.RP.2a
CC.7.RP.2b
CC.7.RP.2d
CC.7.RP.3

Essential question: How can you use graphs to represent and analyze proportional relationships?

1 EXPLORE Graphing Proportional Relationships

Most showerheads that were manufactured before 1994 use 5 gallons of water per minute. Is the relationship between the number of gallons of water and the number of minutes a proportional relationship?

A Complete the table.

Time (min)	1	2	3	7	10
Water Used (gal)	5	10	15	35	50

B Based on the table, is this a proportional relationship? Explain your answer.

Yes; the number of gallons is always five times the number of minutes.

C Plot the data from the table.

D **Draw Conclusions** If you continued the table to include 23 minutes, would the point (23, 125) be on this graph? Why or why not?

No; it would not be on this graph because

23 × 5 = 115, not 125.

Showerhead Water Use

REFLECT

1a. **What If?** If a line was drawn through the plotted points, does it make sense that it would go through the origin? Explain.

Yes; if the showerhead is used for 0 minutes, it will use 0 gallons of water.

1b. Another showerhead uses less water per minute. How would its graph compare to the one you plotted?

The points would be lower for each minute of time.

Unit 2   43   Lesson 3

In addition to using a table to determine if a relationship is proportional, you also can use a graph. A relationship is a proportional relationship if its graph is a straight line through the origin.

2 EXAMPLE Identifying Proportional Relationships

An Internet café charges a one-time $5 service fee and then $2 for every hour of use. Is this relationship a proportional relationship?

A Complete the table.

Time (h)	1	2	5	6	8
Total Cost ($)	7	9	15	17	21

B Plot the data from the table and connect the points with a line.

C The graph of the data is a straight line

The line does (does not) go through the origin.

So, the relationship is not a proportional relationship

Internet Café Charges

TRY THIS!

2a. Plot the data from the table and connect the points with a line.

Canoe Rental (h)	2	5	8	10
Total Cost ($)	5	11	17	21

2b. Is this a proportional relationship? Explain.

No; it is not proportional because the line that goes

through the points does not go through the origin.

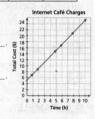

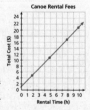

Canoe Rental Fees

© Houghton Mifflin Harcourt Publishing Company

Unit 2   44   Lesson 3

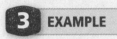
Questioning Strategies

- How can you calculate the constant of proportionality? **Choose a point and divide its *y*-coordinate by its *x*-coordinate.**

- Why do graphs of proportional relationships always go through the origin? **In proportional relationships, one of one quantity would result in none of the other, represented by the point (0, 0).**

Teaching Strategies

Allow students to see how changes in the constant of proportionality affect the graph of the relationship. Have groups of sudents complete tables and compare graphs for different rates. Students will see that a constant of proportionality results in a steeper line.

CLOSE

Essential Question

How can you use graphs to represent and analyze proportional relationships?
Possible answer: A graph that is a straight line through the origin shows a proportional relationship.

Summarize

Have students complete the graphic organizer that they began in Lesson 2. Students can now write the words and sketch the graph for the relationship they previously described with equations and tables.

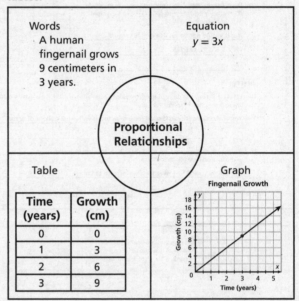

Words	Equation
A human fingernail grows 9 centimeters in 3 years.	$y = 3x$

Proportional Relationships

Table

Time (years)	Growth (cm)
0	0
1	3
2	6
3	9

Graph

Fingernail Growth

PRACTICE

Where skills are taught	Where skills are practiced
① EXPLORE	EXS. 1–2, 5
② EXAMPLE	EXS. 3–5
③ EXAMPLE	EXS. 6–9

You have seen that the equation of a proportional relationship may be written as $y = ax$, where a is a positive number. The constant of proportionality, a, tells you how steep the graph of the relationship is. The greater the value of a, the steeper the line.

3 EXAMPLE Analyzing Graphs

The graph shows the relationship between time in years and the number of centimeters a fingernail grows.

Fingernail Growth

Growth (cm) vs Time (years)

A What does the point (3, 9) represent?

A human fingernail grows 9 centimeters in 3 years.

B What is the constant of proportionality? **3**

C Write an equation for the relationship. **$y = 3x$**

REFLECT

3a. What does the point (0, 0) on the graph represent?

Fingernails grow 0 centimeters in 0 years.

3b. What is the rate at which a fingernail grows? How does this relate to the constant of proportionality?

3 cm per year; it is the same as the constant of proportionality.

PRACTICE

Complete each table. Tell whether the relationship is a proportional relationship. Explain why or why not.

1. A student reads 65 pages per hour.

Time (h)	3	5	9	10
Pages	195	325	585	650

proportional; the number of pages is always 65 times the number of hours.

2. A babysitter makes $7.50 per hour.

Time (h)	2	3	5	8
Earnings	15	22.50	37.50	60

proportional; earnings are always 7.5 times the number of hours.

Tell whether the relationship is a proportional relationship. Explain why or why not.

3.

Chores

Number of Chores vs Age (years)

not proportional; the line will not pass through the origin.

4.

Movie Rentals

Cost ($) vs Number of Movies

proportional; the line will pass through the origin.

5. A train travels at 72 miles per hour. Will the graph of the train's rate of speed show that the relationship between the number of miles traveled and the number of hours is a proportional relationship? Explain.

Yes, the graph will show a proportional relationship because the data for the number of miles traveled and the number of hours will form a straight line and pass through the origin.

The graph shows the relationship between time and the distance run by two horses.

6. How long does it take each horse to run 1 mile?

A: 8 minutes, B: 5 minutes

7. What does the point (0, 0) represent?

At 0 minutes, or the start of the race, each horse has run 0 miles.

Horse Training

Distance (mi) vs Time (min)

8. Write an equation for the relationship between time and distance.

A: $y = \frac{1}{8}x$, B: $y = \frac{1}{5}x$

9. Draw a line on the graph representing a horse that is faster than each of these.

Sample graph shown.

Apply Percents

Essential question: *How do you use percents to solve problems?*

COMMON CORE Standards for Mathematical Content

CC.7.RP.3 Use proportional relationships to solve multistep ratio and percent problems.

Vocabulary

simple interest

percent increase/decrease

Prerequisites

Finding percents

Translating words into mathematical notation

Math Background

Percent means out of 100, so any percent is equivalent to that number of hundredths. To find a percent of a number, you can write the percent as a decimal and multiply the number by 100. Applying percents is a commonly used skill in real-world situations, such as simple interest, tax, gratuities, commissions, fees, and percent error.

INTRODUCE

Bring an item that you recently purchased at a store and the receipt for that purchase. Discuss with the class that the item price is the subtotal and the tax added to the subtotal is a percentage of the subtotal. See if students know what the tax rate is. Explain to students that they will learn how to solve a variety of percent problems such as these.

TEACH

1 EXPLORE

Questioning Strategies

- Is a tip added to or subtracted from the bill? **added to the bill**

- What are two ways you could calculate the total bill? **You can multiply $40 by 0.15 to get the amount of the tip and then add the tip to $40, or you can multiply the bill total by 1.15.**

Avoid Common Errors

Students may forget to add the tip to the original bill to find the total cost. Remind students to review their answer in the context of the situation. The total amount including the tip should be greater than the original bill. If not, students should check their work.

2 EXAMPLE

Questioning Strategies

- To find simple interest on an original amount, what two pieces of information do you need? **the interest rate and the number of years**

- In this case, a large interest rate is good because it is money earned. In what situation would a large interest rate be considered bad? **When you repay a loan, you have to pay the original amount borrowed plus interest. In that case a large interest rate may be considered bad because it is money to be paid, not earned.**

> :::MATHEMATICAL **Highlighting**
> :::PRACTICE **the Standards**
>
> This Example is an opportunity to address Standard 1 (Make sense of problems and persevere in solving them.) Real-world understanding of percents in concepts such as tips and simple interest help students make sense of the mathematical problems set before them. With discussions and examples of how these situations really occur, students can be more successful with them.

Name_____ Class_____ Date_____

2-4

COMMON CORE

CC.7.RP.3

Applying Percents

Essential question: *How do you use percents to solve problems?*

1 **EXPLORE** Finding Total Cost

The bill at a restaurant for the Smith family came to $40. They want to leave a 15% tip. What is the total cost of the meal?

A Find the amount of the tip. Use a bar model.

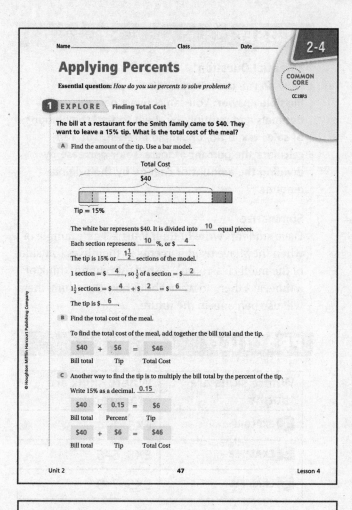

Total Cost

$40

Tip = 15%

The white bar represents $40. It is divided into ___10___ equal pieces.

Each section represents ___10___ %, or $ ___4___

The tip is 15% or ___$1\frac{1}{2}$___ sections of the model.

1 section = $ ___4___, so $\frac{1}{2}$ of a section = $ ___2___

$1\frac{1}{2}$ sections = $ ___4___ + $ ___2___ = $ ___6___

The tip is $ ___6___.

B Find the total cost of the meal.

To find the total cost of the meal, add together the bill total and the tip.

$40	+	$6	=	$46
Bill total		Tip		Total Cost

C Another way to find the tip is to multiply the bill total by the percent of the tip.

Write 15% as a decimal. ___0.15___

$40	×	0.15	=	$6
Bill total		Percent		Tip

$40	+	$6	=	$46
Bill total		Tip		Total Cost

Unit 2   47   Lesson 4

REFLECT

1a. How could the Smith family use mental math to calculate the tip?

Sample answer: To find 10%, move the decimal point in 40 one place to the
left (4). Then, 5% is half of that, which is 2. So 15% is 4 + 2 = $6.

TRY THIS!

1b. Sharon wants to buy a coat that costs $20. The rate of sales tax is 5%. How much is the sales tax? What is her total cost for the coat?

$1; $21

When you place money in a savings account, your money usually earns interest. When you borrow money, you must pay back the original amount of the loan plus interest. **Simple interest** is a fixed percent of the *principal*. The **principal** is the original amount of money deposited or borrowed.

2 **EXPLORE** Finding Simple Interest

Anita deposits $320 into an account that earns 4% simple interest per year. What is the total amount in the account after 3 years?

A Find the amount of interest earned in one year.
Then calculate the amount of interest for 3 years.
Write 4% as a decimal. ___0.04___
Complete the table.

Initial Deposit ($)	×	Interest Rate	=	Interest for 1 year ($)
320	×	0.04	=	12.8

Interest for 1 year ($)	×	3	=	Interest for 3 years ($)
12.8	×	3	=	38.4

B Add the interest for 3 years to the initial deposit to find the total amount in her account after 3 years.

320	+	38.40	=	$358.40
Deposit		Interest		Total

TRY THIS!

2a. **What If?** Anita decides to leave her money in the account. How much will she have in the account after 10 years?

$448

Unit 2   48   Lesson 4

3 EXAMPLE

Questioning Strategies

- What must you determine first in a percent change problem? **the amount and direction of change**

- How do you know if it is a percent increase or decrease? **Percent increase makes the value greater, while percent decrease makes it less.**

Differentiated Instruction

Use cooperative learning to solve percent increase and decrease problems. Start with a problem, and have each person complete one step in the process. Have students exchange roles so each person has a chance to complete each step at least once. This emphasizes that finding percent increase or decrease is a multi-step process.

CLOSE

Essential Question

How do you use percents to solve problems?
Possible answer: You can convert percents to decimals and multiply by them to find the amount of sales tax, a tip, or simple interest. You can calculate the percent of increase or decrease by dividing the amount of change by the original amount.

Summarize

Have students write in their journals an example of when they have used percents in their lives (outside of the math classroom). If students cannot think of a time, ask them to write about how they think they will use percents in the future.

PRACTICE

Where skills are taught	Where skills are practiced
1 EXPLORE	EXS. 1–4
2 EXAMPLE	EXS. 5–6
3 EXAMPLE	EXS. 7–9

2b. Aaron borrows $400 on a 4-year loan. He is charged 5% simple interest per year. How much interest is he charged in the 4 years? What is the total amount Aaron has to pay back?

$80; $480

2c. **What If?** What if Aaron took out a 6-year loan? How much interest would he have to pay back?

$120

Percents can be used to describe an amount of change. **Percent increase** and **percent decrease** show the amount of change in a value. Percent increase describes how much the original amount increases. Percent decrease describes how much the original amount decreases.

$$\text{percent of change} = \frac{\text{amount of change}}{\text{original amount}}$$

3 EXAMPLE   Finding Percent of Change

The price of a pair of shoes increased from $52 to $64. What is the percent increase?

A   Find the amount of change.

64	−	52	=	12
Greater Value		Lesser Value		Amount of Change

B   Find the percent change. Round to the nearest percent.

$$\text{percent of change} = \frac{\text{amount of change}}{\text{original amount}} = \frac{12}{52} = \underline{0.231} \times 100 = \underline{23}\ \%$$

TRY THIS!

3a. The number of students at an elementary school in 2001 was 654. In 2007, there were 520 students. What is the percent decrease in the number of students?

20% decrease

REFLECT

3b. Why will the percent of change always be represented by a positive number?
Sample answer: The greater value minus the lesser value will

always be a positive number.

3c. What does a 100% increase mean?
Sample answer: A 100% increase is an increase equal to the original amount

or, the value doubled.

PRACTICE

1. A ticket to a play costs $50. There is a 5% transaction fee. What is the total cost of the ticket?

$52.50

2. A taxi ride costs $32. Paulie gives the driver a 15% tip. What is the total amount Paulie gives the driver?

$36.80

3. Emily earns $75 per day plus a commission. Her commission is 15%. She sells $600 worth of furniture. How much does she earn for the day?

$165

4. Martin finds a shirt for $20 at a store. The sign says it is 10% off the original price. Martin must also pay 8.5% sales tax. What is the cost of the shirt before and after the sales tax?

$18; $19.53

5. Joe borrowed $2,000 from the bank at a rate of 7% simple interest per year. How much interest did he pay in 5 years?

$700

6. You have $550 in a savings account that earns 3% simple interest each year. How much will be in your account in 10 years?

$715

7. **Error Analysis** A store makes a profit of $1,000 in January. In February sales are up 25%, but in March sales are down 25%. The store manager says that the profit for March is still $1,000. What is his error? What is the actual profit for March?

Feb. sales are up 25% of $1,000, or $1,250, but sales for March are

down 25% of $1,250, not 25% of $1,000. The profit for March is

$1,250 − $312.50, or $937.50.

8. Percent error calculations are used to determine how close to the true values, or how accurate, experimental values really are. The formula is similar to finding percent of change.

$$\text{percent error} = \frac{\text{amount of change}}{\text{actual value}} \times 100$$

In chemistry, Bob records the volume of a liquid as 13.3 ml. The actual volume is 13.6 ml. What is his percent error? Round to the nearest percent.

$\frac{0.3}{13.6} \times 100 = 2.2; 2\%$

9. Complete the table.

Item	Scooter	Bike
Original Price	$45	$110
New Price	$56	$96
Percent Change	24%	13%
Increase or Decrease	Increase	Decrease

Problem Solving Connections
Car or Motorcycle?

 COMMON CORE **Standards for Mathematical Content**

CC.7.NS.3 Solve real-world and mathematical problems involving the four operations with rational numbers.

CC.7.RP.1 Compute unit rates associated with ratios of fractions, including ratios of lengths, areas and other quantities measured in like or different units.

CC.7.RP.2a Decide whether two quantities are in a proportional relationship, e.g., by testing for equivalent ratios in a table or graphing on a coordinate plane and observing whether the graph is a straight line through the origin.

CC.7.RP.2b Identify the constant of proportionality (unit rate) in tables, graphs, equations, diagrams, and verbal descriptions of proportional relationships.

CC.7.RP.2c Represent proportional relationships by equations.

CC.7.RP.2d Explain what a point (x, y) on the graph of a proportional relationship means in terms of the situation, with special attention to the points $(0, 0)$ and $(1, r)$ where r is the unit rate.

CC.7.RP.3 Use proportional relationships to solve multistep ratio and percent problems.

INTRODUCE

Ask students whether they think a car or a motorcycle would win in a race against each other. Discuss what factors would contribute to the victory. Tell students that they will determine whether the fastest car or fastest motorcycle would win a ten-minute race.

TEACH

1 Find Unit Rates

Questioning Strategies
- What units will you use for speed?
  miles per minute
- Will the vehicle with the greater unit rate win? Explain. **Yes, the vehicle with the greater unit rate will win because it will go farther in any amount of time (greater number of miles per minute).**

Avoid Common Errors
Students might find the speed of the vehicles incorrectly. Remind them that speed is a rate of distance divided by time.

2 Make Tables and Write Equations

Questioning Strategies
- How can you find the constant of proportionality? **If you already know the rate you can select a column in the table and divide the distance by the corresponding time in that column.**
- How can you tell what x and y represent? **Substitute one of the pairs of numbers to see if it works in the equation. If not, the variables are reversed.**

Differentiated Instruction
Have students model the situation using counters to represent vehicles and grid paper to indicate units of distance. Have students record the distances in the table for each minute.

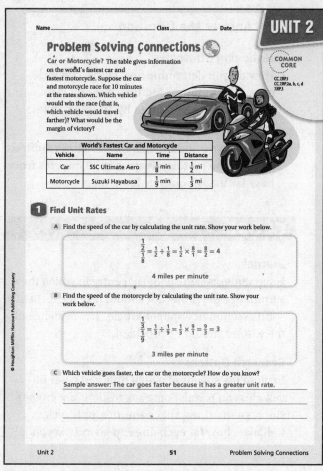

Name_____ Class_____ Date_____

Problem Solving Connections

UNIT 2

COMMON CORE
CC.7.RP.1
CC.7.RP.2a, b, c, d
7.RP.3

Car or Motorcycle? The table gives information on the world's fastest car and fastest motorcycle. Suppose the car and motorcycle race for 10 minutes at the rates shown. Which vehicle would win the race (that is, which vehicle would travel farther)? What would be the margin of victory?

World's Fastest Car and Motorcycle			
Vehicle	Name	Time	Distance
Car	SSC Ultimate Aero	$\frac{1}{8}$ min	$\frac{1}{2}$ mi
Motorcycle	Suzuki Hayabusa	$\frac{1}{9}$ min	$\frac{1}{3}$ mi

1 Find Unit Rates

A Find the speed of the car by calculating the unit rate. Show your work below.

$$\frac{\frac{1}{2}}{\frac{1}{8}} = \frac{1}{2} \div \frac{1}{8} = \frac{1}{2} \times \frac{8}{1} = \frac{8}{2} = 4$$

4 miles per minute

B Find the speed of the motorcycle by calculating the unit rate. Show your work below.

$$\frac{\frac{1}{3}}{\frac{1}{9}} = \frac{1}{3} \div \frac{1}{9} = \frac{1}{3} \times \frac{9}{1} = \frac{9}{3} = 3$$

3 miles per minute

C Which vehicle goes faster, the car or the motorcycle? How do you know?

Sample answer: The car goes faster because it has a greater unit rate.

_____

_____

© Houghton Mifflin Harcourt Publishing Company

Unit 2   51   Problem Solving Connections

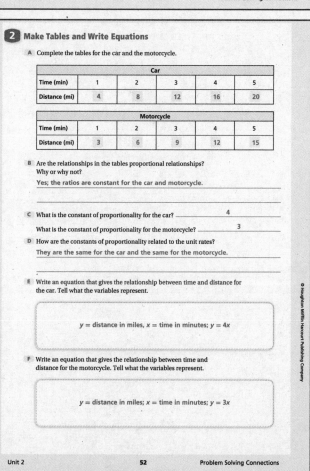

2 Make Tables and Write Equations

A Complete the tables for the car and the motorcycle.

Car					
Time (min)	1	2	3	4	5
Distance (mi)	4	8	12	16	20

Motorcycle					
Time (min)	1	2	3	4	5
Distance (mi)	3	6	9	12	15

B Are the relationships in the tables proportional relationships? Why or why not?

Yes; the ratios are constant for the car and motorcycle.

_____

C What is the constant of proportionality for the car? _____ 4

What is the constant of proportionality for the motorcycle? _____ 3

D How are the constants of proportionality related to the unit rates?

They are the same for the car and the same for the motorcycle.

_____

E Write an equation that gives the relationship between time and distance for the car. Tell what the variables represent.

y = distance in miles, x = time in minutes; $y = 4x$

F Write an equation that gives the relationship between time and distance for the motorcycle. Tell what the variables represent.

y = distance in miles; x = time in minutes; $y = 3x$

© Houghton Mifflin Harcourt Publishing Company

Unit 2   52   Problem Solving Connections

3 Make Graphs

Questioning Strategies

- What determines the steepness of the graph? The unit rate or the constant of proportionality determines the steepness of the graph.

- Can you tell by looking at the graph which vehicle wins? Explain. Yes, the steeper graph represents the vehicle that wins.

> ∴ **MATHEMATICAL PRACTICE** **Highlighting the Standards**
>
> This project is an opportunity to address Standard 3 (Construct viable arguments and critique the reasoning of others.) Students justify their reasoning for their predictions of the winning vehicle. They use rational number calculations, tables, patterns, and graphs to support and critique reasoning.

4 Answer the Question

Questioning Strategies

- How do you determine how far each vehicle goes in 10 minutes? Multiply the unit rate given in miles per minute by 10 to get miles per 10 minutes.

- How can you find the margin of victory? Subtract how far the motorcycle goes in 10 minutes from how far the car goes in 10 minutes.

CLOSE

Journal

Have students write a journal entry in which they summarize the project. It should take the form of a sports section newspaper article. The evidence of the winner should be provided.

Research Options

Explore the speeds at which different types of vehicles can travel. Some suggestions are cruise ships, submarines, space shuttles, or bicycles. Calculate how far each one can go in 10 seconds.

© Houghton Mifflin Harcourt Publishing Company

3 Make Graphs

A Use your tables and/or your equations to graph the relationship for the car and the relationship for the motorcycle. Graph both relationships on the coordinate plane at right.

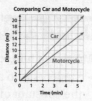

Comparing Car and Motorcycle

B How are the two graphs similar?

They are both straight lines that pass through the origin and both have a

constant rate of change.

C How are the two graphs different?

They pass through different points and do not have the same steepness.

D Do both graphs pass through the origin? Why does this make sense?

Yes; both vehicles start at 0 miles when no time has passed.

E Is it possible to tell which vehicle is faster just by glancing at the graphs? If so, how?

Yes; the steeper line represents the greater unit rate, so the car is the

faster vehicle.

F How can you use the graphs to determine the winner of the race?

Extend the graph to show distances after 10 minutes. The graph would

continue to be steeper and would show that the car drove farther.

4 Answer the Question

A Explain how to find the distance each vehicle travels in 10 minutes using your tables.

Sample answer: Continue the pattern of increasing minutes by 1

and miles per hour by 4 for the car or 3 for the motorcycle.

B Explain how to find the distance each vehicle travels in 10 minutes using your equations.

Substitute 10 for x in each equation and find y.

C Complete the table to help you find the margin of victory.

Race Summary		
Winner of race (circle one)	(Car)	Motorcycle
Loser of race (circle one)	Car	(Motorcycle)
Distance winner travels in 10 minutes	40 miles	
Distance loser travels in 10 minutes	30 miles	
Margin of victory	10 miles	

D **Extend the Ideas** Speeds of cars and motorcycles are most familiar when they are written in miles per hour (mi/h). Use these tables and proportional reasoning to find the speed of each vehicle in miles per hour.

Car				
Time (min)	1	5	10	30	60
Distance (mi)	4	20	40	120	240

60 minutes = 1 hour

Motorcycle				
Time (min)	1	5	10	30	60
Distance (mi)	3	15	30	90	180

Speed of car: _____240_____ mi/h

Speed of motorcycle: _____180_____ mi/h

COMMON CORE   CORRELATION

Standard	Items
CC.7.NS.3	1, 11
CC.7.RP.1	1, 11
CC.7.RP.2a	2, 16
CC.7.RP.2b	4, 5, 7
CC.7.RP.2c	6, 14
CC.7.RP.2d	3, 15
CC.7.RP.3	8, 9, 10, 12, 13

TEST PREP DOCTOR ⊕

Multiple Choice: Item 5

- Students who answered **A** found the reciprocal of the constant of proportionality (hours per mile).
- Students who answered **B** incorrectly read the scale of the x-axis and also found the reciprocal of the constant of proportionality.
- Students who answered **C** read the scale of the x-axis incorrectly.

Multiple Choice: Item 9

- Students who answered **B** may not have estimated 15% of $41 correctly.
- Students who answered **C** may have estimated 10% of $41, not 15%.
- Students who answered **D** found 15% correctly, but did not divide it among the friends.

Free Response: Item 11

- Students who answered **20** may have just multiplied the denominators of both fractions.
- Students who answered $\frac{1}{5}$ found the reciprocal of the unit rate (minutes per gallon).

Free Response: Item 12

- Students who answered **2%** may have found the difference, dropped the zeros from 2,000, and wrote it as a percent.
- Students who answered **4.2%** divided the change by 48,000 instead of by 50,000.
- Students who answered **4% increase** read the problem incorrectly and assumed the population grew over time.

Name _____ Class _____ Date _____

MULTIPLE CHOICE

1. Lauren jogs at a rate of 2 miles every $\frac{2}{5}$ hour. What is her unit rate?

   A. 0.4 mi/h   C. 5 mi/h

   B. 2 mi/h   D. 10 mi/h

2. The tables show the number of pages that several students read over a four-day period. Which table shows a proportional relationship?

   F.
Number of Days	1	2	3	4
Total Pages	16	24	32	40

   G.
Number of Days	1	2	3	4
Total Pages	12	24	36	48

   H.
Number of Days	1	2	3	4
Total Pages	15	20	25	30

   J.
Number of Days	1	2	3	4
Total Pages	8	16	27	36

3. An elevator moves at a constant speed of 20 feet per second. Arturo correctly graphs this proportional relationship on a coordinate plane. Which of the following points lies on Arturo's graph?

   A. (0, 20)   C. (1, 20)

   B. (20, 0)   D. (20, 1)

4. The table below shows a proportional relationship. One of the cells of the table is covered by a drop of ink. What value is covered by the ink?

Time (sec)	3	5	11	17
Distance (ft)	10.2	17	●	57.8

   F. 3.4   H. 23

   G. 18.2   J. 37.4

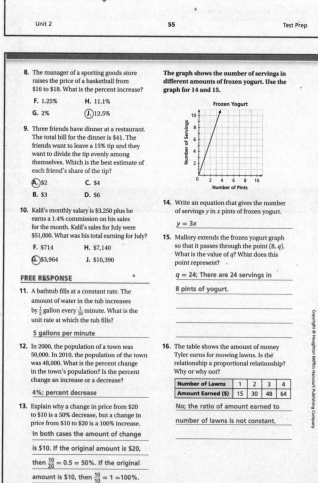

5. What is the constant of proportionality for the proportional relationship shown in the graph?

   Leah's Hike

   $y = 4x$

   A. $\frac{1}{4}$ C. 2

   B. $\frac{1}{2}$ D. 4

6. Two pounds of dried cranberries cost $5.04, 3 pounds of dried cranberries cost $7.56, and 7 pounds of dried cranberries cost $17.64. Which equation gives the total cost y of x pounds of dried cranberries?

   F. $y = 1.68x$ H. $y = 3.04x$

   G. $y = 2.52x$ J. $y = 5.04x$

7. Each yard of a fabric costs $4.35. A table shows the number of yards of fabric and the total cost of the fabric. Which of the following must be true about the data in the table?

   A. The ratio of the total cost to the number of yards is always 4.35.

   B. The ratio of the number of yards to the total cost is always 4.35.

   C. The total cost is always 4.35 greater than the number of yards.

   D. The number of yards is always 4.35 times the total cost.

8. The manager of a sporting goods store raises the price of a basketball from $16 to $18. What is the percent increase?

   F. 1.25%   H. 11.1%

   G. 2%   J. 12.5%

9. Three friends have dinner at a restaurant. The total bill for the dinner is $41. The friends want to leave a 15% tip and they want to divide the tip evenly among themselves. Which is the best estimate of each friend's share of the tip?

   A. $2   C. $4

   B. $3   D. $6

10. Kalil's monthly salary is $3,250 plus he earns a 1.4% commission on his sales for the month. Kalil's sales for July were $51,000. What was his total earning for July?

    F. $714   H. $7,140

    G. $3,964   J. $10,390

FREE RESPONSE

11. A bathtub fills at a constant rate. The amount of water in the tub increases by $\frac{1}{2}$ gallon every $\frac{1}{10}$ minute. What is the unit rate at which the tub fills?

    5 gallons per minute

12. In 2000, the population of a town was 50,000. In 2010, the population of the town was 48,000. What is the percent change in the town's population? Is the percent change an increase or a decrease?

    4%; percent decrease

13. Explain why a change in price from $20 to $10 is a 50% decrease, but a change in price from $10 to $20 is a 100% increase.

    In both cases the amount of change

    is $10. If the original amount is $20,

    then $\frac{10}{20} = 0.5 = 50\%$. If the original

    amount is $10, then $\frac{10}{10} = 1 = 100\%$.

The graph shows the number of servings in different amounts of frozen yogurt. Use the graph for 14 and 15.

Frozen Yogurt

14. Write an equation that gives the number of servings y in x pints of frozen yogurt.

    $y = 3x$

15. Mallory extends the frozen yogurt graph so that it passes through the point $(8, q)$. What is the value of q? What does this point represent?

    q = 24; There are 24 servings in

    8 pints of yogurt.

    _____

    _____

16. The table shows the amount of money Tyler earns for mowing lawns. Is the relationship a proportional relationship? Why or why not?

Number of Lawns	1	2	3	4
Amount Earned ($)	15	30	48	64

    No; the ratio of amount earned to

    number of lawns is not constant.

    _____

UNIT 3

Expressions and Equations

Unit Vocabulary

factor   (3-1)

solution set   (3-4)

UNIT 3

Expressions and Equations

Unit Focus

In this unit you will learn about algebraic expressions, equations, and inequalities. You will learn how to write expressions, equations, and inequalities to represent different real-world scenarios. You will be able to interpret the solutions to these equations and inequalities and adjust the solution sets to make sense in the given scenario. You will be able to determine the rules for when to reverse an inequality symbol when solving an inequality.

Unit at a Glance

COMMON CORE

Lesson		Standards for Mathematical Content
3-1	Algebraic Expressions	CC.7.EE.1
3-2	Rewriting Expressions	CC.7.EE.2, CC.7.RP.3
3-3	Solving Equations	CC.7.EE.4a
3-4	Solving One-Step Inequalities	CC.7.EE.4b
3-5	Solving Two-Step Inequalities	CC.7.EE.4b
3-6	Solving Problems with Expressions, Equations, and Inequalities	CC.7.EE.3
	Problem Solving Connections	
	Test Prep	

Unpacking the Common Core State Standards

Use the table to help you understand the Standards for Mathematical Content that are taught in this unit. Refer to the lessons listed after each standard for exploration and practice.

COMMON CORE Standards for Mathematical Content	What It Means For You
CC.7.RP.3 Use proportional relationships to solve multistep ratio and percent problems. Lesson 3-2	You will apply your understanding of proportional relationships to markups and markdowns.
CC.7.EE.1 Apply properties of operations as strategies to add, subtract, factor, and expand linear expressions with rational coefficients. Lesson 3-1	You will combine, multiply, and factor expressions. The Commutative, Associative, and Distributive Properties will help you simplify expressions.
CC.7.EE.2 Understand that rewriting an expression in different forms in a problem context can shed light on the problem and how the quantities in it are related. Lesson 3-2	Given two quantities, you will express their relationship using a unit rate. Given a specific quantity, you will use unit rates to find a related quantity. You will simplify complex fractions.
CC.7.EE.3 Solve multi-step real-life and mathematical problems posed with positive and negative rational numbers in any form (whole numbers, fractions, and decimals), using tools strategically. Apply properties of operations to calculate with numbers in any form; convert between forms as appropriate; and assess the reasonableness of answers using mental computation and estimation strategies. Lesson 3-6	You will decide whether to use expressions, equations, or inequalities when solving problems. Your prior understanding of arithmetic will be combined with your algebraic skills to solve real-life problems.
CC.7.EE.4a Solve word problems leading to equations of the form $px + q = r$ and $p(x + q) = r$, where p, q, and r are specific rational numbers. Solve equations of these forms fluently. Compare an algebraic solution to an arithmetic solution, identifying the sequence of the operations used in each approach. Lesson 3-3	You will solve multi-step equations by identifying the operations involved and undoing them in the opposite order.
CC.7.EE.4b Solve word problems leading to inequalities of the form $px + q > r$ or $px + q < r$, where p, q, and r are specific rational numbers. Graph the solution set of the inequality and interpret it in the context of the problem. Lessons 3-4, 3-5	You will solve one-step and two-step inequalities and graph their solution sets. You'll be able to describe the solution set in the context of a problem.

Unpacking the Common Core State Standards

This page lists and explains the Standards for Mathematical Content that are addressed in this unit. For information about the Standards for Mathematical Practice, which are integrated throughout the text, see Teacher Edition pages vii–xiii.

UNIT 3

Notes

3-1

Algebraic Expressions

Essential question: *How do you add, subtract, factor, and multiply algebraic expressions?*

COMMON **Standards for**
CORE **Mathematical Content**

CC.7.EE.1 Apply properties of operations as
strategies to add, subtract, factor, and expand linear
expressions with rational coefficients.

Vocabulary
factor

Prerequisites
Writing expressions
Parts of an expression
Evaluating expressions
Equivalent expressions

Math Background
To add expressions, combine like terms. To
subtract expressions, first rewrite the subtraction
as adding the opposite. Then be sure to distribute
the negative sign over the second expression before
combining like terms. To multiply a constant by
an expression, multiply the constant by each term
in the expression. Factoring a constant out of an
expression is the inverse operation of multiplying a
constant by an expression. Find a common factor
and divide each term by that factor. Write the
factored expression as the common factor times the
other factored expression.

INTRODUCE

Connect to prior learning by reviewing prerequisites
for this lesson. Then begin with different colored
counters to represent different variables. Write two
expressions each with two different variables. For
simplicity, make the variables the same as the first
letter in the color that will represent them. Model
the expressions using the counters. Explain that you
cannot combine different colored counters. Add
and subtract the expressions, modeling each by
combining the counters.

TEACH

1 EXPLORE

Questioning Strategies
- How do you know to add the expressions?
  The word "both" indicates addition.
- What are the like terms? The constants are like
  terms, and the terms with *h* are like terms.

▵ **MATHEMATICAL** **Highlighting**
  PRACTICE **the Standards**

This Explore provides an opportunity to
address Standard 4 (Model with mathematics).
Defining variables links the symbols to their
real-world meanings. Substituting values for the
variables allows students to the interpret the
results in the context of the situation. Students
use the sum of expressions to model the
situation, to solve the problem, and to answer
the question in context.

REFLECT

In 1d, students use the Distributive Property to derive
a mathematical justification for combining like terms.

2 EXPLORE

Questioning Strategies
- How do you calculate the amount of money
  collected for adult ticket sales? Multiply *a*, the
  number of adult tickets sold, by $16.60.
- Why do you need parentheses in the final
  expression? To show multiplication of a constant
  and a sum, the parentheses indicate that you
  distribute 0.25 across both terms.

Avoid Common Errors
When multiplying a constant by a sum or difference,
students may only multiply the first term by the
constant. If students make this mistake, have them
first draw arrows from the constant to each term
inside the parentheses. The arrows remind students
to also distribute the multiplication to the other terms.

Unit 3 · 59 · Lesson 1

Name _____ Class _____ Date _____

3-1

Algebraic Expressions

Essential question: *How do you add, subtract, factor, and multiply algebraic expressions?*

COMMON CORE
CC.7.EE.1

1 EXPLORE Combining Expressions

Jill and Kelly work as consultants and get paid per project. Jill is paid a project fee of $25 plus $10 per hour. Kelly is paid a project fee of $18 plus $14 per hour. Write an expression to represent how much a company will pay to hire both consultants for a project.

A Write expressions for how much Jill and Kelly each make per project.

Jill: $ 25 + $ 10 h Kelly: $ 18 + $ 14 h

   Fee + Rate per hour   Fee + Rate per hour

B Add both expressions to represent how much the company will pay to hire both consultants.

Let h represent the number of hours they work together.

$25 + 10h + 18 + 14h$ *Combine their pay rates.*

$= 25 + 18 + 10h + 14h$ *Use the Commutative Property.*

$= 43 + 24h$ *Combine like terms.*

The company will pay $\underline{43 + 24h}$ for both Jill and Kelly to work on their project.

TRY THIS!

1a. How much do Jill and Kelly make individually if they work 10 hours?

   Jill will make $125 and Kelly will make $158.

1b. Combine $\left(3x + \frac{1}{2}\right) - \left(7x - 4\frac{1}{2}\right)$

$= \left(3x + \frac{1}{2}\right) + \left[-\left(7x - 4\frac{1}{2}\right)\right]$ *Subtraction is adding the opposite.*

$= \left(3x + \frac{1}{2}\right) + \left(-7x + 4\frac{1}{2}\right)$ *Distribute the negative sign to each term.*

$= 3x - 7x + \frac{1}{2} + 4\frac{1}{2}$ *Use the Commutative Property.*

$= -4x + 5$ *Combine like terms.*

© Houghton Mifflin Harcourt Publishing Company

Unit 3   59   Lesson 1

REFLECT

1c. What are two different ways to calculate how much a company would pay to hire both Jill and Kelly to work on a 10-hour project?

   Find Jill's and Kelly's pay separately for 10 hours, then add the

   results, or use the expression 43 + 24h for h = 10.

1d. Explain how the Distributive Property allows you to combine the terms 10h and 14h.

   Sample answer: Rewrite 10h and 14h as h(10 + 14), use the

   Distributive Property to get 10h + 14h, or 24h.

2 EXPLORE Using the Distributive Property

Marc is selling tickets for a concert. Adult tickets cost $16.60, and children's tickets cost $12.20. He gets to keep 25% of the money he collects from ticket sales. Write an expression to represent how much Marc gets to keep.

A Let a represent the number of adult tickets he sells.

Let c represent the number of __children's__ tickets he sells.

B The expression 16.60 a + 12.20 c represents the __amount of money Marc collects__

   __from ticket sales.__

C Write 25% as a decimal. __0.25__

D Write an expression to represent 25% of the money he collects.

   $0.25 \times \left(16.60a + 12.20c \right)$

   25% of adult ticket and children ticket

     sales   sales

E Use the Distributive Property to simplify the expression.

   $0.25\left(16.60a\right) + 0.25\left(12.20c\right)$

   $= 4.15a + 3.05c$

TRY THIS!

2. How much does Marc get to keep if he sells 20 adult tickets and 40 children's tickets?

   $205

© Houghton Mifflin Harcourt Publishing Company

Unit 3   60   Lesson 1

© Houghton Mifflin Harcourt Publishing Company

Materials
Algebra tiles

Questioning Strategies
- What are the dimensions of each tile? The *x*-tile is *x* units long and 1 unit wide. The 1-tiles are 1 unit long and 1 unit wide.
- How can you determine the dimensions of your rectangle? Add the lengths of the tiles on each side.
- What do the dimensions of the rectangle represent? The factors

Teaching Strategies
Encourage students to check their work by multiplying the factored expressions to see if the result yields the original expression. This will help students see how the factored expression relates to the original expression.

Essential Question
How do you add, subtract, factor, and multiply algebraic expressions?

Possible answer: Combine like terms to add; to subtract, rewrite subtraction as addition, and combine like terms; to multiply, use the Distributive Property to multiply each term; and to factor, identify a common factor in each term and divide each term by that factor.

Summarize
Have students complete a graphic organizer, such as the one shown here, to describe how to add, subtract, multiply, and factor expressions.

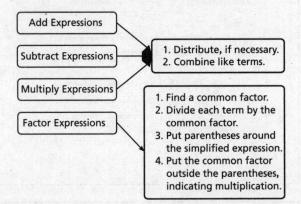

PRACTICE

Where skills are taught	Where skills are practiced
1 EXPLORE	EXS. 1–3
2 EXPLORE	EXS. 4–6
3 EXPLORE	EXS. 7–10

A factor is a number that is being multiplied by another number to get a product. To **factor** is the process of writing a number or an algebraic expression as a product.

3 EXPLORE Factoring Expressions

Factor $4x + 8$.

A Model the expression with algebra tiles.

Use __4__ positive x tiles and __8__ positive one tiles.

B Arrange the tiles to form a rectangle. The total area represents $4x + 8$.
   Sample answer:

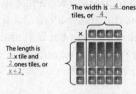

C Since the length multiplied by the width equals area, the length and the width of the rectangle are the factors of $4x + 8$. Find the length and width.

The width is __4__ ones tiles, or __4__

The length is __1__ x tile and __2__ ones tiles, or $x + 2$

D Use the expressions from the length and width of the rectangle to write the area of the rectangle, $4x + 8$, in factored form.

$4(x + 2)$

TRY THIS!

Factor each expression.

3a. $2x + 2$ **3b.** $3x + 9$ **3c.** $5x + 15$ **3d.** $4x + 16$

$2(x + 1)$ $3(x + 3)$ $5(x + 3)$ $4(x + 4)$

REFLECT

3e. How could you use the Distributive Property to check your factoring?

Multiply the factors. The result should match the original expression.

3f. **What If?** How would the model and factors change if the original expression was $4x - 8$?

The 8 positive 1-unit tiles would be negative and the factor of $x + 2$ would change to $x - 2$.

PRACTICE

Add or subtract each expression.

1. $(4.8x + 15.5) + (2.1x - 12.2)$ **2.** $(7x + 8) - (3x + 12)$ **3.** $\left(\frac{1}{2}x + \frac{3}{4}\right) + \left(\frac{1}{2}x - \frac{1}{4}\right)$

$6.9x + 3.3$ $4x - 4$ $x + \frac{1}{2}$

4. Each week, Joey gets paid $10 plus $2 for each chore he does. His sister Julie gets paid $5 plus $3 per chore.

   a. Write an expression for how much their parents pay Joey and Julie each week if they do the same amount of chores.

     $5x + 15$

   b. If Joey and Julie each do 5 chores, how much do they get paid individually? How much do their parents pay altogether?

     Joey: $20; Julie: $20; total: $40

5. A company sets up a food booth and a game booth at the county fair. The fee for the food booth is $100 plus $5 per day. The fee for the game booth is $50 plus $7 per day. How much does the company pay for both booths for 5 days?

   $210

6. A group of 4 people go out to eat. They decide to split the bill so each person pays $\frac{1}{4}$ of the total price. Appetizers are $6 and main dishes are $9. Write an expression to show how much each person pays.

   $\frac{1}{4}(6a + 9m)$

Factor each expression.

7. $24 + 36x$ **8.** $5x - 25$ **9.** $12x + 10$ **10.** $10x - 60$

$12(2 + 3x)$ $5(x - 5)$ $2(6x + 5)$ $10(x - 6)$

Rewriting Expressions

Essential question: *How can you rewrite expressions to help you solve problems?*

© Houghton Mifflin Harcourt Publishing Company

COMMON CORE **Standards for Mathematical Content**

CC.7.RP.3 Use proportional relationships to solve multi-step ratio and percent problems.

CC.7.EE.2 Understand that rewriting an expression in different forms in a problem context can shed light on the problem and how the quantities in it are related.

Prerequisites

Writing percents as fractions and decimals

Math Background

To calculate markups and markdowns, students must first understand that 1 equals a whole, or 100%. Then, markup and markdown can be described as a percentage. This percentage of the price will be added or subtracted from the original price, respectively. A markup will result in a price increase. This increase usually allows a seller to make a profit on a sale. A markdown will result in a price decrease. Sales are an example of markdowns.

INTRODUCE

Have students bring in magazine and newspaper advertisements for sales that include percents. Ask students how they would determine the price from the given information. Explain that students can write an expression for prices so that the price can be calculated with one operation.

TEACH

1 EXPLORE

Questioning Strategies

- When you multiply by a number greater than 1, is the product more or less than the original number? **more**

- What does $1.42s$ represent? **The original cost with a 42% markup included; it is the retail price for the customer.**

Differentiated Instruction

Draw a rectangle to represent one unit, or 100%, on the board. Ask a student to come up to the board, estimate 42% of the bar, and shade it in. Then have another student come and draw a rectangle at the end of the unit rectangle to extend it the same length as the first student shaded in for 42%. Point out that the unit bar is 1, and 42% is the extension. Together the extended rectangle represents 142%, or 1.42.

2 EXPLORE

Questioning Strategies

- When you multiply by a number less than 1, is the product more or less than the original number? **less**

- What does $0.76b$ represent? **The original cost with a 24% markdown included; it is the retail price for the customer.**

Avoid Common Errors

Students may struggle to subtract $1b - 0.24b$. Remind them to write $1b$ as $1.00b$. Another way is to rewrite the expression in percents as $100\%b - 24\%b$. After students find the difference $76\%b$, they can write it as a decimal, if necessary.

CLOSE

Essential Question

How can you rewrite expressions to help you solve problems?
Possible answer: Markups are 1 plus a percentage of the price, and markdowns are 1 minus a percentage of the price. Either can be rewritten as a single term.

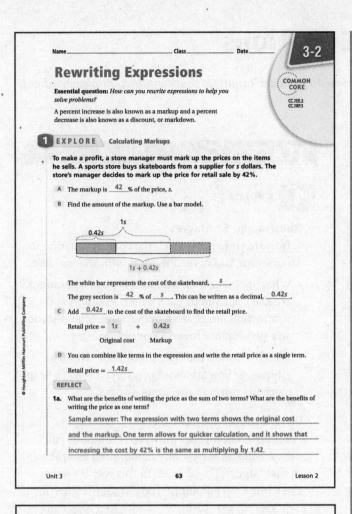

Name _____ Class _____ Date _____

3-2

Rewriting Expressions

COMMON CORE

CC.7EE.2
CC.7RP.3

Essential question: *How can you rewrite expressions to help you solve problems?*

A percent increase is also known as a markup and a percent decrease is also known as a discount, or markdown.

1 EXPLORE Calculating Markups

To make a profit, a store manager must mark up the prices on the items he sells. A sports store buys skateboards from a supplier for *s* dollars. The store's manager decides to mark up the price for retail sale by 42%.

A The markup is __42__% of the price, *s*.

B Find the amount of the markup. Use a bar model.

The white bar represents the cost of the skateboard, __s__.

The grey section is __42__% of __s__. This can be written as a decimal, __0.42s__.

C Add __0.42s__ to the cost of the skateboard to find the retail price.

Retail price = __1s__ + __0.42s__

      Original cost   Markup

D You can combine like terms in the expression and write the retail price as a single term.

Retail price = __1.42s__

REFLECT

1a. What are the benefits of writing the price as the sum of two terms? What are the benefits of writing the price as one term?

Sample answer: The expression with two terms shows the original cost

and the markup. One term allows for quicker calculation, and it shows that

increasing the cost by 42% is the same as multiplying by 1.42.

Unit 3   63   Lesson 2

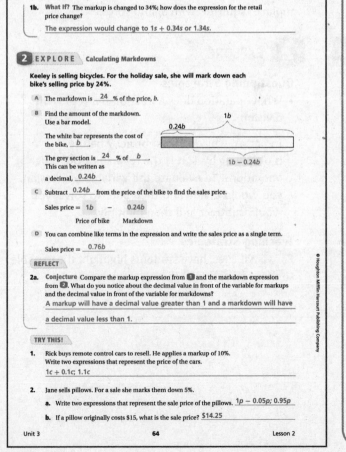

1b. **What If?** The markup is changed to 34%; how does the expression for the retail price change?

The expression would change to 1s + 0.34s or 1.34s.

2 EXPLORE Calculating Markdowns

Keeley is selling bicycles. For the holiday sale, she will mark down each bike's selling price by 24%.

A The markdown is __24__% of the price, *b*.

B Find the amount of the markdown. Use a bar model.

The white bar represents the cost of the bike, __b__.

The grey section is __24__% of __b__. This can be written as a decimal, __0.24b__.

C Subtract __0.24b__ from the price of the bike to find the sales price.

Sales price = __1b__ – __0.24b__

    Price of bike   Markdown

D You can combine like terms in the expression and write the sales price as a single term.

Sales price = __0.76b__

REFLECT

2a. **Conjecture** Compare the markup expression from **1** and the markdown expression from **2**. What do you notice about the decimal value in front of the variable for markups and the decimal value in front of the variable for markdowns?

A markup will have a decimal value greater than 1 and a markdown will have

a decimal value less than 1.

TRY THIS!

1. Rick buys remote control cars to resell. He applies a markup of 10%. Write two expressions that represent the price of the cars.

1c + 0.1c; 1.1c

2. Jane sells pillows. For a sale she marks them down 5%.

a. Write two expressions that represent the sale price of the pillows. 1p – 0.05p; 0.95p

b. If a pillow originally costs $15, what is the sale price? $14.25

Unit 3   64   Lesson 2

Solving Equations

Essential question: *How do you solve equations that contain multiple operations?*

COMMON CORE Standards for Mathematical Content

CC.7.EE.4a Solve word problems leading to equations of the form $px + q = r$ and $p(x + q) = r$, where p, q, and r are specific rational numbers. Solve equations of these forms fluently. Compare an algebraic solution to an arithmetic solution, identifying the sequence of the operations used in each approach.

Prerequisites

Writing equations in a context
Solving one-step equations

Math Background

Solving multi-step equations builds on the foundation of solving one-step equations. In the same way that you solve one-step equations, you use inverse operations to undo the operations and isolate a variable. Remember that sometimes there are many different methods that lead to the solution.

INTRODUCE

Connect to prior learning by having students solve some one-step equations. Then introduce a two-step equation. Have students identify the two operations on the variable in the correct order of operations. Explain that solving multi-step equations requires students to undo these operations in reverse order.

TEACH

1 EXPLORE

Questioning Strategies

- How do you know which part of the equation to cover up? You cover the term with the variable.

- What are inverse operations? Inverse operations are the opposite of each other. Addition and subtraction are inverse operations. Multiplication and division are inverse operations.

- Which solution method should you use? Use whichever you are more comfortable with. Both methods result in the same answer.

Differentiated Instruction

For a variation on Method 1, have students call the variable term by a silly name, such as *squirrel*, so that "squirrel" $- 12 = 23$. In this way it seems like a one-step equation. Have students solve for "squirrel" to get "squirrel" $= 35$. Then they can replace "squirrel" with $5f$ and solve.

2 EXPLORE

Questioning Strategies

- What operation does a fraction bar represent? division

- In part A, why do you subtract 7 before multiplying by 4? It is the reverse of the order of operations. To evaluate the variable expression, you would divide and then add. To solve, you would subtract and then multiply.

Teaching Strategies

For visual cues, have students highlight the variable so they can see what they are trying to isolate.

© Houghton Mifflin Harcourt Publishing Company

Name _____ Class _____ Date _____

3-3

Solving Equations

COMMON CORE

CC.7EE.4a

Essential question: *How do you solve equations that contain multiple operations?*

1 EXPLORE Solving Two-Step Equations

Carrie and Freddy collect stamps. Carrie notes that she has twelve less than five times the number of stamps Freddy has. Carrie has 23 stamps. Let f be the number of stamps that Freddy has.

A Write an equation that represents Carrie's collection. $5f - 12 = 23$

B Method 1: Solve the equation by covering up the term with the variable.

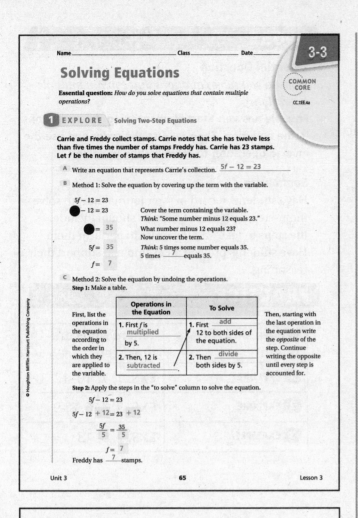

$5f - 12 = 23$

⬤ $- 12 = 23$ Cover the term containing the variable.
Think: "Some number minus 12 equals 23."

⬤ $= 35$ What number minus 12 equals 23?
Now uncover the term.

$5f = 35$ *Think:* 5 times some number equals 35.
5 times ___7___ equals 35.

$f = 7$

C Method 2: Solve the equation by undoing the operations.
Step 1: Make a table.

First, list the operations in the equation according to the order in which they are applied to the variable.

Operations in the Equation	To Solve
1. First f is multiplied by 5.	1. First **add** 12 to both sides of the equation.
2. Then, 12 is subtracted	2. Then **divide** both sides by 5.

Then, starting with the last operation in the equation write the *opposite* of the step. Continue writing the opposite until every step is accounted for.

Step 2: Apply the steps in the "to solve" column to solve the equation.

$5f - 12 = 23$

$5f - 12 + 12 = 23 + 12$

$\dfrac{5f}{5} = \dfrac{35}{5}$

$f = 7$

Freddy has ___7___ stamps.

REFLECT

1a. In what way are these two methods for solving equations similar?

They both add 12 first and then divide by 5.

1b. To solve an equation, you isolate the variable by performing ___inverse___ operations in the ___opposite___ order from the order in which they are applied to the variable in the original equation.

2 EXPLORE Solving Two-Step Equations that Contain Fractions

Use a table to help you solve each equation.

A $22 = \dfrac{n}{4} + 7$

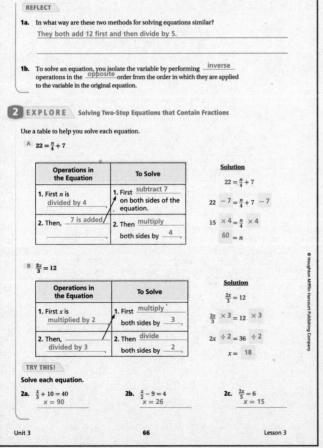

Operations in the Equation	To Solve
1. First n is divided by 4	1. First **subtract 7** on both sides of the equation.
2. Then, **7 is added**	2. Then **multiply** both sides by **4**

Solution

$22 = \dfrac{n}{4} + 7$

$22 - 7 = \dfrac{n}{4} + 7 - 7$

$15 \times 4 = \dfrac{n}{4} \times 4$

$60 = n$

B $\dfrac{2x}{3} = 12$

Operations in the Equation	To Solve
1. First x is multiplied by 2	1. First **multiply** both sides by **3**
2. Then, divided by 3	2. Then **divide** both sides by **2**

Solution

$\dfrac{2x}{3} = 12$

$\dfrac{2x}{3} \times 3 = 12 \times 3$

$2x \div 2 = 36 \div 2$

$x = 18$

TRY THIS!

Solve each equation.

2a. $\dfrac{x}{3} + 10 = 40$
$x = 90$

2b. $\dfrac{x}{2} - 9 = 4$
$x = 26$

2c. $\dfrac{2x}{5} = 6$
$x = 15$

© Houghton Mifflin Harcourt Publishing Company

Questioning Strategies

- What operations are in the variable equation? Addition, then multiplication

- What is the reverse of those operations? Division, then subtraction

---

MATHEMATICAL PRACTICE   **Highlighting the Standards**

This Example provides an opportunity to address Standard 1 (Make sense of problems and persevere in solving them.). Many students struggle to stay focused on the overall goal while performing each step of solving a multi-step equation. Students begin to practice the skill of applying computation skills with a bigger goal in mind. Students also begin to reason differently and see that more than one method works correctly. Finally, with learning to solve multistep equations, students begin to see connections between operations.

CLOSE

Essential Question

How do you solve equations that contain multiple operations?

Possible answer: Start by identifying the operations in the equation. Then reverse the order and use the inverse operation to solve for the variable.

Summarize

Have students record in their journal how to solve multi-step equations. Students should include the steps to take and the order to perform them. Have students provide an example to support their reasoning.

PRACTICE

Where skills are taught	Where skills are practiced
1 EXPLORE	EXS. 1, 7, 10–12
2 EXPLORE	EXS. 3, 4, 6, 8, 9
3 EXAMPLE	EXS. 2, 5, 13

3 EXAMPLE Solving Equations Using the Distributive Property

Kara used the formula $P = 2(\ell + w)$ to find the perimeter of a photograph. She tells Jim that the length is 6 centimeters and the perimeter is 22 centimeters. How can Jim find the width of the photo?

A Rewrite the formula, substituting the values that you know.

$$22 = 2\left(6 + w \right)$$

B Method 1

$$\frac{22}{2} = \frac{2(6 + w)}{2}$$ Since $(6 + w)$ is being __multiplied__ by __2__,

__divide__ _____ by 2 on both sides of the equation.

$$11 = 6 + w$$ Simplify.

$$11 = 6 + w$$ Then, __subtract 6__ _____ from both sides.

$$\underline{-6 \quad -6}$$

$$5 = w$$ Simplify.

C Method 2

$$22 = 2\,(6) + 2\ w$$ Use the Distributive Property.

Distribute __2__ to each term in parenthesis.

$$22 = 12 + 2w$$ Simplify.

$$22 = 12 + 2w$$ Then, __subtract 12__ _____ from both sides.

$$\underline{-12 \quad -12}$$

$$10 = 2w$$ Simplify.

$$\frac{10}{2} = \frac{2w}{2}$$ Now, __divide both sides by 2.__

$$5 = w$$ Simplify.

TRY THIS!

Solve each equation.

3a. $10 = 4(3 + x)$
$x = -\frac{1}{2}$

3b. $40(x - 2) = 200$
$x = 7$

3c. $\frac{1}{2}(2x + 10) = 35$
$x = 30$

REFLECT

3d. How are the two solution methods alike?

Sample answer: They both result in the same answer. In both you have to divide and subtract.

3e. How are the two solution methods different?

Sample answer: You do the operations in different orders. In one equation you use the Distributive Property, and the other you do not.

PRACTICE

Solve each equation.

1. $4x + 12 = 60$
$x = 12$

2. $5(3x - 4) = 40$
$x = 4$

3. $\frac{x}{3} = 33$
$x = 99$

4. $\frac{8x}{2} = 24$
$x = 6$

5. $2(-3x - 4) = 100$
$x = -18$

6. $\frac{-2x}{5} = 2$
$x = -5$

7. For 15 weeks, Sue put the same amount of money in a jar. Then she took $9 out to spend on a friend's birthday present. She had $21 left. How much did she put in each week?
$2

8. Matt gives half of his books to the local library and kept the other half. His best friend gives him 3 more books. He now has 57 books. How many did he have to start?
108 books

9. Half of Allen's test score plus eight equals 50. What did Allen score on his test?
84

10. Carl is paid $10 plus $8 an hour. He was paid $66. How many hours did he work?
7 hours

11. Barry swam three times as many laps as George plus one lap. Barry swam 25 laps. How many laps did George swim?
8 laps

12. Gayle has 3 less than two times as many stickers as Robin. Gayle has 25 stickers. How many does Robin have?
14 stickers

13. Mika used the formula $A = \frac{(b_1 + b_2)h}{2}$ to find the area of a trapezoid. Show 2 ways to find the length of the base, b_1, if the area is 32 cm, the height is 4 cm, and the length of b_2 is 6 cm.

Method 1: $32 = \frac{(b_1 + 6)4}{2}$

$(32)2 = \left(\frac{(b_1 + 6)4}{2}\right)2$

$\frac{64}{4} = \frac{(b_1 + 6)4}{4}$

$16 = b_1 + 6$

$10 = b_1$

Method 2: $32 = \frac{(b_1 + 6)4}{2}$

$32 = \frac{b_1(4) + 6(4)}{2}$

$32(2) = \left(\frac{4b_1 + 24}{2}\right)2$

$64 = 4b_1 + 24$

$64 - 24 = 4b_1 + 24 - 24$

$40 = 4b_1$

$10 = b_1$

$b_1 = $ __10 cm__

Solving One-Step Inequalities

Essential question: How do you solve inequalities that involve one operation?

© Houghton Mifflin Harcourt Publishing Company

COMMON CORE Standards for Mathematical Content

CC.7.EE.4b Solve word problems leading to inequalities of the form $px + q > r$ or $px + q < r$, where p, q, and r are specific rational numbers. Graph the solution set of the inequality and interpret it in the context of the problem.

Vocabulary
solution set

Prerequisites
Solving one-step equations

Graphing on a number line

Using inequality symbols to compare numbers

Math Background
Solving one-step inequalities is similar to solving one-step equations. One major difference is that the solution set to an inequality has more than one value. The other difference is algorithmic: multiplying or dividing by a negative number results in a reversal of the inequality symbol. Graphing solutions to inequalities requires indicating where the solution set lies on a number line. An empty circle indicates that the number is not included in the solution set, and a solid circle indicates that it is included in the solution set.

INTRODUCE

Connect to prior learning by having students graph solutions to simple inequality statements, such as $x > 2$. Then tell students that they will solve one-step inequalities to become simple statements like they are graphing. Students will graph the solutions of one-step inequalities in the same way they graph these simple inequality statements.

TEACH

1 EXPLORE

Questioning Strategies
• What does "at least" mean? A minimum of; this much or more; no less than

• What symbol does the phrase "at least" indicate? ≥ (greater than or equal to)

• How do you know whether to use a solid or empty circle? If the symbol includes "or equal to," then use a solid circle to show that number is included. Otherwise, use an empty circle to show that number is *not* included.

Teaching Strategies
Encourage students to check their answers by substituting a value from the solution set into the original inequality. If that value makes the inequality true, then the solution set is likely correct. If the value does not make the inequality true, then the solution set is wrong.

2 EXPLORE

Questioning Strategies
• What seems to make the new inequality false? Multiplying by a negative number makes it false.

• Does dividing by a negative number make the new inequality false? Explain. Yes, division is defined as multiplication by a reciprocal.

Avoid Common Errors
Students sometimes reverse the sign of the inequality when a negative number is included anywhere. Be sure to emphasize that the inequality symbol is affected only when the number you multiply both sides of the inequality by is a negative number.

3-4

Solving One-Step Inequalities

Essential question: *How do you solve inequalities that involve one operation?*

COMMON
CORE

CC.7EE.4b

1 EXPLORE   Solving Inequalities

Kate took $3 out of her purse, and she still had at least $8 in it. How much did she have to begin?

The phrases *at least* or *at most* can be confusing. *At least* means that amount or more, so use the greater than or equal to ($\geq$) symbol. *At most* means that amount or less, so use the less than or equal to symbol ($\leq$).

A   Write an inequality to represent the amount of money in Kate's purse.

$m - 3 \geq 8$

B   Use inverse operations to solve the inequality.

$m - 3 \geq 8$ Add 3 to each side.
$m - 3 \geq \quad 8$ Simplify.
$\underline{+3 \quad +3}$
$\quad m \geq \ 11$

When graphing an inequality on a number line, use a solid circle to show that the variable can equal that value. Use an empty circle to show that the variable cannot be equal to that value. Since money is not just integer values, you can shade a solid arrow, or ray, to the right.

C   Graph the solutions on a number line.

D   What does the solution tell you?

Kate had at least $11 in her purse before she took out $3.

TRY THIS!

Solve. Then graph the solution.

1a. $x + 4 < 9$

$\underline{\quad x < 5 \quad}$

REFLECT

1b.   Choose a value in the shaded area of the number line from **C** . Substitute it into the original inequality from **A** . Does this value make the inequality true?

Sample answer: yes; 12 − 3 = 9 and 9 is greater than 8

1c.   Now choose a value outside the shaded area of the number line from **C** . Substitute it in the original inequality. Does this value make the inequality in **A** true?

Sample answer: no; 10 − 3 = 7 and 7 is not greater than or equal to 8

1d.   **Conjecture** What does the shaded part of the inequality show?

The solutions to the inequality.

A value that can be substituted for the variable to make the inequality a true statement is part of the **solution set**. Therefore, 12 is part of the solution set, whereas 10 is not part of the solution set. So, Kate could have had $12 in her purse.

2 EXPLORE   Inequality Signs

A   Complete the tables.

Inequality	Multiply each side by:	New Inequality	New Inequality is True or False?
3 < 4	2	6 < 8	true
2 ≥ −3	3	6 ≥ −9	true
−1 ≤ 6	5	−5 ≤ 30	true
5 > 2	−1	−5 > −2	false
1 ≤ 7	−5	−5 ≤ −35	false
−8 > −10	−8	64 > 80	false

Inequality	Divide each side by:	New Inequality	New Inequality is True or False?
4 < 8	4	1 < 2	true
12 ≥ −15	3	4 ≥ −5	true
−16 ≤ 12	−4	4 ≤ −3	false
15 > 5	−5	−3 > −1	false

B   When both sides of an inequality are multiplied or divided by a ___negative___ number, the inequality is no longer true.

Questioning Strategies

- What operation do you see in this inequality? **The inequality has multiplication.**

- What operation will you use to solve the inequality? **Division is the inverse operation of multiplication.**

- Do you need to reverse the inequality sign? Explain. **No, division by a positive number does not reverse the inequality symbol.**

TRY THIS

Have students solve $-3c < \neg60$, $-3c < 60$, and $3c < -60$. Lead students to recognize that when solving $-3c < -60$ or $-3c < 60$, they will need to reverse the inequality symbol, but when solving $3c < -60$, they will not.

CLOSE

Essential Question

How do you solve inequalities that contain one operation?

Possible answer: Use the inverse operation and solve in the same way that you solve equations. However, multiplying or dividing both sides by a negative number reverses the inequality symbol.

Summarize

Have the students create a chart with two columns: sign not reversed, sign reversed. Have them write inequalities that belong in each column.

Sign not Reversed	Sign Reversed
$x + 3 < 9$	$-2x \leq -10$
$4x \geq -12$	$\frac{x}{-2} > 1$

PRACTICE

Where skills are taught	Where skills are practiced
1 EXPLORE	EXS. 1, 4, 7
2 EXPLORE	EXS. 2–3, 6
3 EXAMPLE	EX. 5

C Complete the tables.

Inequality	Multiply each side by:	New Inequality	Reverse the Inequality Symbol	Reversed symbol makes it True or False?
$5 > 2$	-1	$-5 > -2$	$-5 < -2$	true
$1 \le 7$	-5	$-5 \le -35$	$-5 \ge -35$	true
$-8 > -10$	-8	$64 > 80$	$64 < 80$	true

Inequality	Divide each side by:	New Inequality	Reverse the Inequality Symbol	Reversed symbol makes it True or False?
$-16 \le 12$	-4	$4 \le -3$	$4 \ge -3$	true
$15 > 5$	-5	$-3 > -1$	$-3 < -1$	true

REFLECT

2a. **Conjecture** When both sides of an inequality are multiplied or divided by a negative number, you must <u>reverse the inequality symbol</u> to make the statement true.

Properties of Inequalities
- You can add or subtract the same number on both sides of an inequality and the statement will still be true.
- You can multiply or divide both sides of an inequality by the same positive number, and the statement will still be true.
- If you multiply or divide both sides of an inequality by the same negative number, you must reverse the inequality symbol for the statement to still be true.

3 EXAMPLE Solving Real-World Inequalities

Michael bought three cans of paint. The bill was less than $60. How much was each can of paint?

A First, write an inequality to represent the situation. Then solve.

$3c < 60$ *Let c represent the cost of the paint.*

$\dfrac{3c}{3} < \dfrac{60}{3}$ *Divide each side by* __3__.

$c < 20$ *Simplify.*

B What does the solution tell you? Does it make sense for the cost of each paint can to be $0, or less that $0? Explain.

Each can was less than $20. Since a can of paint must cost more than $0, and prices are not negative, it does not make sense for a can to be $0 or less.

C Graph the solution set.

-5 0 5 10 15 20 25

REFLECT

3. Why did you not reverse the inequality sign?

I divided by a positive number, not a negative number.

PRACTICE

Solve each inequality.

1. $3x \ge -12$ **2.** $-4x > 16$ **3.** $\dfrac{x}{-2} > -6$ **4.** $3.5x \le 14$

$x \ge -4$ $x < -4$ $x < 12$ $x \le 4$

5. Karen divided her books onto 6 shelves. There were at least 14 books per shelf. How many books does she have? Write an inequality to represent the situation, then solve.

$\dfrac{b}{6} \ge 14$; $b \ge 84$; Karen has at least 84 books

6. **Error Analysis** A student's solution to the inequality $\dfrac{x}{-9} > 5$ was $x > -45$. What error did the student make in the solution?

The student did not reverse the inequality symbol. The answer should be $x < -45$.

7. Lina bought 4 smoothies at a health food store. The bill was less than $16.

a. Write and solve an inequality to represent the cost of each smoothie.

$4s < 16$; $s < 4$; the cost of each smoothie was less than $4

b. Is the graph of the solution set a solid ray or individual points? Explain.

The solution set is graphed as a solid line because the cost of each smoothie can be any amount, not just whole number amounts.

c. Does it make sense for the cost of each smoothie to be $0 or less than $0? Explain.

Each smoothie must cost more than $0, and prices are not negative so it does not make sense for a smoothie to be $0 or less.

d. Graph the solution set.

-1 0 1 2 3 4 5

Solving Two-Step Inequalities

Essential question: *How do you solve inequalities that involve multiple operations?*

© Houghton Mifflin Harcourt Publishing Company

COMMON CORE Standards for Mathematical Content

CC.7.EE.4b Solve word problems leading to inequalities of the form $px + q > r$ or $px + q < r$, where p, q, and r are specific rational numbers. Graph the solution set of the inequality and interpret it in the context of the problem.

Prerequisites
Solving one-step inequalities

Math Background
Solving two-step inequalities is similar to solving two-step equations. The solution method is much the same, with the only difference being multiplying or dividing by a negative number reverses the inequality symbol. The graph of the solution is the same as the graph for one-step inequalities.

INTRODUCE

Present the following situation to students: "You win at most $30 plus $10 times your age." Ask students what "at most" means. Then add the following information: "You won at most $150. What is your age?" Help students write and solve the inequality, finding the age to be 12.

TEACH

1 EXPLORE

Questioning Strategies
- What does the solution $x \geq 16$ represent? **It is the least number of sales needed to earn $100.**

- Is it OK to substitute 16 for x in the original inequality to check your solution? **It is OK and it should make the inequality true, but it cannot tell you whether the inequality symbol is correct because 16 forms the boundary point.**

Avoid Common Errors
Students sometimes substitute an equals sign ($=$) for the inequality symbol when solving inequalities. Remind them to watch their symbols carefully. This includes remembering which operations reverse the inequality symbol.

Teaching Strategies
Have students highlight the key words or phrases in each problem. This will help students correctly set up their inequalities.

2 EXAMPLE

Questioning Strategies
- How do you know which operation to perform first? **Use the inverse operations of those in the inequality you are solving. Use the reverse order of the order of operations.**

- Why does the inequality symbol reverse? **Both sides were multiplied by a negative number.**

- Why does the graph of the solution include an empty circle? **The solution does not include the value −12.**

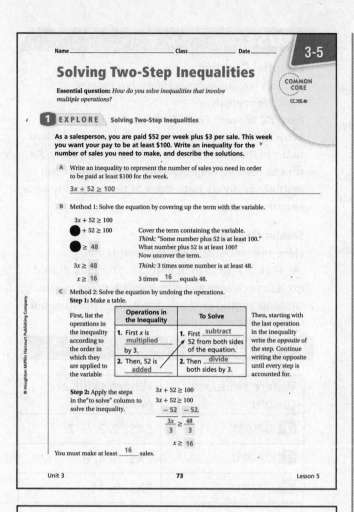

Name _____ Class _____ Date _____

3-5

Solving Two-Step Inequalities

COMMON
CORE
CC.7EE.4b

Essential question: *How do you solve inequalities that involve multiple operations?*

1 EXPLORE Solving Two-Step Inequalities

As a salesperson, you are paid $52 per week plus $3 per sale. This week you want your pay to be at least $100. Write an inequality for the number of sales you need to make, and describe the solutions.

A Write an inequality to represent the number of sales you need in order to be paid at least $100 for the week.

$3x + 52 \geq 100$

B Method 1: Solve the equation by covering up the term with the variable.

$3x + 52 \geq 100$

● $+ 52 \geq 100$ Cover the term containing the variable.
   Think: "Some number plus 52 is at least 100."

● ≥ 48 What number plus 52 is at least 100?
   Now uncover the term.

$3x \geq 48$ *Think:* 3 times some number is at least 48.

$x \geq 16$ 3 times __16__ equals 48.

C Method 2: Solve the equation by undoing the operations.
Step 1: Make a table.

First, list the operations in the inequality according to the order in which they are applied to the variable

Operations in the Inequality	To Solve
1. First *x* is __multiplied__ by 3.	1. First __subtract__ 52 from both sides of the equation.
2. Then, 52 is __added__	2. Then __divide__ both sides by 3.

Then, starting with the last operation in the inequality write the *opposite* of the step. Continue writing the opposite until every step is accounted for.

Step 2: Apply the steps in the "to solve" column to solve the inequality.

$3x + 52 \geq 100$
$3x + 52 \geq 100$
$\quad -52 \quad -52$
$\dfrac{3x}{3} \geq \dfrac{48}{3}$
$x \geq 16$

You must make at least __16__ sales.

Unit 3   73   Lesson 5

© Houghton Mifflin Harcourt Publishing Company

REFLECT

1a. How can you check your solution?

Substitute a number greater than 16 to see if you earn more than $100.

1b. Would the graph of the solution set be a ray or individual points? Explain your answer.

Since you cannot make a fraction of a sale, this graph would be

individual points, with each point on a whole number.

2 EXAMPLE Solving Two-Step Inequalities Containing Fractions

Solve $\frac{x}{4} - 5 < -2$. Then graph the solution set.

A Complete the table and solution steps.

Operations in the Inequality	To Solve
1. First *x* is divided by −4	1. First __add 5__ to both sides of the inequality.
2. Then, 5 is subtracted	2. Then __multiply__ both sides by __−4__ and reverse the inequality symbol.

Solution
$\frac{x}{4} - 5 < -2$
$\frac{x}{4} - 5 < -2$
$\quad +5 \quad +5$
$\frac{x}{4}(-4) > 3(-4)$
$x > -12$

B Graph the solution on a number line. Put an __empty__ circle on −12, since the inequality sign is greater than, not greater than or equal to. Then, the ray goes to the __right__.

−14 −13 −12 −11 −10 −9 −8

TRY THIS!

Solve each inequality.

2a. $-13 > \frac{x}{8} - 3$ **2b.** $40 \leq -3x + 10$ **2c.** $-\frac{x}{3} + 5 < -10$
$-80 > x$ $x \leq -10$ $x > 45$

REFLECT

2d. How is solving inequalities different from solving equations?

You must reverse the inequality if you multiply or divide by

a negative number.

Unit 3   74   Lesson 5

© Houghton Mifflin Harcourt Publishing Company

Questioning Strategies

• Why is the solution a set of points on the number line? Since the variable represents the number of sweaters, the realistic set of numbers possibly represented by this variable is the set of whole numbers (positive integers and 0). The actual solution is a subset of the set of whole numbers.

• How do you know when it makes sense to include 0 in the solution set? Consider what the variable represents. For example, when the variable represents a person's age, it does not make sense to include negative numbers or 0, but it does make sense to include all real numbers greater than 0, up to about 100.

MATHEMATICAL PRACTICE **Highlighting the Standards**

This example is an opportunity to address Standard 6 (Attend to precision.) When writing and solving an inequality, students must carefully choose a symbol(s) to represent the actual situation. Students must also consider whether the boundary point is or is not included in the solution set. When multiplying or dividing, students must consider whether the operation reverses the inequality symbol. And finally, students must consider their interpretation of the solution in context. In this case, the solution only logically consists of whole numbers, or positive integers and 0.

CLOSE

Essential Question

How do you solve inequalities that involve multiple operations?

Possible answer: First identify what operations occur in the inequality. Use the inverse operations to undo the operations or solve the inequality. Be sure to reverse the inequality symbol when you multiply or divide both sides of the inequality by a negative number.

Summarize

Have the students solve the inequality $\frac{x}{-1} + 41 > -12$ in their journals. Students should explain each step and why they are doing it. Finally, students should graph their solution, pointing out the critical parts of the graph.

PRACTICE

Where skills are taught	Where skills are practiced
1 EXPLORE	EXS. 1–2, 5–7
2 EXAMPLE	EXS. 3–4, 8
3 EXAMPLE	EXS. 9–11

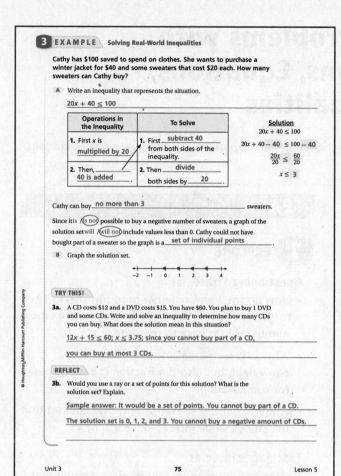

3 EXAMPLE Solving Real-World Inequalities

Cathy has $100 saved to spend on clothes. She wants to purchase a winter jacket for $40 and some sweaters that cost $20 each. How many sweaters can Cathy buy?

A Write an inequality that represents the situation.

$20x + 40 \leq 100$

Operations in the Inequality	To Solve
1. First x is multiplied by 20	1. First subtract 40 from both sides of the inequality.
2. Then, 40 is added	2. Then divide both sides by 20.

Solution
$20x + 40 \leq 100$
$20x + 40 - 40 \leq 100 - 40$
$\frac{20x}{20} \leq \frac{60}{20}$
$x \leq 3$

Cathy can buy no more than 3 sweaters.

Since it is (is not) possible to buy a negative number of sweaters, a graph of the solution set will (will not) include values less than 0. Cathy could not have bought part of a sweater so the graph is a set of individual points.

B Graph the solution set.

-2 -1 0 1 2 3 4

TRY THIS!

3a. A CD costs $12 and a DVD costs $15. You have $60. You plan to buy 1 DVD and some CDs. Write and solve an inequality to determine how many CDs you can buy. What does the solution mean in this situation?

$12x + 15 \leq 60; x \leq 3.75$; since you cannot buy part of a CD, you can buy at most 3 CDs.

REFLECT

3b. Would you use a ray or a set of points for this solution? What is the solution set? Explain.

Sample answer: It would be a set of points. You cannot buy part of a CD.
The solution set is 0, 1, 2, and 3. You cannot buy a negative amount of CDs.

Unit 3   75   Lesson 5

PRACTICE

Solve each inequality. Round to the nearest hundredth, if necessary.

1. $10x + 4 \geq -6$
$x \geq -1$

2. $-3x - 21 > 16$
$x < -12\frac{1}{3}$

3. $\frac{x}{2} + 1 \geq 4\frac{1}{2}$
$x \geq 7$

4. $\frac{x}{-5} + 11 < 15$
$x > -20$

5. $1.5x - 2 \leq 16$
$x \leq 12$

6. $0.2 > -1.2x - 5.1$
$x > -4.42$

Solve each inequality. Then graph the solution set.

7. $-5x - 17 \leq 38$
$x \geq -11$

-12 -11 -10 -9 -8 -7 -6 -5 -4 -3 -2 -1 0

8. $42 < -\frac{y}{9} + 30$
$-108 > y$

-113 -112 -111 -110 -109 -108 -107

9. Dominique has $5.00. Bagels cost $0.60 each and a small container of cream cheese costs $1.50.

a. How many bagels can Dominique buy if she also buys one small container of cream cheese? Explain your answer.

She can buy at most 5 bagels. The answer to the inequality is 5.83 but since you cannot buy part of a bagel, she can only buy at most 5 bagels.

b. Graph the solution set.

-2 -1 0 1 2 3 4 5

Yasmine and Alex each have $200 to spend on clothes. Use the table for 10–11.

Item	Price ($)
Short-sleeve shirt	15
Long-sleeve shirt	20
Pair of jeans	30
Jacket	50

10. Yasmine decides to purchase a jacket and some long-sleeve shirts. How many long-sleeve shirts can she buy?

$50 + 20x \leq 200; x \leq 7.5; 7$ shirts

11. Alex wants to buy a jacket, 2 long-sleeve shirts, and some short-sleeve shirts. Can she buy at least 8 short-sleeve shirts? Explain.

$90 + 15x \leq 200; x \leq 7.33$; no, she can only afford to buy 7.3 short-sleeve shirts and since she cannot buy part of a shirt she can buy at most 7.

Unit 3   76   Lesson 5

Notes

© Houghton Mifflin Harcourt Publishing Company

Solving Problems with Expressions, Equations, and Inequalities

Essential question: *How can you solve problems by using expressions, equations, and inequalities?*

Standards for Mathematical Content

CC.7.EE.3 Solve multi-step real-life and mathematical problems posed with positive and negative rational numbers in any form (whole numbers, fractions, and decimals), using tools strategically. Apply properties of operations to calculate with numbers in any form; convert between forms as appropriate; and assess the reasonableness of answers using mental computation and estimation strategies.

Prerequisites

Writing and simplifying algebraic expressions
Solving equations and inequalities

Math Background

Students combine all the skills from this unit to solve real-world problems. It is important to be able to use all these skills flexibly with an assortment of number types when solving real-world problems. Estimating solutions before finding exact solutions will help alert students when a computation or algorithmic mistake has been made.

INTRODUCE

Review with students the lessons in this unit and make sure that students are familiar with and know how to use a bar model. Ask students to share times when they have used estimation in their life outside of school. Tell students that they will be using estimation to solve real-world problems and then solving the problem for the exact answers. Remind students to use their estimations as a check to see if their exact answers are reasonable.

TEACH

 **1 EXPLORE**

Questioning Strategies

- How do you know whether to round 18.9 to 19 or to 20? **You round 18.9 to 20 because it is a whole number that is easy to compute.**

- Why do you change 20% to $\frac{1}{5}$? **They are equivalent, but also the fraction is easier to use for computation.**

- What does 0.189(41) represent? **The amount that the stock's value increased, 18.9% of 41.**

Teaching Strategies

Be sure to discuss other real-world examples that are similar to this one. Students may associate this concept with markups or sales tax.

2 EXPLORE

Questioning Strategies

- Why did you write a two-step equation? **Because the amount of wall that the picture does not take up (the difference) must be divided in halves so the picture can be centered.**

- Why do you use an equation rather than an inequality? **There is only one spot where the picture is perfectly centered. An inequality would indicate that there is more than one solution.**

Avoid Common Errors

Students sometimes forget to include the idea of distance on both sides in their equation. Centering a picture on the wall requires that you consider the distances from both sides of it to the wall, and that those distances be equal.

© Houghton Mifflin Harcourt Publishing Company

Name_____ Class_____ Date_____

3-6

Solving Problems with Expressions, Equations, and Inequalities

COMMON CORE
CC.7EE.3

Essential question: *How can you solve problems by using expressions, equations, and inequalities?*

1 EXPLORE Solving Problems Using Expressions

At the beginning of the year, a stock was worth $41. By the end of the year, its value had increased 18.9%.

A Estimate the value of the stock at the end of the year. Use a bar model.

Round 41 to ⟨40⟩ and 18.9 to 20. As a fraction, 20% is written as $\frac{1}{5}$.

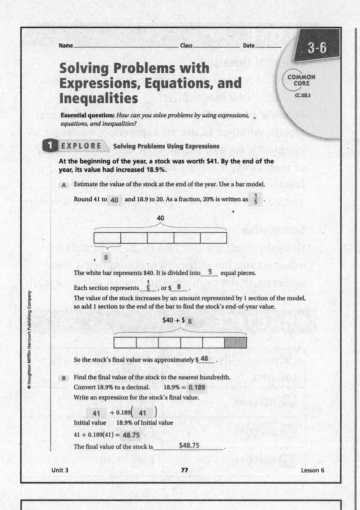

The white bar represents $40. It is divided into ⟨5⟩ equal pieces.

Each section represents $\frac{1}{5}$, or $ ⟨8⟩.

The value of the stock increases by an amount represented by 1 section of the model, so add 1 section to the end of the bar to find the stock's end-of-year value.

$40 + $ ⟨8⟩

So the stock's final value was approximately $ ⟨48⟩.

B Find the final value of the stock to the nearest hundredth.
Convert 18.9% to a decimal.   18.9% = 0.189
Write an expression for the stock's final value.

⟨41⟩ + 0.189(⟨41⟩)
Initial value   18.9% of Initial value

41 + 0.189(41) = ⟨48.75⟩
The final value of the stock is _____⟨$48.75⟩_____.

Unit 3   77   Lesson 6

REFLECT

1a. Was your estimate reasonable? Explain.

Yes; $48 is close to $48.75.

1b. Recall that the final retail value of a markup could be written as a single term. What is a single term that can be used to find the exact value of the stock?

1.189(41)

2 EXPLORE Solving Problems Using Equations

Carl is hanging a picture, and he wants to center it on the wall. The picture is $18\frac{1}{2}$ inches long, and the wall is $60\frac{3}{4}$ inches long.

$60\frac{3}{4}$ inches

x inches   x inches
$18\frac{1}{2}$ inches

A Estimate how many inches from each side of the wall the picture should be placed. ⟨about 21 inches⟩

B Use the diagram to write an equation to find the exact distance from each side the picture needs to be placed.

$60\frac{3}{4}$	=	x	+	x	+	$18\frac{1}{2}$
Total length of wall		Distance from side of wall		Distance from side of wall		Total length of picture

Combine like terms and solve the equation for the variable.

$$60\frac{3}{4} = 2x + 18\frac{1}{2}$$
$$-18\frac{1}{2} \qquad\qquad -18\frac{1}{2}$$
$$\frac{42\frac{1}{4}}{2} = \frac{2x}{2}$$
$$21\frac{1}{8} = x$$

C The picture should be placed ⟨$21\frac{1}{8}$ inches⟩ from each side of the wall.

REFLECT

2a. Was your estimate reasonable? Explain your answer.

21 is close to $21\frac{1}{8}$, so the estimate was reasonable.

2b. What If? If the picture were 24 inches wide, how would the amount of space on either side of the wall change?

The distance on the sides would decrease to $18\frac{3}{8}$ inches.

Unit 3   78   Lesson 6

Questioning Strategies

- What does 53,000x represent? **The amount of increase in the population.**

- How can you estimate what percent 2,000 is of 53,000? **Use 50,000 for 53,000; $\frac{2,000}{50,000} = \frac{1}{25}$, or 4%.**

- How do you use the table feature in a graphing calculator to estimate the solution? **Enter 53,000 + 53,000x as Y1. Set up the table to substitute x-values in increments of 0.01. Then display the table to see x-values and y-values. The y-values pass 55,000 when x is between 0.03 and 0.04, or between 3% and 4%.**

MATHEMATICAL PRACTICE · **Highlighting the Standards**

This Explore provides an opportunity to address Standard 5 (Use appropriate tools strategically.) Students use number sense to estimate the solution. Students then use the table feature of a graphing calculator to narrow down the estimate. Using the graphing calculator tool, students are also able to see the general behavior of the function near the solution.

CLOSE

Essential Question

How can you solve problems by using expressions, equation, and inequalities?

Possible answer: The context of the problem will dictate whether to use an expression, equation, or inequality. An expression does not state equality or inequality; it merely expresses operations. Equations will have one exact answer, and inequalities will often have many possible answers.

Summarize

Have the students describe in their journals how using estimation to solve a problem helps them understand the problem and how to solve it exactly.

PRACTICE

Where skills are taught	Where skills are practiced
1 EXPLORE	EXS. 2, 5–7
2 EXPLORE	EXS. 3–4
3 EXPLORE	EXS. 1, 8

3 EXPLORE Solving Problems Using Inequalities

A town has a population of 53,000. The mayor wants to know what percent increase would be necessary for the town's population to be greater than 55,000.

A Write an inequality that represents the situation.

53,000	+	53,000x	>	55,000
Current population		Increase in population		Target population

B The population needs to increase by 2,000. Estimate what percent 2,000 is of the current population, 53,000. ____4%____

C Use your graphing calculator to help you estimate the percent increase. Enter the expression on the left side of your inequality for Y_1. Set your table to start at 0, and have a step value of 0.01, or 1%.

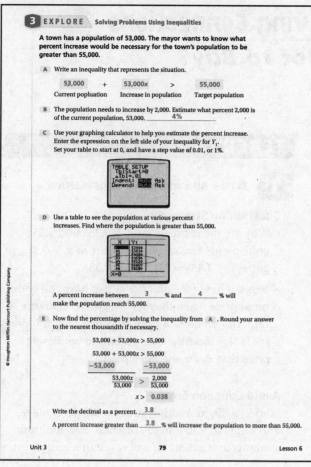

```
TABLE SETUP
 TblStart=0
 ΔTbl=.01
Indpnt: Auto Ask
Depend: Auto Ask
```

D Use a table to see the population at various percent increases. Find where the population is greater than 55,000.

```
 X      Y1
 0     53000
.01    53530
.02    54060
.03    54590
.04    55120
.05    55650
.06    56180
X=0
```

A percent increase between ___3___ % and ___4___ % will make the population reach 55,000.

E Now find the percentage by solving the inequality from A . Round your answer to the nearest thousandth if necessary.

$$53,000 + 53,000x > 55,000$$
$$53,000 + 53,000x > 55,000$$
$$\underline{-53,000 \qquad\qquad -53,000}$$
$$\frac{53,000x}{53,000} > \frac{2,000}{53,000}$$
$$x > 0.038$$

Write the decimal as a percent. ___3.8___

A percent increase greater than ___3.8___ % will increase the population to more than 55,000.

REFLECT

3a. How could the table be used to get a better estimate?

Sample answer: With smaller increments in x-values, it could be more accurate.

3b. Did you get an exact answer by solving the inequality?

Sample answer: No, it had to be rounded, so it is also an estimate.

PRACTICE

1. Mary got $\frac{8}{10}$ questions right on her test. With what percentage increase could her test have been at least a 90?

_____12.5% or more_____

2. Joe's balance in his checking account is $132. At the end of the month, it is 15.3% higher. What is his balance at the end of the month?

_____$152.20_____

3. Diane is centering a $3\frac{1}{2}$-inch-long picture on a 12-inch-wide scrapbook page. How far from the side edges should she put the picture?

_____$4\frac{1}{4}$ inches_____

4. The quarterback was sacked x yards from his own goal as the first quarter ended. He walked to the other end of the field and lined up on the other x yard line. He walked $41\frac{3}{4}$ yards between the two yard lines. How far from his end zone was he sacked?

_____$29\frac{1}{8}$ yards_____

5. Last year, Mr. Jones made $30,000. His boss just informed him that he will be receiving at least an 11.2% raise for this year. How much will he make this year?

_____$33,360 or more_____

6. In March, a share of stock was worth $55. Six months later the value of the stock decreased by 7.2%. Find the final value of the stock.

_____$51.04_____

7. There were 348 students in the school last year. The school expects a 7.25% increase in enrollment this year. How many students do they expect to be in the school this year?

_____373 students_____

8. A company has 350 workers. The president of the company wants to know what percent increase in employment would be necessary for the number of workers to be greater than 375.

_____7.1%_____

Problem Solving Connections
To Buy or Not to Buy?

© Houghton Mifflin Harcourt Publishing Company

COMMON CORE Standards for Mathematical Content

CC.7.RP.3 Use proportional relationships to solve multi-step ratio and percent problems.

CC.7.EE.1 Apply properties of operations as strategies to add, subtract,... linear expressions...

CC.7.EE.2 Understand that rewriting an expression in different forms in a problem context can shed light on the problem and how the quantities in it are related.

CC.7.EE.3 Solve multi-step real-life and mathematical problems... Apply properties of operations to calculate with numbers in any form...

CC.7.EE.4a Solve word problems leading to equations of the form $px + q = r$ and $p(x + q) = r$, where p, q, and r are specific rational numbers...

CC.7.EE.4b Solve word problems leading to inequalities of the form $px + q > r$ or $px + q < r$, where p, q, and r are specific rational numbers... and interpret it in the context of the problem.

Materials
Calculator

INTRODUCE

Ask students how they decide where to buy something. They will probably indicate that the store with the lowest price is one factor. Other factors like location, may also be discussed. Then, ask students to imagine being in the store. How can they determine whether or not they can afford an item? Explain that this project will lead them through that process.

TEACH

1 **Write and Evaluate Expressions**

Questioning Strategies
• Why are the expressions $x + 0.35x$ and $1.35x$ equivalent? **You can factor x out of $x + 0.35x$ to get $x(1 + 0.35) = x(1.35)$, or $1.35x$**

• Explain how *Fine and Fancy* can have the better retail price when they have a greater markup rate. **The wholesale price that they buy the dress for is significantly lower than the wholesale price that *Beau and Belle* pays.**

Avoid Common Errors
Students might multiply only by the percentage, and forget to add it to the original cost. Remind students that a markup will result in a greater price.

2 **Write and Solve Equations**

Questioning Strategies
• What is sales tax? **It is a percentage of the total merchandise cost that is added to the merchandise cost to give you a final total amount. Before-tax totals are also called subtotals.**

• How can you figure the amount of sales tax on a purchase? **Subtract the sub-total from the total price and then divide the difference by the sub-total.**

Teaching Strategies
You may need to discuss sales tax in greater detail. Some students may be familiar with the term but not know how it is calculated.

Name _____ Class _____ Date _____

Problem Solving Connections 🌐

To Buy or Not To Buy? *Beau and Belle* and *Fine and Fancy* sell formal attire to the students at Wallace High School. Charlene has been looking at one dress in particular. She hears that both stores will be having a big sale. Will she be able to purchase the dress with her $65 budget limit?

COMMON CORE
CC.7EE.1, CC.7EE.2,
CC.7EE.3,
CC.7EE.4a, b,
CC.7RP.3

Formal Wear Stores	
Store	Percent Markup
Beau and Belle	35
Fine and Fancy	47

1 Write and Evaluate Expressions

A Write an expression that represents the cost of the dress after the markup at *Beau and Belle*.

$$x + 0.35x \text{ or } 1.35x$$

B *Beau and Belle* buys the dress Charlene wants at a wholesale market for $55. What price will they charge their customers? Show your work below.

$$55 + 0.35(55) \quad \text{or} \quad 1.35(55)$$
$$55 + 19.25 \qquad\qquad 74.25$$
$$74.25$$
The store will charge $74.25 for the dress.

C Write an expression that represents the cost of the dress after the markup at *Fine and Fancy*.

$$x + 0.47x \text{ or } 1.47x$$

D *Fine and Fancy* buys the same dress at another wholesale market for $48. What price will they charge their customers? Show your work below.

$$48 + 0.47(48) \quad \text{or} \quad 1.47(48)$$
$$48 + 22.56 \qquad\qquad 70.56$$
$$70.56$$
The store will charge $70.56 for the dress.

E At which retail store is the price less expensive? _____ Fine and Fancy _____

2 Write and Solve Equations

Charlene asks each store to give her the total price she would have to pay after sales tax.

Formal Wear Stores	
Store	Total Price ($)
Beau and Belle	76.48
Fine and Fancy	76.91

A How does sales tax impact the price of the dress?

It increases the amount that the customer has to pay.

B Write an equation that could be used to determine the amount of sales tax charged at *Beau and Belle*.

$$74.25 + 74.25x = 76.48$$

C Find the sales tax rate. Show your work below.

$$74.25 + 74.25x = 76.48$$
$$\underline{-74.25} \qquad\quad \underline{-74.25}$$
$$\frac{74.25x}{74.25} = \frac{2.23}{74.25}$$
$$x \approx 0.03$$
The sales tax rate is about 3% for the dress.

D Write an equation that could be used to determine the amount of sales tax charged at *Fine and Fancy*.

$$70.56 + 70.56x = 76.91$$

E Find the sales tax rate. Show your work below.

$$70.56 + 70.56x = 76.91$$
$$\underline{-70.56} \qquad\quad \underline{-70.56}$$
$$\frac{70.56x}{70.56} = \frac{6.35}{70.56}$$
$$x \approx 0.089$$
The sales tax rate is about 9% for the dress.

F Charlene is looking at a pair of earrings that costs $10. Find the total cost of the earrings if there is a 15% discount and the sales tax is 8%. Does it matter if the discount is taken before or after the sales tax is added? Show your work below.

Discount first: $10 - 10(0.15)$ Sales tax first: $10 + 10(0.08)$
$$10 - 1.5 = 8.5 \qquad\qquad\qquad 10 + 0.80 = 10.80$$
$$8.5 + 8.5(0.08) \qquad\qquad\qquad 10.80 - 10.80(0.15)$$
$$8.5 + 0.68 = 9.18 \qquad\qquad\qquad 10.80 - 1.62 = 9.18$$

It does not matter if the discount is taken before or after the sales tax is added. The price will be the same.

3 Write and Solve Inequalities

Questioning Strategies

- How do markups and markdowns differ? **Markups increase the price and markdowns lower the price.**

- Which inequality symbol should be used to indicate that Charlene wants to stay within a budget? **If Charlene needs to stay within a budget, then the price needs to stay low. If we are solving for a markdown, then the markdown needs to be high in order to lower the price. Use a > or ≥ symbol.**

- How can you tell if a discount is enough for her to buy the item? **It will be enough if it satisfies the solution inequality, $x \geq 0.1501$ or 15%.**

Technology

It may benefit students to use a spreadsheet to set up final price calculations. Students would be able to easily change the percentages to make new calculations on a spreadsheet. One column can show the original cost, and then the markup. The following columns can show the discount, sales tax, and the final price. Students should program formulas so that they can enter different values in each column and still find the final price.

4 Answer the Question

Questioning Strategies

- Twenty percent off is the same as paying what percent? **80%**

- What would be one reason that she may purchase the more expensive dress? **Personal preference or salesperson's influence**

CLOSE

Journal

Have students write a journal entry in which they summarize the project. Students should identify the steps that they took to find the final price, and how they determined which dress to buy.

3 Write and Solve Inequalities

A Write an inequality that can be used to calculate how much of a markdown *Beau and Belle* must take for Charlene to stay within her budget.

$$76.48 - 76.48x \le 65$$

B Find the percent markdown Charlene hopes for at *Beau and Belle*.

$$76.48 - 76.48x \le 65$$
$$\underline{-76.48} \qquad \underline{-76.48}$$
$$\frac{-76.48x}{-76.48} \le \frac{-11.48}{-76.48}$$
$$x \ge 0.1501$$

She needs a markdown greater than or equal to 15.01%.

C Write an inequality that calculates how much of a markdown *Fine and Fancy* must take for Charlene to stay within her budget.

$$76.91 - 76.91x \le 65$$

D Find the percent markdown she hopes for at *Fine and Fancy*.

$$76.91 - 76.91x \le 65$$
$$\underline{-76.91} \qquad \underline{-76.91}$$
$$\frac{-76.91x}{-76.91} \le \frac{-11.91}{-76.91}$$
$$x \ge 0.15485$$

She needs a markdown greater than or equal to 15.49%.

E *Beau and Belle* has a sale with a 12% discount.
Find the final price of the dress after the discount. _____ $67.30

F Is the 12% discount enough? Explain using the answer to **B** .

No, the price is still more than $65. The inequality shows that the

markdown must be greater than 15.01%, so 12% is not enough.

G *Fine and Fancy* has a sale with a 15.5% discount.
Find the final price of the dress after the discount. _____ $64.99

H Is the 15.5% discount enough to make the dress fit within Charlene's budget? Explain using the answer to **D** .

Yes, the price is less than $65. The inequality shows that the markdown must be

greater than or equal to 15.49%, and 15.5% is greater.

4 Answer the Question

A Explain how Charlene will know if she can buy the dress.

Sample answer: Charlene must check the percent discount at each store if they

have a sale. The discount must be greater than the percent she calculated to

stay under her budget.

B Both stores advertise a special 20% off sale. Write two expressions that represent the price after a 20% markdown.

$p - 0.2p$ or $0.8p$

C Complete the table to help you find the final price at each store.

Store	Cost	Markup	Retail Price	Special Sale Markdown	Sale Price	Sales Tax	Final Price
Beau and Belle	$55	35%	$74.25	20%	$59.40	3%	$61.18
Fine and Fancy	$48	47%	$70.56	20%	$56.45	9%	$61.53

D What store has the best price for Charlene?

Beau and Belle

E If Charlene wants to purchase her dress and the earrings she looked at on sale, is she able to do so on her budget?

No, the dress plus the earrings will cost her more than her $65 budget.

F Charlene's mother says she will give her a $10 loan at a simple interest rate of 2%. Complete the table to find the amount of interest Charlene pays in 1 month.

Loan ($)	×	Interest Rate	=	Interest for a Month
10	×	0.02	=	0.20

G What is the total amount Charlene will have to pay her mother back if she pays off the loan in 1 month? 3 months?

$10.20; $10.60

H Describe some reasons why Charlene might choose to buy the dress at one store over the other.

Sample answer: Charlene might choose the lower price, the convenience

of the store location, or the better customer service.

Notes

Standard	Items
CC.7.RP.3	1, 7
CC.7.EE.1	3, 7, 13
CC.7.EE.2	1, 3, 7, 13, 14
CC.7.EE.3	1–17
CC.7.EE.4a	5, 9, 11, 12
CC.7.EE.4b	2, 4, 6, 8, 10, 15, 16 , 17

TEST PREP DOCTOR ✚

Multiple Choice: Item 1
- Students who answered **A** correctly translated the expression, but did not factor it. They needed to factor out a 2.
- Students who answered **B** may have tried to factor the expression, but did not factor 4 from the second term.
- Students who answered **C** may have factored 2 out twice.

Multiple Choice: Item 9
- Students who answered **A** forgot to multiply the percent x by 22.
- Students who answered **B** are finding the percent of 30 that gives 22.
- Students who answered **D** did not understand how to find a percent increase.

Free Response: Item 16
- Students who answered $7s + 4$ added the number of Shelly's wristbands and the number of Katia's wristbands.
- Students who answered $3s + 4$ did not subtract $2s + 3$ correctly from $5s + 1$.
- Students who answered $5s + 1$ did not subtract the two expressions.

Free Response: Item 17
- Students who answered **0 or 1** did not put the the expression for the cost of the pencils into the inequality.
- Students who answered **at most 166** did not add the cost of the notebooks and pens to the inequality.
- Students who answered **at most 20** did not add the cost of the pens to the inequality.

Name _____ Class _____ Date _____

MULTIPLE CHOICE

1. Maya has read two less than four times the number of books Theo has read. What factored expression represents the number of books, x, Maya has read?

    A. $4x - 2$ **C.** $2(x - 1)$

    B. $4(x - 2)$ **(D.)** $2(2x - 1)$

2. Hannah has $175 to spend. She buys $120 worth of non-taxable items. Some other items are taxable at 6%. Which inequality shows how much she can spend on taxable items before tax is applied?

    F. $x \le \$3.30$ **(H.)** $x \le \$51.89$

    G. $x \le \$45.09$ **J.** $x \le \$165.09$

3. Let p represent the price of a shirt. Joe has to pay sales tax of 10%. Which expression represents the total amount that Joe pays?

    A. p **C.** $10p$

    (B.) $1.1p$ **D.** $p + 10$

4. A mover notes the weights of a table and 4 chairs and records $t + 4c \ge 100$ on his invoice. What is he communicating?

    F. The table and 4 chairs each weigh more than 100 pounds.

    G. The table and 4 chairs weigh at most 100 pounds.

    H. The table and 4 chairs weigh around 100 pounds, give or take a little.

    (J.) The table and 4 chairs weigh at least 100 pounds.

5. Martha buys tennis rackets for $45 dollars. She marks them up 25% before selling them. What is the retail price of the tennis racket?

    A. $11.25   **(C.)** $56.25

    B. $54.00   **D.** $112.50

6. Brad bought a skateboard for $2 less than half its original price. If he paid $21.50, which skateboard did he buy?

Skateboard	Price ($)
Go Green	45
Speedster	47
Up and Down	43
With the Flow	41

    F. Go Green   **H.** Up and Down

    (G.) Speedster   **J.** With the Flow

7. Eric sells movie tickets. Adult tickets cost $8 and children's tickets cost $5. He keeps 15% of his sales. Which expression represents how much he keeps?

    (A.) $1.2a + 0.75c$ **C.** $15(8a + 5c)$

    B. $8a + 5c$ **D.** $0.15(13ac)$

8. Ken has $18 to spend on two models of the solar system and supplies to paint them. The two models cost the same amount. His paint supplies cost $4.62. Which expression indicates how much he can spend on each model?

    (F.) $x \le \$6.69$ **H.** $x \le \$13.38$

    G. $x \ge \$6.69$ **J.** $x \ge \$13.38$

9. Mrs. Hughes' class has 22 students. Her principal tells her that her class will increase to 30 students. Which equation can be used to find the percent increase?

    A. $22 + x = 30$ **(C.)** $22 + 22x = 30$

    B. $22 = 30x$ **D.** $30 - 22x = x$

10. Which inequality can be used to find how many $1.25 snack packs can be purchased for $10.00?

    F. $1.25s \ge 10.00$ **H.** $\frac{s}{1.25} \ge 10.00$

    (G.) $1.25s \le 10.00$ **J.** $\frac{s}{1.25} \le 10.00$

11. The price of mailing a small package is $0.32 for the first ounce and $0.21 for each additional ounce. Sandra paid $1.16 to mail her package. How much did it weigh?

    A. 4 ounces   **C.** 6 ounces

    (B.) 5 ounces   **D.** 7 ounces

12. A bench is being centered on a wall. The wall is 2.7 m long and the bench is 1.8 m wide. Which equation can be used to determine how much of the wall should be on each side of the bench?

    F. $2.7 - 1.8x = 2$

    G. $1.8x - 2 = 2.7$

    H. $2x - 1.8 = 2.7$

    (J.) $2.7 - 2x = 1.8$

13. Shawn sells sunglasses for s dollars. For his winter sale, he marks them down by 33%. Which expression represents the sale price of the sunglasses?

    A. $0.33s$ **(C.)** $0.67s$

    B. $0.66s$ **D.** $1.33s$

FREE RESPONSE

14. Henry is putting a new baseboard around his room. He used the formula $P = 2(\ell + w)$ to find the perimeter. The perimeter is $72\frac{1}{2}$ feet. He remembers that the width was $16\frac{1}{2}$ feet. Show two different ways to find the length of the other wall.

$72\frac{1}{2} = 2\left(\ell + 16\frac{1}{2}\right); 72\frac{1}{2} = 2\ell + 33;$

$39\frac{1}{2} = 2\ell; 19\frac{3}{4} = \ell; 72\frac{1}{2} = 2\left(\ell + 16\frac{1}{2}\right);$

$36\frac{1}{4} = \ell + 16\frac{1}{2}; 19\frac{3}{4} = \ell$

_____

_____

15. A baseball stadium has seats in the three areas listed in the table.

Type of Seat	Number of Seats
Lower Deck	10,238
Upper Deck	26,142
Box level	721

Suppose all the box level seats during a game are filled. Write and solve an inequality to determine how many people could be sitting in the other seats.

$721 + p \le 37,101; p \le 36,380;$ the

number of people sitting in the seats

could be between 0 and 36,380.

16. Katia has one more than five times the number of wristbands that Shelly has. Rae has three more than twice the number that Shelly has. What expression would show how many more wristbands Katia has than Rae? Show your work.

Let s = the number of wristbands

Shelly has; Katia = $5s + 1$, Rae = $2s +$

$3; 5s + 1 - (2s + 3) = 5s + 1 - 2s - 3;$

$5s - 2s + 1 - 3 = 3s - 2$

17. Lacey has $20 to spend on school supplies. Notebooks cost $2.50, pens cost $0.50 and pencils cost $0.12. Lacey needs 7 notebooks for her classes and also wants to get 4 pens. How many pencils cans she buy? Explain.

$19.50 + 0.12p \le 20; 0.12p \le 0.5;$

$p \le 4.166...$; Lacey can buy at most

4 pencils, she can not buy part of

a pencil or a negative amount of

pencils so she can buy, 0, 1, 2, 3, or 4.

Modeling Geometric Figures

Unit Vocabulary

adjacent angles   (4-4)

complementary angles   (4-4)

congruent angles   (4-4)

cross section   (4-3)

intersection   (4-3)

scale   (4-1)

scale drawing   (4-1)

supplementary angles   (4-4)

vertical angles   (4-4)

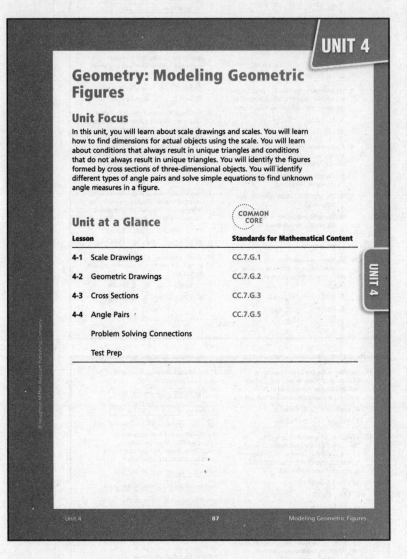

UNIT 4

Geometry: Modeling Geometric Figures

Unit Focus

In this unit, you will learn about scale drawings and scales. You will learn how to find dimensions for actual objects using the scale. You will learn about conditions that always result in unique triangles and conditions that do not always result in unique triangles. You will identify the figures formed by cross sections of three-dimensional objects. You will identify different types of angle pairs and solve simple equations to find unknown angle measures in a figure.

Unit at a Glance

COMMON CORE

Lesson		Standards for Mathematical Content
4-1	Scale Drawings	CC.7.G.1
4-2	Geometric Drawings	CC.7.G.2
4-3	Cross Sections	CC.7.G.3
4-4	Angle Pairs	CC.7.G.5
	Problem Solving Connections	
	Test Prep	

UNIT 4

Unit 4   87   Modeling Geometric Figures

Unpacking the Common Core State Standards

Use the table to help you understand the Standards for Mathematical Content that are taught in this unit. Refer to the lessons listed after each standard for exploration and practice.

COMMON CORE Standards for Mathematical Content	What It Means For You
CC.7.G.1 Solve problems involving scale drawings of geometric figures, including computing actual lengths and areas from a scale drawing and reproducing a scale drawing at a different scale. Lesson 4-1	You will learn how to calculate actual measurements from a scale drawing. You will draw geometric figures at different scales.
CC.7.G.2 Draw (freehand, with ruler and protractor, and with technology) geometric shapes with given conditions. Focus on constructing triangles from three measures of angles or sides, noticing when the conditions determine a unique triangle, more than one triangle, or no triangle. Lesson 4-2	You will draw triangles given certain sets of conditions, such as the measures of two angles and the included side, the lengths of all three sides, or the lengths of two sides and the measure of the angle that is not included between the two sides.
CC.7.G.3 Describe the two-dimensional figures that result from slicing three-dimensional figures, as in plane sections of right rectangular prisms and right rectangular pyramids. Lesson 4-3	You will identify the figures formed by cross sections. You will also sketch cross sections of three-dimensional figures.
CC.7.G.5 Use facts about supplementary, complementary, vertical, and adjacent angles in a multi-step problem to write and solve simple equations for an unknown angle in a figure. Lesson 4-4	You will learn about supplementary, complementary, vertical, and adjacent angles. You will solve simple equations to find the measure of an unknown angle in a figure.

Unpacking the Common Core State Standards

This page lists and explains the Standards for Mathematical Content that are addressed in this unit. For information about the Standards for Mathematical Practice, which are integrated throughout the text, see Teacher Edition pages vii–xiii.

UNIT 4

Notes

Scale Drawings

Essential question: *How can you use scale drawings to solve problems?*

COMMON CORE Standards for Mathematical Content

CC.7.G.1 Solve problems involving scale drawings of geometric figures, including computing actual lengths and areas from a scale drawing and reproducing a scale drawing at a different scale.

Vocabulary

Scale drawing

Scale

Prerequisites

Ratios and rates

Solving proportions

Math Background

A scale drawing is a drawing that shows an object with its measurements in proportion to the true measurements of the object. A scale is the ratio that shows how a length in a scale drawing relates to the actual object. The scale is usually denoted as a ratio with two numbers separated by a colon. The colon is read as "to". For example, 1:20 means 1 unit on the drawing equals 20 units for the real object, or 1 to 20. Likewise, 1 cm:1 m means 1 cm on the drawing equals 1 m on the real object.

INTRODUCE

To introduce scale drawings, show a map of your school. Point out the scale and tell students that every scale drawing is associated with a scale. Use maps of your local area, and have some students find the school or their home on the map. Discuss how to use the scale to find the actual distance between two places that are shown on the map.

TEACH

1 EXPLORE

Questioning Strategies

- What kind of pattern can you use to complete the table? Possible answer: In each row, you can use skip counting, repeated addition, or multiples. The first row contains multiples of 4; the second row contains multiples of 3.

- How can you find the answer to 1b? Possible answer: You can solve a proportion. $\frac{4}{3} = \frac{?}{33}$

MATHEMATICAL PRACTICE **Highlighting the Standards**

This Explore provides an opportunity to address Standard 2 (Reason abstractly and quantitatively.). Students must work with a pattern that leads to the solution of the problem. They must first solve for the values in the second row of the table by reasoning from the number pattern in the first row. In solving the Try This problems, students also use reasoning to determine if their solutions make sense.

---

2 EXAMPLE

Questioning Strategies

- How could you find the actual dimensions in the room without first finding the number of meters represented by 1 centimeter? You could solve a proportion using the given scale each time.

- Why is it useful to find the number of meters represented by 1 cm? You can use it as a multiplier to convert centimeter-dimensions in the drawing to meter-dimensions in the room.

Differentiated Instruction

If students do not see that they are solving proportions to find the lengths of the sides of the room, have them rewrite each proportion without the units. This may help students recognize proportions and remember how to solve for the unknown information.

© Houghton Mifflin Harcourt Publishing Company

Scale Drawings

Name _____ Class _____ Date _____

Essential question: *How can you use scale drawings to solve problems?*

COMMON CORE

CC.7.G.1

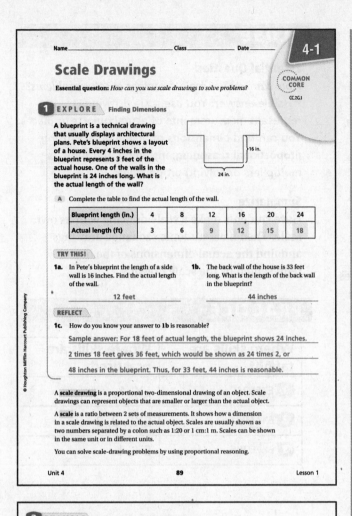

1 EXPLORE   Finding Dimensions

A blueprint is a technical drawing that usually displays architectural plans. Pete's blueprint shows a layout of a house. Every 4 inches in the blueprint represents 3 feet of the actual house. One of the walls in the blueprint is 24 inches long. What is the actual length of the wall?

A   Complete the table to find the actual length of the wall.

Blueprint length (in.)	4	8	12	16	20	24
Actual length (ft)	3	6	9	12	15	18

TRY THIS!

1a. In Pete's blueprint the length of a side wall is 16 inches. Find the actual length of the wall.

12 feet

1b. The back wall of the house is 33 feet long. What is the length of the back wall in the blueprint?

44 inches

REFLECT

1c. How do you know your answer to **1b** is reasonable?

Sample answer: For 18 feet of actual length, the blueprint shows 24 inches.

2 times 18 feet gives 36 feet, which would be shown as 24 times 2, or

48 inches in the blueprint. Thus, for 33 feet, 44 inches is reasonable.

A **scale drawing** is a proportional two-dimensional drawing of an object. Scale drawings can represent objects that are smaller or larger than the actual object.

A **scale** is a ratio between 2 sets of measurements. It shows how a dimension in a scale drawing is related to the actual object. Scales are usually shown as two numbers separated by a colon such as 1:20 or 1 cm:1 m. Scales can be shown in the same unit or in different units.

You can solve scale-drawing problems by using proportional reasoning.

Unit 4   89   Lesson 1

2 EXAMPLE   Using a Scale Drawing to Find Area

The figure at the right is a scale drawing of a large rectangular room. What is the area of the actual room?

Set up proportions to help you solve the problem.

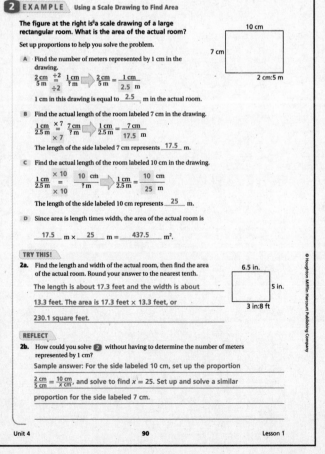

A   Find the number of meters represented by 1 cm in the drawing.

$$\frac{2\ cm}{5\ m} \overset{\div 2}{\underset{\div 2}{=}} \frac{1\ cm}{?\ m} \Rightarrow \frac{2\ cm}{5\ m} = \frac{1\ cm}{2.5\ m}$$

1 cm in this drawing is equal to   2.5   m in the actual room.

B   Find the actual length of the room labeled 7 cm in the drawing.

$$\frac{1\ cm}{2.5\ m} \overset{\times 7}{\underset{\times 7}{=}} \frac{7\ cm}{?\ m} \Rightarrow \frac{1\ cm}{2.5\ m} = \frac{7\ cm}{17.5\ m}$$

The length of the side labeled 7 cm represents   17.5   m.

C   Find the actual length of the room labeled 10 cm in the drawing.

$$\frac{1\ cm}{2.5\ m} \overset{\times 10}{\underset{\times 10}{=}} \frac{10\ cm}{?\ m} \Rightarrow \frac{1\ cm}{2.5\ m} = \frac{10\ cm}{25\ m}$$

The length of the side labeled 10 cm represents   25   m.

D   Since area is length times width, the area of the actual room is

   17.5   m ×   25   m =   437.5   m².

TRY THIS!

2a. Find the length and width of the actual room, then find the area of the actual room. Round your answer to the nearest tenth.

The length is about 17.3 feet and the width is about

13.3 feet. The area is 17.3 feet × 13.3 feet, or

230.1 square feet.

REFLECT

2b. How could you solve 2 without having to determine the number of meters represented by 1 cm?

Sample answer: For the side labeled 10 cm, set up the proportion

$\frac{2\ cm}{5\ cm} = \frac{10\ cm}{x\ cm}$, and solve to find $x = 25$. Set up and solve a similar

proportion for the side labeled 7 cm.

Unit 4   90   Lesson 1

© Houghton Mifflin Harcourt Publishing Company

Questioning Strategies

- Using the original scale, how many meters does the width of the rectangle in the drawing represent? **It represents 18 meters.**

- Using the original scale, how many meters does the length of the rectangle in the drawing represent? **It represents 24 meters.**

- How can you convert the actual measurements to the new scale? **Divide each measurement by 6 meters.**

Avoid Common Errors

Students may think that using a larger scale creates a larger picture. Have students find a couple more measurements using both scales. Ask students what 4 centimeters represent in each scale. What measurement does 8 centimeters represent in each scale? After working with several sample measurements, students should reason that the new scale will result in a smaller drawing.

CLOSE

Essential Question

How can you use scale drawings to solve problems?
Possible answer: You use scale drawings to represent measurements of actual objects or places. You can find dimensions of actual objects using proportional reasoning; including unit rates as multipliers or solving proportions.

Summarize

Have students make a scale drawing with its own scale. Then have students exchange drawings and find the actual dimensions of the object represented by the scale drawing.

PRACTICE

Where skills are taught	Where skills are practiced
1 EXPLORE	EX. 1
2 EXAMPLE	EXS. 2, 3
3 EXPLORE	EX. 4

© Houghton Mifflin Harcourt Publishing Company

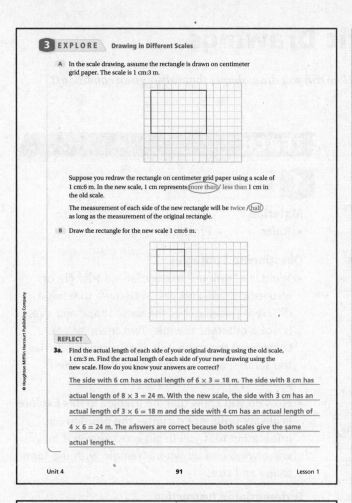

3 EXPLORE Drawing in Different Scales

A In the scale drawing, assume the rectangle is drawn on centimeter grid paper. The scale is 1 cm:3 m.

Suppose you redraw the rectangle on centimeter grid paper using a scale of 1 cm:6 m. In the new scale, 1 cm represents (more than)/ less than 1 cm in the old scale.

The measurement of each side of the new rectangle will be twice / (half) as long as the measurement of the original rectangle.

B Draw the rectangle for the new scale 1 cm:6 m.

REFLECT

3a. Find the actual length of each side of your original drawing using the old scale, 1 cm:3 m. Find the actual length of each side of your new drawing using the new scale. How do you know your answers are correct?

The side with 6 cm has actual length of 6 × 3 = 18 m. The side with 8 cm has

actual length of 8 × 3 = 24 m. With the new scale, the side with 3 cm has an

actual length of 3 × 6 = 18 m and the side with 4 cm has an actual length of

4 × 6 = 24 m. The answers are correct because both scales give the same

actual lengths.

PRACTICE

The scale of a room in a blueprint is 3 in:5 ft. A wall in the same blueprint is 18 in. Complete the table.

Blueprint length (in.)	3	6	9	12	15	18
Actual length (ft)	5	10	15	20	25	30

a. How long is the actual wall? _____ The wall is 30 feet long.

b. A window in the room has an actual width of 2.5 feet. Find the width of the window in the blueprint. _____ 1.5 in.

2. The scale in the drawing is 2 in.:4 ft. What are the length and width of the actual room? Find the area of the actual room.

The length is 28 feet and the width is 14 feet.

The area is 28 feet × 14 feet, or 392 square feet.

14 in.

7 in.

3. The scale in the drawing is 2 cm:5 m. What are the length and width of the actual room? Find the area of the actual room.

The length is 25 meters and the width is

15 meters. The area is 25 meters × 15 meters, or

375 square meters.

10 cm

6 cm

4. In the scale drawing below, assume the rectangle is drawn on centimeter grid paper. The scale is 1 cm:4 m.

a. Redraw the rectangle on centimeter grid paper using a scale of 1 cm:6 m.

b. What is the actual length and width of the rectangle using the original scale? What is the actual dimensions using the new scale?

Length is 36 m and width is 24 m using both scales.

Geometric Drawings

Essential question: *How can you draw shapes that satisfy given conditions?*

....
COMMON Standards for
CORE Mathematical Content
....

CC.7.G.2 Draw (freehand, with ruler and protractor, and with technology) geometric shapes with given conditions. Focus on constructing triangles from three measures of angles or sides, noticing when the conditions determine a unique triangle, more than one triangle, or no triangle.

Prerequisites
Measuring line segments and angles
Properties of triangles

Math Background
Students will construct triangles based on different conditions and using different tools. Some sets of conditions will determine a unique triangle. In this lesson, students will find that the length of two sides and the measure of the angle between the two sides describes a unique triangle. Also, knowing the three sides of a triangle will result in a unique triangle, as long as the three sides connect to make a triangle. Students will find that there are no unique triangles for knowing the lengths of the two sides and the measure of an angle not included between the two sides. This lesson will have students explore these sets of conditions and other sets (SAS and AAA) in the practice set.

INTRODUCE

Connect to previous learning by first reviewing the definition and properties of a triangle. Then review with students how to draw and measure line segments and angles. Explain to students that they will learn to construct triangles and learn what information they need in order to do so.

TEACH

1 EXPLORE

Materials
• Ruler   • Protractor

Questioning Strategies
• What is a "unique" triangle? It is a triangle of a specific shape and size. A triangle that has a different position, but the same shape and size, is not a different triangle. Two triangles are considered the same unique triangle if they have the same shape and size, regardless of their positions or orientations.

• How do you know that the triangle in this Explore is always unique? No matter the position or orientation that you begin constructing it in, you will always end up with a triangle with the same shape and size.

Differentiated Instruction
To help students understand that the uniqueness of a triangle does not depend on its position or orientation, have students cut out a triangle shape and move it around on their desktop. Point out that no matter where the triangle cut-out is located or arranged, it is still the same shape and size.

2 EXPLORE

Materials
• Ruler   • Protractor   • Compass

Questioning Strategies
• How do you know that the given information does not describe one unique triangle? When you use the compass to find where the second and third segments will meet in step 3, you find there are two possibilities. Both possibilities satisfy the given information.

Notes

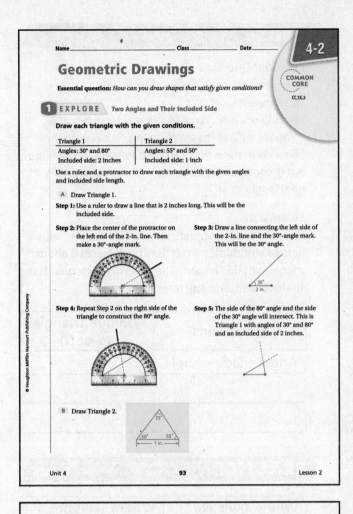

Name _____ Class _____ Date _____

4-2

Geometric Drawings

COMMON CORE

CC.7.G.2

Essential question: *How can you draw shapes that satisfy given conditions?*

1 EXPLORE Two Angles and Their Included Side

Draw each triangle with the given conditions.

Triangle 1	Triangle 2
Angles: 30° and 80°	Angles: 55° and 50°
Included side: 2 inches	Included side: 1 inch

Use a ruler and a protractor to draw each triangle with the given angles and included side length.

A Draw Triangle 1.

Step 1: Use a ruler to draw a line that is 2 inches long. This will be the included side.

Step 2: Place the center of the protractor on the left end of the 2-in. line. Then make a 30°-angle mark.

Step 3: Draw a line connecting the left side of the 2-in. line and the 30°-angle mark. This will be the 30° angle.

Step 4: Repeat Step 2 on the right side of the triangle to construct the 80° angle.

Step 5: The side of the 80° angle and the side of the 30° angle will intersect. This is Triangle 1 with angles of 30° and 80° and an included side of 2 inches.

B Draw Triangle 2.

Unit 4   93   Lesson 2

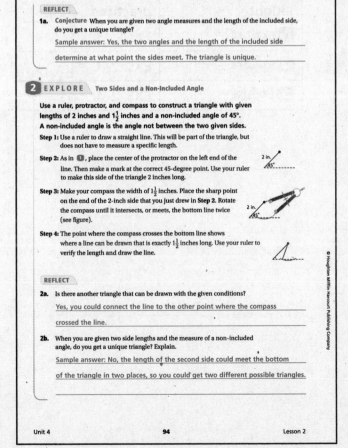

REFLECT

1a. **Conjecture** When you are given two angle measures and the length of the included side, do you get a unique triangle?

Sample answer: Yes, the two angles and the length of the included side

determine at what point the sides meet. The triangle is unique.

2 EXPLORE Two Sides and a Non-Included Angle

Use a ruler, protractor, and compass to construct a triangle with given lengths of 2 inches and $1\frac{1}{2}$ inches and a non-included angle of 45°. A non-included angle is the angle not between the two given sides.

Step 1: Use a ruler to draw a straight line. This will be part of the triangle, but does not have to measure a specific length.

Step 2: As in **1**, place the center of the protractor on the left end of the line. Then make a mark at the correct 45-degree point. Use your ruler to make this side of the triangle 2 inches long.

Step 3: Make your compass the width of $1\frac{1}{2}$ inches. Place the sharp point on the end of the 2-inch side that you just drew in **Step 2**. Rotate the compass until it intersects, or meets, the bottom line twice (see figure).

Step 4: The point where the compass crosses the bottom line shows where a line can be drawn that is exactly $1\frac{1}{2}$ inches long. Use your ruler to verify the length and draw the line.

REFLECT

2a. Is there another triangle that can be drawn with the given conditions?

Yes, you could connect the line to the other point where the compass

crossed the line.

2b. When you are given two side lengths and the measure of a non-included angle, do you get a unique triangle? Explain.

Sample answer: No, the length of the second side could meet the bottom

of the triangle in two places, so you could get two different possible triangles.

Unit 4   94   Lesson 2

© Houghton Mifflin Harcourt Publishing Company

© Houghton Mifflin Harcourt Publishing Company

© Houghton Mifflin Harcourt Publishing Company

Unit 4   94   Lesson 2

MATHEMATICAL PRACTICE — Highlighting the Standards

Explores 2 and 3 provide an opportunity to address Standard 5 (Use appropriate tools strategically.). Students use geometric tools and software in order to make conjectures about whether or not they create a unique triangle. Students must work precisely because the activities involve drawing angles with specific measures.

3 EXPLORE

Questioning Strategies
- Do three given lengths always create a triangle? **No, the three sides may not always connect.**

- If three given sides make a triangle, is the triangle always unique? **Yes**

Teaching Strategies
If geometry software is not available, have students use a ruler to draw each side separately. Have students cut out and label each segment, then manipulate the segments to form a triangle.

CLOSE

Essential Question
How can you draw shapes that satisfy given conditions?
Possible answer: You can use a ruler, protractor, compass, and software to help you draw shapes. Some conditions result in unique triangles, while other conditions create more than one triangle, or no triangle at all.

Summarize
Have students complete a chart like the one shown here to summarize what they have learned about triangles in this lesson. The first row is started. Have students add as many rows as needed.

Conditions	Unique Triangle (Y or N)
Angle – Side - Angle	

PRACTICE

Where skills are taught	Where skills are practiced
1 EXPLORE	EX. 1
2 EXPLORE	EXS. 2–4
3 EXPLORE	EXS. 2–4

3 EXPLORE   Drawing Three Sides

Use geometry software to draw a triangle whose sides have the following lengths: 2 units, 3 units, and 4 units.

Step 1: Draw three line segments of 2, 3, and 4 units of length.

Step 2: Let $\overline{AB}$ be the base of the triangle. Place endpoint C on top of endpoint B and endpoint E on top of endpoint A. These will become two of the vertices of the triangle.

Step 3: Using the endpoints C and E as fixed vertices, rotate endpoints F and D to see if they will meet in a single point.

The line segments of 2, 3, and 4 units (do)/do not form a triangle.

TRY THIS!

3a. Repeat Steps 2 and 3, but start with a different base length. Do the line segments make the exact same triangle as the original?

Yes, the line segments make the same size and shape triangle as the original.

3b. Use geometry software to draw a triangle with given sides of 2, 3, and 6 units. Do these line segments form a triangle?

No, these line segments do not connect to form a triangle.

REFLECT

3c. Conjecture When you are given three side lengths that form a triangle, do you get a unique triangle or more than one triangle?

You get a unique triangle. The triangle can only be formed one way with that

particular size and shape or no triangle can be formed at all.

PRACTICE

1. On a separate piece of paper, draw a triangle that has side lengths of 3 cm and 6 cm with an included angle of 120°. Determine if the given information makes a unique triangle, more than one triangle, or no triangle.

The given conditions will make a unique triangle ; check students' work.

2. Use geometry software to determine if the given side lengths can be used to form one unique triangle, more than one triangle, or no triangle.

	Construction 1	Construction 2	Construction 3	Construction 4
Side 1 (units)	5	8	20	1
Side 2 (units)	5	9	20	1
Side 3 (units)	10	10	20	7
Triangle Formation?	No triangle	One	One	No triangle

3. On a separate piece of paper, draw a triangle that has degrees of 30°, 60°, and 90°. Measure the side lengths. Check student's work.

a. Can you draw another triangle with the same angles but different side lengths?

Sample answer: Yes, I can draw several triangles of different sizes

that have 30°, 60°, and 90° angles.

b. If you are given 3 angles in one triangle, will the triangle be unique?

No, several differently sized triangles can be drawn with the

same angles.

4. Draw a freehand sketch of a triangle with three angles that have the same measure. Explain how you made your drawing.

Sample answer: Since a triangle has 180°,

I drew angles that were about 60° then

connected them with lines that were

about the same length.

Cross Sections

Essential question: How can you identify cross sections of three-dimensional figures?

© Houghton Mifflin Harcourt Publishing Company

COMMON CORE **Standards for Mathematical Content**

CC.7.G.3 Describe the two-dimensional figures that result from slicing three-dimensional figures, as in plane sections of right rectangular prisms and right rectangular pyramids.

Prerequisites

Intersection

Cross section

Math Background

A cross section can be thought of as a "slice" of a three-dimensional object. The slice is a plane that "cuts" into the three-dimensional object. The intersection of the plane and the object creates a two-dimensional shape, such as a square or a circle.

INTRODUCE

Connect to previous learning by reviewing names of shapes, such as square, triangle, rectangle, pentagon, hexagon, and octagon. Draw each shape on the board and have students identify the shape by the number of sides.

TEACH

1 EXPLORE

Questioning Strategies

• Does a cross section always have to be horizontal or vertical? No, it could be at another angle.

• Does a cross section of a rectangular prism have to intersect opposite sides? No, the plane can intersect adjacent faces, such as when cutting off a corner of a prism.

Teaching Strategies

Use boxes to model rectangular prisms. Cut slots into the boxes to represent the angles of the cross sections and have students slide paper into the slots to help find the shapes of the various cross sections.

2 EXPLORE

Questioning Strategies

• Name different ways that you can form a cross section with a pyramid. You can form a horizontal or vertical cross section. The plane can also intersect at an angle.

• Why does the horizontal cross section of the pyramid form the shape of a square? The bottom of the pyramid is a square.

Teaching Strategies

Having actual models of a square pyramid and a cylinder will help students understand how to find the different cross sections. Encourage students to use a piece of paper as the plane to help them visualize the intersection of the plane and the solid.

MATHEMATICAL PRACTICE **Highlighting the Standards**

This Explore provides an opportunity to address Standard 1 (Make sense of problems and persevere in solving them.). Students will have to consider different ways of visualizing the cross section before sketching it. It may take time for students to get used to visualizing in three dimensions, and students will be challenged in drawing the cross sections.

CLOSE

Essential Question

How can you identify cross sections of three-dimensional figures?

Possible answer: You visualize the shape of an intersection created by a flat plane cutting into a three-dimensional object.

Summarize

Have students write the answer to the following question in their journals: *What is a cross section?*

Name_____ Class_____ Date_____

Cross Sections

Essential question: *How can you identify cross sections of three-dimensional figures?*

An **intersection** is a point or set of points common to two or more geometric figures. A **cross section** is the intersection of a three-dimensional figure and a plane. Below are two examples of cross sections.

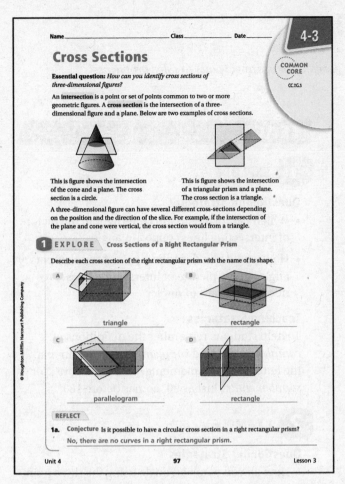

This is figure shows the intersection of the cone and a plane. The cross section is a circle.

This is figure shows the intersection of a triangular prism and a plane. The cross section is a triangle.

A three-dimensional figure can have several different cross-sections depending on the position and the direction of the slice. For example, if the intersection of the plane and cone were vertical, the cross section would from a triangle.

1 EXPLORE Cross Sections of a Right Rectangular Prism

Describe each cross section of the right rectangular prism with the name of its shape.

A — triangle

B — rectangle

C — parallelogram

D — rectangle

REFLECT

1a. **Conjecture** Is it possible to have a circular cross section in a right rectangular prism?

No, there are no curves in a right rectangular prism.

2 EXPLORE Describing Cross Sections

A right rectangular pyramid is shown.

A The shape of the base is a ___rectangle___

The shape of each side is a ___triangle___

B Circle the cross sections that are possible.

square   (rectangle)   (triangle)   circle   (trapezoid)

C Sketch the cross sections of the right rectangular pyramid below.

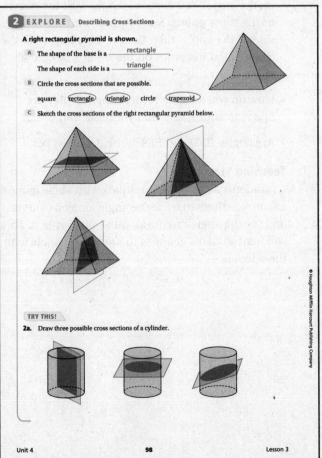

TRY THIS!

2a. Draw three possible cross sections of a cylinder.

4-4 Angle Pairs

Essential question: *How can you use angle pairs to solve problems?*

COMMON CORE Standards for Mathematical Content

CC.7.G.5 Use facts about supplementary, complementary, vertical, and adjacent angles in a multi-step problem to write and solve simple equations for an unknown angle in a figure.

Vocabulary
congruent angles
supplementary angles
complementary angles
adjacent angles
vertical angles

Prerequisites
Lines and angles
Measuring angles

Math Background
Students will work with special angles. Congruent angles have the same measure. A pair of angles is supplementary if they have a sum of 180°. A pair of angles is complementary if they have a sum of 90°. Adjacent angles share one side without overlapping. Vertical angles are the non-adjacent angles formed by intersecting lines. They lie opposite of each other at the point of intersection.

INTRODUCE

Connect to previous learning by reviewing angle measurement. Have students use their protractors to draw angles of 43°, 125°, and 180°. Then have students draw three angles with three different measures. Have students switch drawings and then measure each other's angles with their protractors.

TEACH

1 EXPLORE

Questioning Strategies
- Which pair of angles are congruent in the picture of intersecting lines? **opposite angles**
- How would you describe a pair of supplementary angles in the picture of intersecting lines? **any side-by-side pair of angles**

Teaching Strategies
To help students remember the definitions of *complementary* and *supplementary*, explain that the letter *c* for complementary comes before *s* for *supplementary* just as 90° comes before 180°.

2 EXAMPLE

Questioning Strategies
- How do you name an angle using the three points on the angle? **You name an angle with the names of the three points. Start with a point on one side of the angle; then the vertex is always in the middle; and the point on the other side of the angle is last.**
- How do you identify vertical angles? **They are opposite angles formed by intersecting lines.**
- Are angles *BFD* and *EFA* vertical angles? **yes**

Teaching Strategies
As students answer the questions with angle names, encourage them to trace the angle along its letters and say the angle's name aloud as they write it. This will help students get used to naming an angle with three letters.

4-4

Name _____ Class _____ Date _____

Angle Pairs

Essential question: *How can you use angle pairs to solve problems?*

COMMON CORE

CC.7.G.5

Recall that two rays with a common endpoint form an angle. The two rays form the sides of the angle, and the common endpoint marks the vertex. You can name an angle several ways: by its vertex, by a point on each ray and the vertex, or by a number.

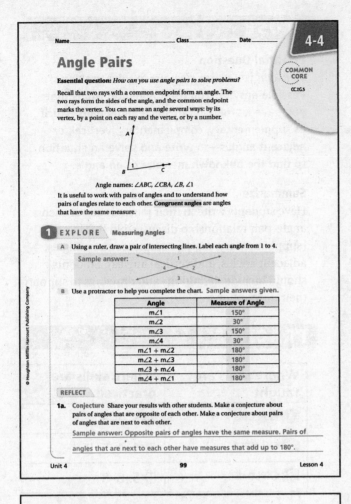

Angle names: ∠ABC, ∠CBA, ∠B, ∠1

It is useful to work with pairs of angles and to understand how pairs of angles relate to each other. **Congruent angles** are angles that have the same measure.

1 EXPLORE   Measuring Angles

A   Using a ruler, draw a pair of intersecting lines. Label each angle from 1 to 4.

Sample answer:

B   Use a protractor to help you complete the chart. Sample answers given.

Angle	Measure of Angle
m∠1	150°
m∠2	30°
m∠3	150°
m∠4	30°
m∠1 + m∠2	180°
m∠2 + m∠3	180°
m∠3 + m∠4	180°
m∠4 + m∠1	180°

REFLECT

1a. Conjecture Share your results with other students. Make a conjecture about pairs of angles that are opposite of each other. Make a conjecture about pairs of angles that are next to each other.

Sample answer: Opposite pairs of angles have the same measure. Pairs of

angles that are next to each other have measures that add up to 180°.

Unit 4   99   Lesson 4

Vertical angles are the opposite angles formed by two intersecting lines. Vertical angles are congruent because the angles have the same measure. **Adjacent angles** are pairs of angles that share a vertex and one side but do not overlap.

Complementary angles are two angles whose measures have a sum of 90°. **Supplementary angles** are two angles whose measures have a sum of 180°. You have discovered in Explore 1 that adjacent angles formed by two intersecting lines are supplementary.

2 EXAMPLE   Identifying Angles and Angle Pairs

Use the diagram below.

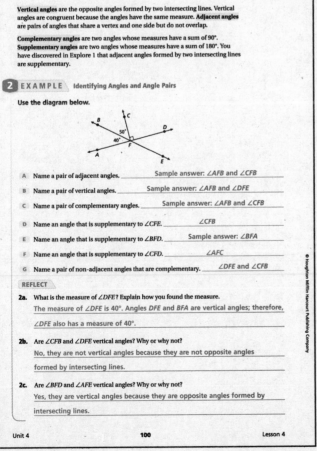

A   Name a pair of adjacent angles. _____ Sample answer: ∠AFB and ∠CFB

B   Name a pair of vertical angles. _____ Sample answer: ∠AFB and ∠DFE

C   Name a pair of complementary angles. _____ Sample answer: ∠AFB and ∠CFB

D   Name an angle that is supplementary to ∠CFE. _____ ∠CFB

E   Name an angle that is supplementary to ∠BFD. _____ Sample answer: ∠BFA

F   Name an angle that is supplementary to ∠CFD. _____ ∠AFC

G   Name a pair of non-adjacent angles that are complementary. _____ ∠DFE and ∠CFB

REFLECT

2a. What is the measure of ∠DFE? Explain how you found the measure.

The measure of ∠DFE is 40°. Angles *DFE* and *BFA* are vertical angles; therefore,

∠DFE also has a measure of 40°.

2b. Are ∠CFB and ∠DFE vertical angles? Why or why not?

No, they are not vertical angles because they are not opposite angles

formed by intersecting lines.

2c. Are ∠BFD and ∠AFE vertical angles? Why or why not?

Yes, they are vertical angles because they are opposite angles formed by

intersecting lines.

Unit 4   100   Lesson 4

Questioning Strategies

- What fact about angles do you use to find the angle measure in part A? **The two angles are supplementary.**

- Do you need to solve for x in part B? **No, because the measure of angle *EHF* equals $2x$, not x.**

Teaching Strategies

Encourage students to write an equation to solve for the measure of an angle in an angle pair relationship. Students will write an equation to represent the angle pair relationship and substitute the information that they are given to solve for the unknown.

MATHEMATICAL PRACTICE **Highlighting the Standards**

This Explore provides an opportunity to address Standard 3 (Construct viable arguments and critique the reasoning of others.). Students write and solve equations by analyzing geometric figures. Students use reasoning to draw conclusions from given information and known relationships.

CLOSE

Essential Question

How can you use angle pairs to solve problems?
Possible answer: You use the relationships that you have learned about some angle pairs—such as supplementary, complementary, vertical, or adjacent angles—to write and solve an equation to find the unknown measure of an angle.

Summarize

Have students write in their journals about each angle-pair relationship discussed in this lesson (supplementary angles, complementary angles, adjacent angles, and vertical angles). Students should include definitions and drawings to support their descriptions.

PRACTICE

Where skills are taught	Where skills are practiced
1 EXPLORE	EXS. 1–8
2 EXAMPLE	EXS. 1–5, 9
3 EXPLORE	EXS. 6–8

3 EXAMPLE Finding Angle Measures

Find the measure of each angle.

A ∠BDC

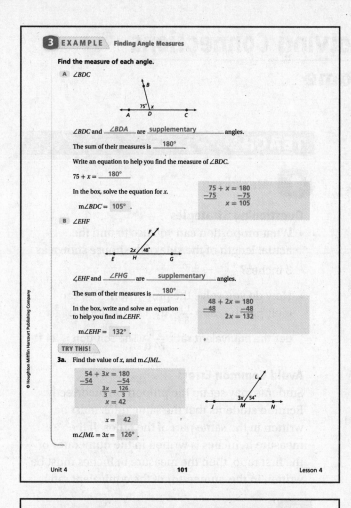

∠BDC and __∠BDA__ are __supplementary__ angles.

The sum of their measures is __180°__.

Write an equation to help you find the measure of ∠BDC.

$75 + x =$ __180°__

In the box, solve the equation for x.

m∠BDC = __105°__.

$$75 + x = 180$$
$$\underline{-75 \quad\quad -75}$$
$$x = 105$$

B ∠EHF

∠EHF and __∠FHG__ are __supplementary__ angles.

The sum of their measures is __180°__.

In the box, write and solve an equation to help you find m∠EHF.

m∠EHF = __132°__.

$$48 + 2x = 180$$
$$\underline{-48 \quad\quad -48}$$
$$2x = 132$$

TRY THIS!

3a. Find the value of x, and m∠JML.

$$54 + 3x = 180$$
$$\underline{-54 \quad\quad -54}$$
$$\frac{3x}{3} = \frac{126}{3}$$
$$x = 42$$

x = __42__

m∠JML = 3x = __126°__.

Unit 4   101   Lesson 4

PRACTICE

For 1–5, use the figure.

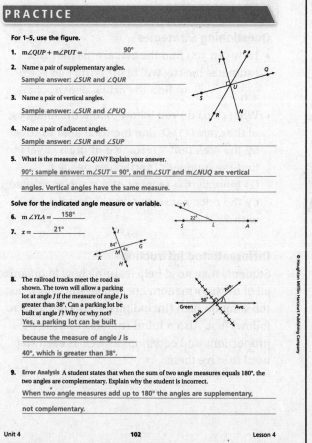

1. m∠QUP + m∠PUT = __90°__

2. Name a pair of supplementary angles.
   Sample answer: ∠SUR and ∠QUR

3. Name a pair of vertical angles.
   Sample answer: ∠SUR and ∠PUQ

4. Name a pair of adjacent angles.
   Sample answer: ∠SUR and ∠SUP

5. What is the measure of ∠QUN? Explain your answer.
   90°; sample answer: m∠SUT = 90°, and m∠SUT and m∠NUQ are vertical
   angles. Vertical angles have the same measure.

Solve for the indicated angle measure or variable.

6. m∠YLA = __158°__

7. x = __21°__

8. The railroad tracks meet the road as shown. The town will allow a parking lot at angle J if the measure of angle J is greater than 38°. Can a parking lot be built at angle J? Why or why not?
   Yes, a parking lot can be built
   because the measure of angle J is
   40°, which is greater than 38°.

9. **Error Analysis** A student states that when the sum of two angle measures equals 180°, the two angles are complementary. Explain why the student is incorrect.
   When two angle measures add up to 180° the angles are supplementary,
   not complementary.

Unit 4   102   Lesson 4

UNIT 4

Problem Solving Connections
Buying a Home

COMMON
CORE **Standards for Mathematical Content**

CC.7.G.1 Solve problems involving scale drawings of geometric figures, including computing actual lengths and areas from a scale drawing and reproducing a scale drawing at a different scale.

CC.7.G.2 Draw (freehand, with ruler and protractor, and with technology) geometric shapes with given conditions. Focus on constructing triangles from three measures of angles or sides, noticing when the conditions determine a unique triangle, more than one triangle, or no triangle.

CC.7.G.3 Describe the two-dimensional figures that result from slicing three-dimensional figures, as in plane sections of right rectangular prisms and right rectangular pyramids.

CC.7.G.5 Use facts about supplementary, complementary, vertical, and adjacent angles in a multi-step problem to write and solve simple equations for an unknown angle in a figure.

Materials:
- Straightedge
- Compass
- Protractor

Or

- Geometry software

INTRODUCE

Explain to students that they will work with scale drawings and models in this project. They will calculate actual measurements from measurements presented in scale drawings and models.

TEACH

1 Measuring

Questioning Strategies
- What proportion can you use to find the actual length of the side of the house shown as 3 inches? $\frac{1 \text{ in.}}{8 \text{ ft}} = \frac{3 \text{ in.}}{x}$
- How do you solve the proportion? **You can multiply the ratio $\frac{1 \text{ in.}}{8 \text{ ft}}$ by 1 in the form of $\frac{3}{3}$ to get the equivalent ratio $\frac{3 \text{ in.}}{24 \text{ ft}}$. The solution is 24 ft.**

Avoid Common Errors
Students may set up the proportion incorrectly. Remind students that the same units must be written in the same part of the ratios. If the measure in inches is written in the numerator of the first ratio, then the measure in inches must be written in the numerator of the equivalent ratio.

2 Decorating

Questioning Strategies
- How can you find the actual area that Tina estimates the rug will fit in? **Write and solve $\frac{1 \text{ in.}}{8 \text{ ft}} = \frac{1.5 \text{ in.}}{x}$ to find the actual dimensions.**
- What steps do you follow to find the total cost of the grass? **(1) Divide the total area to cover by the area that 1 rectangle of grass covers to find the number of rectangles needed. (2) Multiply the number of rectangles needed by the price per rectangle. (3) Find the total with 8% tax.**

Differentiated Instruction
Students may need help learning how to organize all of the information. Encourage students to list the solution plan (including the specific steps to follow) first. Also remind students to write the proportions and equations as well as each step used to solve them.

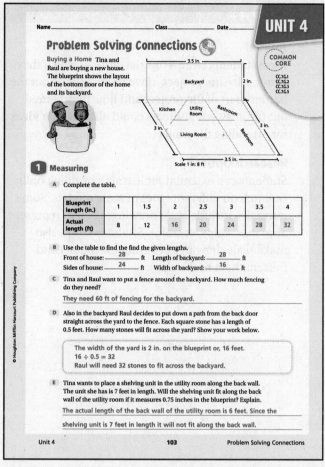

Name_____ Class_____ Date_____

UNIT 4

Problem Solving Connections 🌐

Buying a Home Tina and Raul are buying a new house. The blueprint shows the layout of the bottom floor of the home and its backyard.

COMMON
CORE
CC.7.G.1
CC.7.G.2
CC.7.G.3
CC.7.G.5

Blueprint labels: 3.5 in., Backyard, 2 in., Kitchen, Utility Room, Bathroom, 3 in., 3 in., Living Room, Bedroom, 3.5 in., Scale 1 in: 8 ft

1 Measuring

A Complete the table.

Blueprint length (in.)	1	1.5	2	2.5	3	3.5	4
Actual length (ft)	8	12	16	20	24	28	32

B Use the table to find the find the given lengths.

Front of house: __28__ ft Length of backyard: __28__ ft

Sides of house: __24__ ft Width of backyard: __16__ ft

C Tina and Raul want to put a fence around the backyard. How much fencing do they need?

They need 60 ft of fencing for the backyard.

D Also in the backyard Raul decides to put down a path from the back door straight across the yard to the fence. Each square stone has a length of 0.5 feet. How many stones will fit across the yard? Show your work below.

> The width of the yard is 2 in. on the blueprint or, 16 feet.
> 16 ÷ 0.5 = 32
> Raul will need 32 stones to fit across the backyard.

E Tina wants to place a shelving unit in the utility room along the back wall. The unit she has is 7 feet in length. Will the shelving unit fit along the back wall of the utility room if it measures 0.75 inches in the blueprint? Explain.

The actual length of the back wall of the utility room is 6 feet. Since the

shelving unit is 7 feet in length it will not fit along the back wall.

Unit 4   103   Problem Solving Connections

---

2 Decorating

A Tina wants to put a large rug in the living room. The rug is shown at right. Tina estimates she can place a rug in an $1\frac{1}{2}$ in.-by-$1\frac{1}{2}$ in. area in the living room.

Find the actual area of the rug that Tina thinks will fit in the living room. Determine if her rug can be placed in the living room. Show your work.

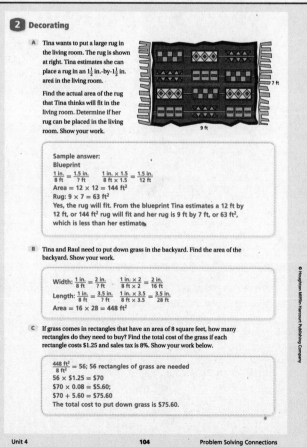

Rug labels: 7 ft, 9 ft

> Sample answer:
> Blueprint
> $\frac{1\text{ in.}}{8\text{ ft}} = \frac{1.5\text{ in.}}{? \text{ ft}}$ $\frac{1\text{ in.} \times 1.5}{8\text{ ft} \times 1.5} = \frac{1.5\text{ in.}}{12\text{ ft}}$
> Area = 12 × 12 = 144 ft²
> Rug: 9 × 7 = 63 ft²
> Yes, the rug will fit. From the blueprint Tina estimates a 12 ft by 12 ft, or 144 ft² rug will fit and her rug is 9 ft by 7 ft, or 63 ft², which is less than her estimate.

B Tina and Raul need to put down grass in the backyard. Find the area of the backyard. Show your work.

> Width: $\frac{1\text{ in.}}{8\text{ ft}} = \frac{2\text{ in.}}{?\text{ ft}}$ $\frac{1\text{ in.} \times 2}{8\text{ ft} \times 2} = \frac{2\text{ in.}}{16\text{ ft}}$
> Length: $\frac{1\text{ in.}}{8\text{ ft}} = \frac{3.5\text{ in.}}{?\text{ ft}}$ $\frac{1\text{ in.} \times 3.5}{8\text{ ft} \times 3.5} = \frac{3.5\text{ in.}}{28\text{ ft}}$
> Area = 16 × 28 = 448 ft²

C If grass comes in rectangles that have an area of 8 square feet, how many rectangles do they need to buy? Find the total cost of the grass if each rectangle costs $1.25 and sales tax is 8%. Show your work below.

> $\frac{448\text{ ft}^2}{8\text{ ft}^2}$ = 56; 56 rectangles of grass are needed
> 56 × $1.25 = $70
> $70 × 0.08 = $5.60;
> $70 + 5.60 = $75.60
> The total cost to put down grass is $75.60.

Unit 4   104   Problem Solving Connections

3 Building

Questioning Strategies

- How do you know that the table with a 1-ft side facing the bedroom will fit into this corner? **The 2-ft side is long enough to reach from the wall against the bathroom to the wall against the living room.**

- How do you know that the table with a 2-ft side facing the bedroom will *not* fit into this corner? **The 1-ft side is *not* long enough to reach from the wall against the bathroom to the wall against the living room.**

Teaching Strategies

Students may use geometry software to construct the triangular tables as described, or they may construct the triangular tables by hand. Either approach will help students understand which information results in a unique triangle.

Gardening

Questioning Strategies

- Does information about the lengths of three sides of a triangle define a unique triangle? **yes**

- How can Raul make sure that a cross section of the cube forms an equilateral triangle? **He makes the slice intersect with the three edges of the cube at the same distance from the vertex of the cube.**

Avoid Common Errors

Allow students to model the cross sections with three-dimensional models. It may be easier for students to describe the answers if their models have labels and names for the edges, faces, and vertices.

Journal

Have students write a journal entry in which they summarize the project. Have them write about the hardest part of the project and how they figured out the answers. Students could also include ideas for extending the project.

Research Options

Students can extend their learning by doing online research on different types of scale models. Some examples include scale drawings used to represent airplanes, ships, or trains. Students could also make scale drawings of familiar locations and present them to the class.

3 Building

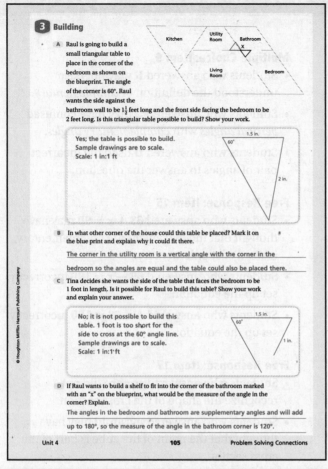

A Raul is going to build a small triangular table to place in the corner of the bedroom as shown on the blueprint. The angle of the corner is 60°. Raul wants the side against the bathroom wall to be $1\frac{1}{2}$ feet long and the front side facing the bedroom to be 2 feet long. Is this triangular table possible to build? Show your work.

> Yes; the table is possible to build.
> Sample drawings are to scale.
> Scale: 1 in:1 ft

B In what other corner of the house could this table be placed? Mark it on the blue print and explain why it could fit there.

The corner in the utility room is a vertical angle with the corner in the

bedroom so the angles are equal and the table could also be placed there.

C Tina decides she wants the side of the table that faces the bedroom to be 1 foot in length. Is it possible for Raul to build this table? Show your work and explain your answer.

> No; it is not possible to build this table. 1 foot is too short for the side to cross at the 60° angle line.
> Sample drawings are to scale.
> Scale: 1 in:1 ft

D If Raul wants to build a shelf to fit into the corner of the bathroom marked with an "x" on the blueprint, what would be the measure of the angle in the corner? Explain.

The angles in the bedroom and bathroom are supplementary angles and will add

up to 180°, so the measure of the angle in the bathroom corner is 120°.

4 Gardening

A Raul finds some wooden planks of wood in the backyard with lengths 6 feet, 6.5 feet, and 8 feet. Tina decides she wants to make a triangular garden in the yard. Use geometry software to show whether these planks form a triangle for her to use as an outline for her garden.

> Yes, the planks will make a triangular outline for her garden. Students should use geometry software to construct a triangle with side lengths of 6, 6.5, and 8 units.

B If Tina can form a triangle, will it only be one shape and size or can she make a different shape and size out of the planks?

Tina will only be able to make one shape and size of triangle

with the planks she has.

C Raul also finds a block of wood in the shape of a 6 feet cube. He is going to use the wood to cut the top of a patio table. Could he cut a cross section of the block to form an equilateral triangle? What about a triangle that is not equilateral? Show your work below.

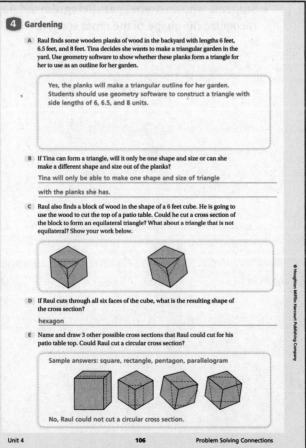

D If Raul cuts through all six faces of the cube, what is the resulting shape of the cross section?

hexagon

E Name and draw 3 other possible cross sections that Raul could cut for his patio table top. Could Raul cut a circular cross section?

> Sample answers: square, rectangle, pentagon, parallelogram
>
> No, Raul could not cut a circular cross section.

© Houghton Mifflin Harcourt Publishing Company

COMMON CORE CORRELATION

Standard	Items
CC.7.G.1	4, 12–14
CC.7.G.2	16, 19
CC.7.G.3	4, 6, 17, 18
CC.7.G.5	2–3, 5, 7–11, 15

TEST PREP DOCTOR ⊕

Multiple Choice: Item 3

- Students who answered **B** incorrectly subtracted 88° from 90°.
- Students who answered **C** may not fully understand the definition of *complementary*.
- Students who answered **D** may have subtracted 88° from 180°.

Multiple Choice: Item 4

- Students who answered **F** picked 1 inch from the scale in the statement of the problem.
- Students who answered **H** may have confused 5 inches with 5 miles in the statement of the problem.
- Students who answered **J** did not calculate the number of inches correctly.

Multiple Choice: Item 9

- Students who answered **B** may not have understood the definition of *complementary*.
- Students who answered **C** may have confused *vertical angles* with *complementary angles*.
- Students who answered **D** used the incorrect pair of angles to answer the question.

Free Response: Item 15

- Students who answered $63 + x = 90$ may have thought that the two angles are complementary, instead of supplementary.
- Students who answered $63 - x = 180$ incorrectly set up the equation.
- Students who answered $x - 63 = 180$ incorrectly set up the equation.

Free Response: Item 17

- Students who answered **square** did not recognize the shape of the cross section.
- Students who answered **pyramid** may have thought that the point of the cube is part of the cross section.
- Students who answered **parallelogram** did not recognize the shape of the cross section.

Name _____ **Class** _____ **Date** _____

MULTIPLE CHOICE

1. Which of the following could be a horizontal cross-section of a cylinder?
   - **A.** hexagon
   - **C.** circle
   - **B.** triangle
   - **D.** octagon

2. If two angles are supplementary, what is the sum of their measures?
   - **F.** 30°
   - **H.** 180°
   - **G.** 90°
   - **J.** 360°

3. What is the measure of the angle that is complementary to the angle shown?

   - **A.** 2°
   - **C.** 90°
   - **B.** 12°
   - **D.** 92°

4. A map has a scale of 1 inch to 5 miles. The distance from Yuri's home to school is 10 miles. How many inches is Yuri's home from school on the map?
   - **F.** 1 inch
   - **H.** 5 inches
   - **G.** 2 inches
   - **J.** 10 inches

5. Angle D is a vertical angle to ∠F. The measure of ∠D is 53°. What is the measure of ∠F?
   - **A.** 3°
   - **C.** 43°
   - **B.** 37°
   - **D.** 53°

6. Which of the following could NOT be a cross section of a rectangular prism?
   - **F.** rectangle
   - **H.** parallelogram
   - **G.** circle
   - **J.** triangle

Use the figure for problems 7–11.

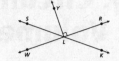

7. Which pair of angles are adjacent angles?
   - **A.** ∠SLW and ∠RLK
   - **B.** ∠SLW and ∠WLK
   - **C.** ∠SLY and ∠WLK
   - **D.** ∠YLR and ∠YLK

8. Which pair of adjacent angles are supplementary angles?
   - **F.** ∠RLK and ∠YLR
   - **G.** ∠SLY and ∠YLR
   - **H.** ∠RLK and ∠WLK
   - **J.** ∠SLW and ∠WLR

9. Which pair of angles are complementary angles?
   - **A.** ∠YLS and ∠RLK
   - **B.** ∠YLR and ∠YLS
   - **C.** ∠SLW and ∠RLK
   - **D.** ∠WLK and ∠RLK

10. The measure of ∠RLK is 38°. What is the measure of ∠SLY?
    - **F.** 52°
    - **H.** 142°
    - **G.** 62°
    - **J.** 218°

11. The sum of which two angle measures equals the measure of ∠WLK?
    - **A.** ∠SLY and ∠YLR
    - **B.** ∠SLW and ∠YLR
    - **C.** ∠RLK and ∠SLY
    - **D.** ∠RLK and ∠YLR

The figure is a scale drawing of a rectangular room. The scale is 2 cm:4 m. Use the figure for problems 12–14.

12. What is the length of the actual room?
    - **F.** 2 meters
    - **G.** 6 meters
    - **H.** 12 meters
    - **J.** 24 meters

13. What is the width of the actual room?
    - **A.** 6 meters
    - **B.** 12 meters
    - **C.** 18 meters
    - **D.** 24 meters

14. What is the area of the actual room?
    - **F.** 72 square meters
    - **G.** 144 square meters
    - **H.** 288 square meters
    - **J.** 576 square meters

FREE RESPONSE

Use the figure for problems 15 and 16.

15. Write and solve an equation to find the measure of ∠TSU.

    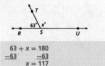

    $63 + x = 180$
    $-63 \quad\quad -63$
    $x = 117$

    m∠TSU is 117°.

16. Name two ways to describe angles TSU and TSR. Explain.

    Angles TSU and TSR are adjacent angles because they share a vertex and one side but do not overlap. They are also supplementary angles because they form a 180° angle.

17. What shape describes the cross section in the cube below?

    triangle

18. Name 2 other cross sections shapes that can be made from the cube.

    Sample answers: square, rectangle, pentagon, trapezoid, hexagon, parallelogram

19. Draw a triangle with angle measures of 32°, and 45°, and an included side with a length of 2 inches.

    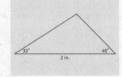

Notes

Geometry: Circumference, Area, and Volume

Unit Vocabulary

circumference   (5-1)

diameter   (5-1)

radius   (5-1)

UNIT 5

Geometry: Circumference, Area, and Volume

Unit Focus

While you have worked with and found areas of triangles and quadrilaterals, now you will find the area of circles and composite figures. You will also discover a relationship between the ratio of the circumference to the diameter of a circle. This relationship is represented by the Greek letter, π. Then, you will apply your understanding of area to solve area and surface area problems. In addition, you will find the volume of different prisms.

Unit at a Glance

COMMON CORE

Lesson	Standards for Mathematical Content
5-1 Circumference of a Circle	CC.7.G.4
5-2 Area of a Circle	CC.7.G.4
5-3 Solving Area Problems	CC.7.G.6
5-4 Solving Surface Area Problems	CC.7.G.6
5-5 Solving Volume Problems	CC.7.G.6
Problem Solving Connections	
Test Prep	

Unit 5   109   Geometry: Circumference, Area, and Volume

Unpacking the Common Core State Standards

This page lists and explains the Standards for Mathematical Content that are addressed in this unit. For information about the Standards for Mathematical Practice, which are integrated throughout the text, see Teacher Edition pages vii–xiii.

Unpacking the Common Core State Standards

Use the table to help you understand the Standards for Mathematical Content that are taught in this unit. Refer to the lessons listed after each standard for exploration and practice.

COMMON CORE Standards for Mathematical Content	What It Means For You
CC.7.G.4 Know the formulas for the area and circumference of a circle and use them to solve problems; give an informal derivation of the relationship between the circumference and area of a circle. Lessons 5-1, 5-2	Given any circle, you will be able to find its circumference and area. You will understand the difference between area and circumference and their formulas. You will also learn the relationship between the circumference and area of a circle. Then, you will solve problems by applying your knowledge of circles.
CC.7.G.6 Solve real-world and mathematical problems involving area, volume, and surface area of two- and three-dimensional objects composed of triangles, quadrilaterals, polygons, cubes, and right prisms. Lessons 5-3, 5-4, 5-5	You will solve problems by using formulas to find the areas, surface areas, and volumes of two- and three-dimensional figures. They may be simple or composite figures made up of triangles, quadrilaterals, polygons, cubes, and right prisms.

Notes

_____

_____

_____

_____

_____

_____

_____

_____

_____

_____

5-1

Circumference of a Circle

Essential question: *How do you find the circumference of a circle?*

COMMON CORE Standards for Mathematical Content

CC.7.G.4 Know the formulas for area and circumference of a circle and use them to solve problems; give an informal derivation of the relationship between the circumference and area of a circle.

Vocabulary
diameter

radius

circumference

Prerequisites
definition of circle

Math Background
The circumference of a circle is like the perimeter of a polygon in the sense that it is a one-dimensional measure of distance around the figure. The formula for the circumference of a circle is $C = \pi d$, where C is circumference and d is diameter. The irrational number π is the constant value of the ratio of circumference to diameter, or $\frac{C}{d}$, in any circle. The irrational number π is usually approximated with 3.14 or $\frac{22}{7}$. Another formula for circumference comes from the fact that the diameter is twice the length of the radius: $C = 2\pi r$.

INTRODUCE

Discuss with students how they might approximate the distance around a circular object (e.g., cup, bottle, or can) with a ruler. Tell students that in this lesson, they will learn how to better approximate that distance around circular objects.

TEACH

1 EXPLORE

Questioning Strategies
- Why is a measuring tape better to use than a ruler? **The measuring tape can mold around a circular object because it is not rigid like a ruler.**
- How is the ratio $\frac{C}{d}$ alike for each object? **It is a little more than 3 for each circular object.**

> MATHEMATICAL PRACTICE **Highlighting the Standards**
>
> This Explore is an opportunity to address Standard 5 (Use appropriate tools strategically). Students use a measuring tape, rather than a ruler, to measure around circular objects. The measurements using a measuring tape are more accurate than with a ruler. The increased level of accuracy allows students to learn about the irrational number π through measurement and observation.

2 EXAMPLE

Questioning Strategies
- What are two formulas for the circumference of a circle? $C = \pi d$ and $C = 2\pi r$
- Which formula would you use for this example? Why? **Possible answer: Use $C = 2\pi r$ because the radius is given.**
- How could you use the other formula? **Double the radius to get the diameter, then use $C = \pi d$.**
- Why is your answer for the circumference actually an approximation? **The circumference is actually an approximation because π is approximated in the calculation.**

© Houghton Mifflin Harcourt Publishing Company

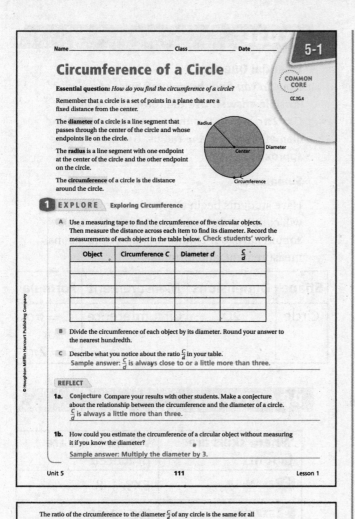

Name_____ Class_____ Date_____

5-1

Circumference of a Circle

COMMON CORE
CC.7.G.4

Essential question: *How do you find the circumference of a circle?*

Remember that a circle is a set of points in a plane that are a fixed distance from the center.

The **diameter** of a circle is a line segment that passes through the center of the circle and whose endpoints lie on the circle.

The **radius** is a line segment with one endpoint at the center of the circle and the other endpoint on the circle.

The **circumference** of a circle is the distance around the circle.

1 EXPLORE   Exploring Circumference

A Use a measuring tape to find the circumference of five circular objects. Then measure the distance across each item to find its diameter. Record the measurements of each object in the table below. Check students' work.

Object	Circumference C	Diameter d	$\frac{C}{d}$

B Divide the circumference of each object by its diameter. Round your answer to the nearest hundredth.

C Describe what you notice about the ratio $\frac{C}{d}$ in your table.

Sample answer: $\frac{C}{d}$ is always close to or a little more than three.

REFLECT

1a. **Conjecture** Compare your results with other students. Make a conjecture about the relationship between the circumference and the diameter of a circle.

$\frac{C}{d}$ is always a little more than three.

1b. How could you estimate the circumference of a circular object without measuring it if you know the diameter?

Sample answer: Multiply the diameter by 3.

Unit 5   111   Lesson 1

The ratio of the circumference to the diameter $\frac{C}{d}$ of any circle is the same for all circles. The ratio is called *pi*, or π. As you calculated in **1**, the value of π is close to 3. You can approximate π as 3.14 or $\frac{22}{7}$. You can use this ratio to find a formula for circumference.

For any circle, $\frac{C}{d} = \pi$. Solve the equation for C to give an equation for the circumference of a circle in terms of the diameter.

$\frac{C}{d} = \pi$ The ratio of <u>circumference</u> to <u>diameter</u> is *pi*.

$\frac{C}{d} \times d = \pi \times d$ Multiply both sides by <u>d</u>.

$C = \underline{\pi d}$ Simplify.

Since the diameter is the same as two times the radius, you can also substitute 2*r* in the equation for *d*.

$d = 2r$ The diameter is two times the <u>radius</u>.

$C = \pi(2r)$ Substitute for *d*.

$C = 2\pi r$ Use the Commutative Property.

The two equivalent formulas for circumference are:

$C = \underline{\pi d}$ and $C = \underline{2\pi r}$

2 EXAMPLE   Finding the Circumference of a Circle

Find the circumference of the circle to the nearest hundredth. Use 3.14 for π.

The <u>radius</u> of the circle is 3 cm. Use the formula that includes the radius, <u>$C = 2\pi r$</u>

$C = 2\pi \ r$ *Use the formula.*

$C = 2\pi \ 3$ *Substitute 3 for r.*

$C \approx 2(3.14)(3)$ *Substitute 3.14 for π.*

$C \approx 18.84$ *Multiply.*

The circumference is about <u>18.84</u> cm.

REFLECT

2a. What value of *pi* could you use to estimate the circumference? <u>3</u>

2b. How do you know your answer is reasonable?

Sample answer: Using 3 for *pi*, $2 \times 3 \times 3 = 18$, which is close to the answer.

2c. When would it be logical to use $\frac{22}{7}$ instead of 3.14 for *pi*?

It would be logical to use $\frac{22}{7}$ when the radius or diameter is a multiple of 7.

Unit 5   112   Lesson 1

© Houghton Mifflin Harcourt Publishing Company

Notes

Unit 5   **112**   Lesson 1

Questioning Strategies

• What information are you given? circumference and speed of the boat traveling along the diameter

• How can you find the diameter with the information you are given? Substitute 942 ft for the circumference in $C = \pi d$, and solve for d.

• Is the length of the diameter the answer to the question asked in this problem? No, the question asks for the time it takes the boat to cross.

• How can you find the answer to the question asked in the problem? Use the relationship between distance, rate, and time: $d = rt$. The distance is 300 ft and the rate is 4 ft/s.

Teaching Strategies

Discuss with students plans for solving this multi-step problem. Make sure they understand the information given and the information requested. Remind students of the relationship between distance, rate, and time ($d = rt$), if necessary.

CLOSE

Essential Question

How do you find the circumference of a circle?
Possible answer: Use the formula $C = \pi d$ or $C = 2\pi r$, where C is the circumference, d is the diameter, and r is the radius. Use 3.14 or $\frac{22}{7}$ to approximate π.

Summarize

Have students begin a formula chart they will continue throughout this unit. The table should have four columns: shape, dimensions, measurement, and formula.

Shape	Dimensions	Measurement	Formula
Circle	2D	Circumference	$C = \pi d$ or $C = 2\pi r$

PRACTICE

Where skills are taught	Where skills are practiced
2 EXAMPLE	EXS. 1–8
3 EXPLORE	EXS. 9–12

3 EXPLORE   Using Circumference

The circumference of a circular pond is 942 feet. A model boat is moving directly across the pond, along the diameter, at a rate of 4 feet per second. How long does it take the boat to get to the other side?

A Make a diagram.

Sketch the pond, and label what you know and what you need to find.

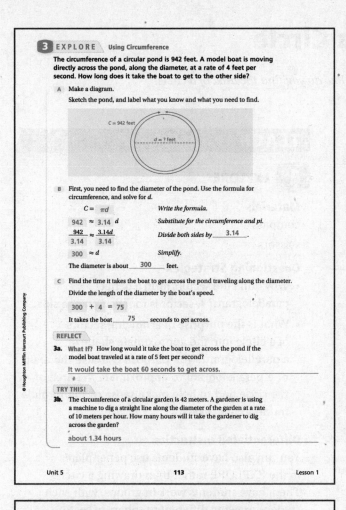

B First, you need to find the diameter of the pond. Use the formula for circumference, and solve for *d*.

$C =$	πd	*Write the formula.*
$942 \approx$	$3.14\ d$	*Substitute for the circumference and pi.*
$\dfrac{942}{3.14} \approx$	$\dfrac{3.14d}{3.14}$	*Divide both sides by* ____3.14____ .
$300 \approx$	d	*Simplify.*

The diameter is about ____300____ feet.

C Find the time it takes the boat to get across the pond traveling along the diameter.

Divide the length of the diameter by the boat's speed.

$300 \div 4 = 75$

It takes the boat ____75____ seconds to get across.

REFLECT

3a. **What If?** How long would it take the boat to get across the pond if the model boat traveled at a rate of 5 feet per second?

It would take the boat 60 seconds to get across.

TRY THIS!

3b. The circumference of a circular garden is 42 meters. A gardener is using a machine to dig a straight line along the diameter of the garden at a rate of 10 meters per hour. How many hours will it take the gardener to dig across the garden?

about 1.34 hours

PRACTICE

Find the circumference of each circle to the nearest tenth, if necessary. Use 3.14 or $\frac{22}{7}$ for π.

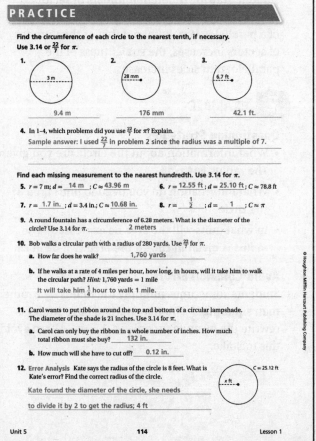

1.   3 m   2.   28 mm   3.   6.7 ft

9.4 m   176 mm   42.1 ft.

4. In 1–4, which problems did you use $\frac{22}{7}$ for π? Explain.

Sample answer: I used $\frac{22}{7}$ in problem 2 since the radius was a multiple of 7.

Find each missing measurement to the nearest hundredth. Use 3.14 for π.

5. $r = 7$ m; $d =$ ___14 m___ ; $C \approx$ ___43.96 m___

6. $r =$ ___12.55 ft___ ; $d =$ ___25.10 ft___; $C \approx 78.8$ ft

7. $r =$ ___1.7 in.___ ; $d = 3.4$ in.; $C \approx$ ___10.68 in.___

8. $r = \frac{1}{2}$; $d =$ ___1___ ; $C \approx \pi$

9. A round fountain has a circumference of 6.28 meters. What is the diameter of the circle? Use 3.14 for π. ___2 meters___

10. Bob walks a circular path with a radius of 280 yards. Use $\frac{22}{7}$ for π.

a. How far does he walk? ___1,760 yards___

b. If he walks at a rate of 4 miles per hour, how long, in hours, will it take him to walk the circular path? *Hint:* 1,760 yards = 1 mile

It will take him $\frac{1}{4}$ hour to walk 1 mile.

11. Carol wants to put ribbon around the top and bottom of a circular lampshade. The diameter of the shade is 21 inches. Use 3.14 for π.

a. Carol can only buy the ribbon in a whole number of inches. How much total ribbon must she buy? ___132 in.___

b. How much will she have to cut off? ___0.12 in.___

12. **Error Analysis** Kate says the radius of the circle is 8 feet. What is Kate's error? Find the correct radius of the circle.

Kate found the diameter of the circle, she needs

to divide it by 2 to get the radius; 4 ft

$C = 25.12$ ft

x ft

© Houghton Mifflin Harcourt Publishing Company

Area of a Circle

Essential question: *How do you find the area of a circle?*

COMMON CORE **Standards for Mathematical Content**

CC.7.G.4 Know the formulas for area and circumference of a circle and use them to solve problems; give an informal derivation of the relationship between the circumference and area of a circle.

Prerequisites

Circumference of a circle

Area of a parallelogram

Math Background

Area is a measure of the space inside a two-dimensional figure and is measured in square units. The formula for the area of a circle is $A = \pi r^2$, where A is area and r is the radius. You can use the sectors of a circle to develop this formula. Using all the sectors of a cut up circle, you can form the approximate shape of a parallelogram in which the base is half the circumference ($\frac{1}{2}C$) and the height is the radius (r). Then the area can be approximated using the formula for area of a parallelogram. Students do this in Explore 1.

INTRODUCE

Use circular fruit, such as oranges and grapes, to create circle stamps of different sizes. Have students stamp each on a sheet of paper, in order, from smallest to largest. Ask how they know which is smallest and which is largest. Remind them that this is the area of the stamp. Then, ask them how much bigger the largest stamp is than the smallest. Explain that in this lesson, they will be able to calculate and compare the actual areas of the stamps.

TEACH

1 EXPLORE

Materials

compass

scissors

Questioning Strategies

- Why don't the sectors form a perfect parallelogram? A sector is rounded on one side.

- What is the purpose of arranging sectors of a circle into the approximate shape of a parallelogram? The purpose is to use the area of a parallelogram to approximate the area of the circle and to help make sense of the formula for area of a circle.

Differentiated Instruction

You can also have students use paper plates in the EXPLORE rather than drawing a circle. Then, have students work in groups, with each student drawing different numbers of sectors. Have them put the sectors together in the shape of a parallelogram. Point out that as the number of sectors increases, the straightness of the parallelogram sides increases.

2 EXAMPLE

Questioning Strategies

- What information about the circle are you given? The radius is 4 cm.

- What information do you need to find? area of the circle

- In what units will the area be expressed? The radius is given in cm, so the area will be in cm^2.

Avoid Common Errors

Students sometimes multiply the radius by 2 rather than squaring it. You may want to have students rewrite the formula for area as $A = \pi \cdot r \cdot r$ to avoid this mistake.

Name_____ Class_____ Date_____

5-2

Area of a Circle

Essential question: *How do you find the area of a circle?*

COMMON CORE

CC.7.G.4

1 EXPLORE Finding the Area of a Circle

You can use what you know about circles and *pi* to help find the formula for the area of a circle.

Step 1: Use a compass to draw a circle and cut it out.

Step 2: Fold the circle three times as shown to get equal wedges.

Step 3: Unfold and shade one-half of the circle.

Step 4: Cut out the wedges and fit the pieces together to form a figure that looks like a parallelogram.

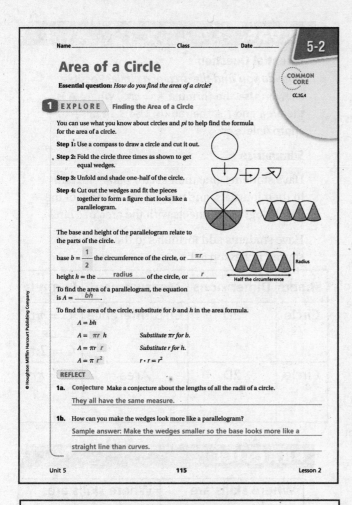

The base and height of the parallelogram relate to the parts of the circle.

base $b = \dfrac{1}{2}$ the circumference of the circle, or $\dfrac{\pi r}{}$

height $h = $ the ___radius___ of the circle, or ___r___

To find the area of a parallelogram, the equation is $A = $ ___bh___

To find the area of the circle, substitute for *b* and *h* in the area formula.

$A = bh$

$A = \pi r \; h$ *Substitute πr for b.*

$A = \pi r \; r$ *Substitute r for h.*

$A = \pi \, r^2$ $r \cdot r = r^2$

REFLECT

1a. **Conjecture** Make a conjecture about the lengths of all the radii of a circle.

They all have the same measure.

1b. How can you make the wedges look more like a parallelogram?

Sample answer: Make the wedges smaller so the base looks more like a

straight line than curves.

Unit 5   115   Lesson 2

Area of a Circle

The area of a circle is equal to π times the radius squared.

$A = \pi r^2$

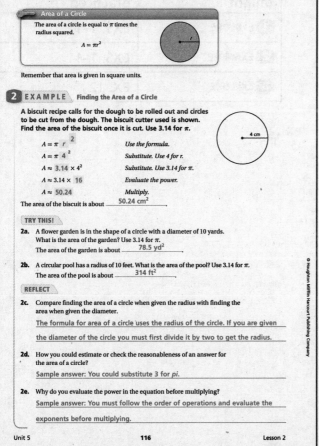

Remember that area is given in square units.

2 EXAMPLE Finding the Area of a Circle

A biscuit recipe calls for the dough to be rolled out and circles to be cut from the dough. The biscuit cutter used is shown. Find the area of the biscuit once it is cut. Use 3.14 for π.

4 cm

$A = \pi \; r^2$ *Use the formula.*

$A = \pi \; 4^2$ *Substitute. Use 4 for r.*

$A \approx 3.14 \times 4^2$ *Substitute. Use 3.14 for π.*

$A \approx 3.14 \times 16$ *Evaluate the power.*

$A \approx 50.24$ *Multiply.*

The area of the biscuit is about ___50.24 cm^2___

TRY THIS!

2a. A flower garden is in the shape of a circle with a diameter of 10 yards. What is the area of the garden? Use 3.14 for π.

The area of the garden is about ___78.5 yd^2___

2b. A circular pool has a radius of 10 feet. What is the area of the pool? Use 3.14 for π.

The area of the pool is about ___314 ft^2___

REFLECT

2c. Compare finding the area of a circle when given the radius with finding the area when given the diameter.

The formula for area of a circle uses the radius of the circle. If you are given

the diameter of the circle you must first divide it by two to get the radius.

2d. How you could estimate or check the reasonableness of an answer for the area of a circle?

Sample answer: You could substitute 3 for *pi*.

2e. Why do you evaluate the power in the equation before multiplying?

Sample answer: You must follow the order of operations and evaluate the

exponents before multiplying.

Unit 5   116   Lesson 2

Questioning Strategies

- What does it mean to solve $C = 2\pi r$ for r? It means to get the variable r on one side of the equation so you can have an expression that is equal to r.

- What do you substitute for r in the area formula? Substitute the expression for r that resulted from solving $C = 2\pi r$ for r.

- How do you find the square of $\frac{C}{2\pi}$? Square the numerator and the denominator. Be sure that you square both parts of the denominator. $\left(\frac{C}{2\pi}\right)^2 = \frac{C^2}{2^2\pi^2}$

- How can you use your results to find the area of a circle with a given circumference? Substitute the given circumference for C in the formula you derived for area: $A = \frac{C^2}{4\pi}$.

Teaching Strategies

Encourage students to keep their expressions in terms of π. Then, when manipulating the equation, treat π like a variable. If an approximate answer is needed, encourage them to substitute 3.14 for π at the very end of the calculations.

CLOSE

Essential Question

How do you find the area of a circle? Possible answer: Use the formula $A = \pi r^2$, where A is the area and r is the radius. Use 3.14 or $\frac{22}{7}$ to approximate π.

Summarize

Have students glue their sector parallelograms in their journals, and explain for the area of the parallelogram connects with the area of a circle.

Have students add formulas to the chart they started in Lesson 5-1.

Shape	Dimensions	Measurement	Formula
Circle	2D	Circumference	$C = \pi d$ or $C = 2\pi r$
Circle	2D	Area	$C = \pi r^2$

PRACTICE

Where skills are taught	Where skills are practiced
1 EXPLORE	EXS. 1–11
2 EXAMPLE	EXS. 1–11
3 EXPLORE	EX. 12

You can use what you know about circumference and area of circles to find a relationship between them.

3 EXPLORE Finding the Relationship between Circumference and Area

Find the relationship between the circumference and area of a circle.

Start with a circle that has radius r.

Solve the equation $C = 2\pi r$ for r.

$$r = \frac{C}{2\pi}$$

Substitute your expression for r in the formula for area of a circle.

$$A = \pi \left(\frac{C}{2\pi} \right)^2$$

Square the term in the parenthesis.

$$A = \pi \left(\frac{C^2}{2^2 \cdot \pi^2} \right)$$

Evaluate the power.

$$A = \frac{\pi \cdot C^2}{4 \cdot \pi^2}$$

Simplify.

$$A = \frac{C^2}{4 \cdot \pi}$$

Solve for C^2.

$$C^2 = 4 \ \pi \ A$$

The circumference of the circle squared is equal to ___four times _pi_ times the area.___

REFLECT

3a. Does this formula work for a circle with a radius of 3 inches? Show your work below.

Yes; $A = \pi r^2$ $C = 2\pi r$ $C^2 \overset{?}{=} 4\pi A$
$= \pi \times 3^2$ $= 2\pi 3$ $18.84^2 \overset{?}{=} 4 \times 3.14 \times 28.26$
$= 9\pi$ $= 6\pi$ $354.9456 = 354.9456$
≈ 28.26 ≈ 18.84

TRY THIS!

Find the area of the circles given the circumference. Give your answers in terms of π.

3b. $C = 8\pi$; $A = $ ___16π square units___

3c. $C = \pi$; $A = $ ___$\frac{\pi}{4}$ square units___

3d. $C = 2\pi$; $A = $ ___π square units___

Unit 5   117   Lesson 2

PRACTICE

Find the area of each circle to the nearest tenth, if necessary. Use 3.14 for π.

1.
153.9 m²

2.
452.2 mm²

3.
314 yd²

4.
78.5 ft²

5.
32.2 cm²

6.
213.7 in²

7. A clock face has a radius of 8 inches. What is the area of the clock face? Round your answer to the nearest hundredth.
200.96 in²

8. A DVD has a diameter of 12 centimeters. What is the area of the DVD? Round your answer to the nearest hundredth.
113.04 cm²

9. A company makes steel lids that have a diameter of 13 inches. What is the area of each lid? Round your answer to the nearest hundredth.
132.67 in²

10. A circular garden has an area of 64π square yards. What is the circumference of the garden? Give your answer in terms of π.
16π yd

11. **Reasoning** A small silver dollar pancake served at a restuarant has a circumference of 2π inches. A regular pancake has a circumference of 4π inches. Is the area of the regular pancake twice the area of the silver dollar pancake? Explain.
No, the area of the regular pancake is 4 times as large as the area of the silver dollar pancake.

12. **Critical Thinking** Describe another way to find the area of a circle when given the circumference.
Sample answer: First find the radius of the circle by using the formula $C = 2\pi r$. Then substitute the radius into the formula for the area of a circle.

Unit 5   118   Lesson 2

Notes

Solving Area Problems

Essential question: How do you find the area of composite figures?

COMMON CORE Standards for Mathematical Content

CC.7.G.6 Solve real-world and mathematical problems involving area, volume, and surface area of two- and three-dimensional objects composed of triangles, quadrilaterals, polygons, cubes, and right prisms.

Prerequisites

Area of polygons

Math Background

The concept of area, the measure of total space inside a two-dimensional figure, measured in square units, is the foundation of this lesson. Finding the area of composite figures requires finding the sum of the areas of figures that compose it.

INTRODUCE

Have students draw a capital letter in block-letter style on graph paper. The letter must contain line segments only (no curves) and each part of the letter must have a width of one unit. Ask students to think of ways to divide the letter into smaller polygons. Students should draw the divisions and identify which shapes they used. For example, the letter F is shown.

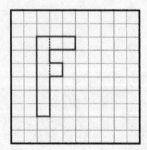

TEACH

1 EXPLORE

Questioning Strategies

- How do you know which way to divide up a composite figure? It does not matter, as long as it includes all areas of the composite figure and you know how to find the area of each individual piece.

- What pieces do you see in this composite figure? Possible answers: Triangles, rectangles, squares

> **MATHEMATICAL PRACTICE** **Highlighting the Standards**
>
> This Explore is an opportunity to address Standard 1 (Make sense of problems and persevere in solving them). Students may choose to divide the shape in a way that makes sense to them. There are many correct solution methods in this type of problem, but most solutions are multi-step. Students will need to persevere to find the area.

2 EXAMPLE

Questioning Strategies

- What is the height of the parallelogram? The height is 1.5 cm,.

- Which measurements are not used to find the area of the composite figure? 3 cm, 4 cm, and 2 cm,

- Could you divide this composite figure differently? Possible answer: Yes, you could divide it into a parallelogram, rectangle and two triangles.

Avoid Common Errors

Be sure that students remember how to find the height of a parallelogram or trapezoid. The height always forms a right angle with the base(s). Have students highlight the base and height before beginning calculations.

© Houghton Mifflin Harcourt Publishing Company

Solving Area Problems

5-3

Name_____ Class_____ Date_____

Essential question: *How do you find the area of composite figures?*

COMMON CORE
CC.7G.6

1 EXPLORE Area of a Composite Figure

Aaron was plotting the shape of his garden on grid paper. While it was an irregular shape, it was perfect for his yard. Each square on the grid represents 1 square meter.

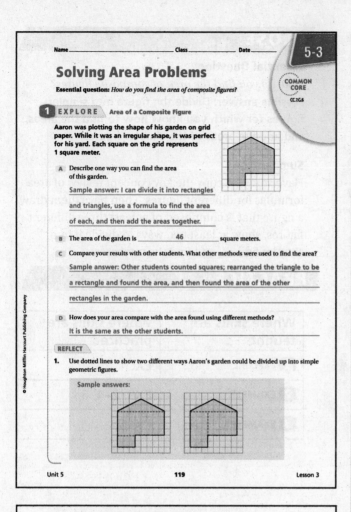

A Describe one way you can find the area of this garden.

Sample answer: I can divide it into rectangles

and triangles, use a formula to find the area

of each, and then add the areas together.

B The area of the garden is _____46_____ square meters.

C Compare your results with other students. What other methods were used to find the area?

Sample answer: Other students counted squares; rearranged the triangle to be

a rectangle and found the area, and then found the area of the other

rectangles in the garden.

D How does your area compare with the area found using different methods?

It is the same as the other students.

REFLECT

1. Use dotted lines to show two different ways Aaron's garden could be divided up into simple geometric figures.

Sample answers:

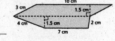

A composite figure is made up of simple geometric shapes. To find the area of composite figures and other irregular shaped figures, divide it into simple, non-overlapping figures. Find the area of each simpler figure, and then add them together to find the total area of the composite figure.

Use the chart below to review some common area formulas.

Shape	Area Formula
triangle	$A = \frac{1}{2}bh$
square	$A = s^2$
rectangle	$A = \ell w$
parallelogram	$A = bh$
trapezoid	$A = \frac{1}{2}h(b_1 + b_2)$

2 EXAMPLE Finding the Area of a Composite Figure

Find the area of the figure.

A Into what two figures can you divide this composite figure?

parallelogram and trapezoid

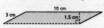

B Find the area of each shape.

Area of the Parallelogram

The base of the parallelogram is __10__ cm.
The height of the parallelogram is __1.5__ cm.
Use the formula.

$A = bh$

$A = $ __10__ · __1.5__

$A = $ __15__

The area of the parallelogram is __15__ cm².

Area of the Trapezoid

The bottom base of the trapezoid is
__7__ cm.
The top base the trapezoid is __10__ cm, since it is the same length as the base of the parallelogram.
The height of the trapezoid is __1.5__ cm.
Use the formula.

$A = \frac{1}{2}h(b_1 + b_2)$

$A = \frac{1}{2}$ 1.5 (__7__ + __10__)

$A = \frac{1}{2}$ 1.5 (__17__)

$A = $ __12.75__

The area of the trapezoid is __12.75__ cm².

Questioning Strategies

- What are the dimensions of each square on the grid? **1 yard by 1 yard, or 1 square yard**

- Do you need to find the lengths of the diagonal sides of the parallelogram or triangle? **No, they are not needed to find the area.**

- How do you find the cost of the carpet? **Multiply the number of square yards (area) by the cost per square yard.**

Teaching Strategies

Discuss several real-world examples in which the cost is expressed as dollars per square unit, such as flooring, fertilizer, paint, or wallpaper. Discuss how to find the amount of materials needed and the total costs. Students should begin to see a pattern where you multiply the cost by the number of square units needed.

CLOSE

Essential Question

How do you find the area of composite figures?
Possible answer: Divide the figure into simpler figures for which you know how to find the areas, and add the areas of the simpler figures.

Summarize

Have students copy the key concept review of area formulas for different figures. Then have them draw a figure that is composed of at least three different figures, show at least two ways to divide it into simpler figures, and find the total area.

PRACTICE

Where skills are taught	Where skills are practiced
1 EXPLORE	EX. 1
2 EXAMPLE	EXS. 2–4, 6
3 EXAMPLE	EX. 5

C Find the area of the composite figure.

$$\underset{\text{Area of parallelogram}}{15} + \underset{\text{Area of trapezoid}}{12.75} = \underset{\text{Area of composite shape}}{27.75 \text{ cm}^2}$$

REFLECT

2a. Describe another way to divide the shape into simpler figures.

Sample answer: two triangles, a rectangle, and a trapezoid

2b. If you divide the composite figure into different shapes, what is the area? What does this tell you?

27.75 cm²; it does not matter how you divide the figure, the area

is still the same.

3 EXAMPLE Calculating Cost Based on Area

A banquet room is being carpeted. A floor plan of the room is shown at right. Each unit length represents 1 yard. Carpet costs $23.50 per square yard. How much will it cost to carpet the room?

A Divide the figure into simpler shapes: a parallelogram, a rectangle, and a triangle. Show the divisions on the floor plan with dotted lines. Count the units to find the dimensions.

B Find the area of the parallelogram. **C** Find the area of the rectangle.

$A = bh$ $A = \ell w$

$A = \boxed{4} \cdot \boxed{2}$ $A = \boxed{6} \cdot \boxed{4}$

$A = \boxed{8}$ square yards $A = \boxed{24}$ square yards

D Find the area of the triangle.

$A = \frac{1}{2}bh$

$A = \frac{1}{2} \boxed{1} \cdot \boxed{2}$

$A = \boxed{1}$ square yard

E The area of the composite figure is $\underline{\quad 33 \quad}$ yd².

F To calculate the cost to carpet the room, multiply $\underline{\quad \text{area} \quad}$ by the $\underline{\text{cost per square yard}}$

The cost to carpet the banquet room is $\underline{\$775.50}$.

Unit 5   **121**   Lesson 3

REFLECT

3. Describe how you can estimate the cost to carpet the room.

Sample answer: Draw a bigger rectangle around the room, and overestimate

the area, then round the price of carpet to $20. This would give an

overestimate of the cost.

PRACTICE

Find the area of each figure. Use 3.14 for π.

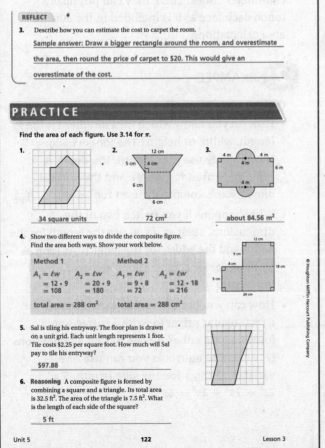

1.

34 square units

2.
12 cm
5 cm   4 cm
6 cm
6 cm

72 cm²

3.
4 m   4 m
4 m   6 m
4 m

about 84.56 m²

4. Show two different ways to divide the composite figure. Find the area both ways. Show your work below.

Method 1		Method 2	
$A_1 = \ell w$	$A_2 = \ell w$	$A_1 = \ell w$	$A_2 = \ell w$
$= 12 \cdot 9$	$= 20 \cdot 9$	$= 9 \cdot 8$	$= 12 \cdot 18$
$= 108$	$= 180$	$= 72$	$= 216$

total area = 288 cm²   total area = 288 cm²

5. Sal is tiling his entryway. The floor plan is drawn on a unit grid. Each unit length represents 1 foot. Tile costs $2.25 per square foot. How much will Sal pay to tile his entryway?

$97.88

6. **Reasoning** A composite figure is formed by combining a square and a triangle. Its total area is 32.5 ft². The area of the triangle is 7.5 ft². What is the length of each side of the square?

5 ft

Unit 5   **122**   Lesson 3

Solving Surface Area Problems

Essential question: *How do you find the surface area of a figure made of prisms?*

COMMON CORE **Standards for Mathematical Content**

CC.7.G.6 Solve real-world and mathematical problems involving area, volume, and surface area of two- and three-dimensional objects composed of triangles, quadrilaterals, polygons, cubes, and right prisms.

Prerequisites

Nets and surface area

Math Background

Surface area is the sum of the areas of all the faces of a three-dimensional figure. To visualize the faces and their dimensions, you can use a net. A net is the two-dimensional representation of a three-dimensional figure. It looks like the wrapping around a three-dimensional figure that is peeled off and lying flat. You can find the surface area of a three-dimensional figure by adding the areas of all the faces.

INTRODUCE

Have students each bring an empty small box from home (examples: raisin box, cereal box, shoe box). Ask them to identify the parts of the box you see when the box is closed. Tell them that this is called the surface of the box. Have students measure and find the area of each face of the surface, and add those areas to find the total surface area. It may help to cut it into a net first. Remind them to find the area of only the surface, not extra flaps that cannot be seen when the box is closed. Tell students that in this lesson, they will learn formulas for surface area.

TEACH

1 EXPLORE

Questioning Strategies

- How are the two figures different? They are both cubes, except one cube is missing a unit cube at the vertex.

- How does the missing unit cube at the vertex change the surface? Removing the unit cube from the vertex creates an inverted corner on the cube.

- How does the missing unit cube at the vertex change the surface area? The inverted corner exposes the same number of faces as the corner with the unit cube in place, so the surface area is the same.

Differentiated Instruction

Allow students to build these figures with centimeter cubes. Then, they can physically touch each face as it is included in the surface area calculations.

2 EXAMPLE

Questioning Strategies

- How do you know which measurement is the length, width, or height? The longest edge is commonly used for length, the depth is commonly used for width, and the vertical dimension is commonly used for height.

- What happens if you switch two of the dimensions, such as if you use the length for the width and the width for the length? As long as all three factor combinations are used, it will not matter.

- How can you use the surface-area formula for a rectangular prism to write a surface-area formula for a cube? A cube has all 3 dimensions (ℓ, w, and h) equal, so you can use one variable. Using s for any side length, $S = 2s^2 + 2s^2 + 2s^2 = 6s^2$.

© Houghton Mifflin Harcourt Publishing Company

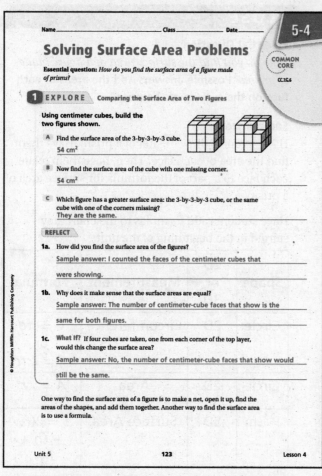

5-4

Name _____ Class _____ Date _____

Solving Surface Area Problems

COMMON CORE
CC.7G.6

Essential question: How do you find the surface area of a figure made of prisms?

1 EXPLORE Comparing the Surface Area of Two Figures

Using centimeter cubes, build the
two figures shown.

A   Find the surface area of the 3-by-3-by-3 cube.

    54 cm²

B   Now find the surface area of the cube with one missing corner.

    54 cm²

C   Which figure has a greater surface area: the 3-by-3-by-3, or the same
    cube with one of the corners missing?
    They are the same.

REFLECT

1a. How did you find the surface area of the figures?

Sample answer: I counted the faces of the centimeter cubes that

were showing.

1b. Why does it make sense that the surface areas are equal?

Sample answer: The number of centimeter-cube faces that show is the

same for both figures.

1c. What If? If four cubes are taken, one from each corner of the top layer,
would this change the surface area?

Sample answer: No, the number of centimeter-cube faces that show would

still be the same.

One way to find the surface area of a figure is to make a net, open it up, find the
areas of the shapes, and add them together. Another way to find the surface area
is to use a formula.

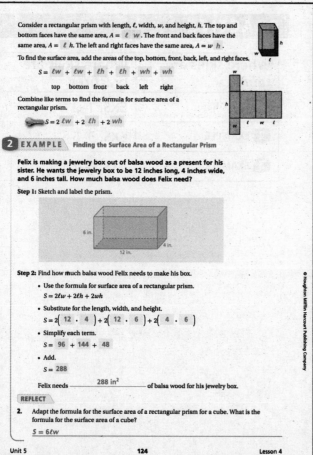

Consider a rectangular prism with length, ℓ, width, w, and height, h. The top and
bottom faces have the same area, $A = \ell\, w$. The front and back faces have the
same area, $A = \ell\, h$. The left and right faces have the same area, $A = w\, h$.

To find the surface area, add the areas of the top, bottom, front, back, left, and right faces.

$S = \ell w + \ell w + \ell h + \ell h + wh + wh$

   top bottom front back left right

Combine like terms to find the formula for surface area of a
rectangular prism.

$S = 2\,\ell w + 2\,\ell h + 2\,wh$

2 EXAMPLE Finding the Surface Area of a Rectangular Prism

Felix is making a jewelry box out of balsa wood as a present for his
sister. He wants the jewelry box to be 12 inches long, 4 inches wide,
and 6 inches tall. How much balsa wood does Felix need?

Step 1: Sketch and label the prism.

6 in.
12 in.
4 in.

Step 2: Find how much balsa wood Felix needs to make his box.

- Use the formula for surface area of a rectangular prism.
  $S = 2\ell w + 2\ell h + 2wh$
- Substitute for the length, width, and height.
  $S = 2(12 \cdot 4) + 2(12 \cdot 6) + 2(4 \cdot 6)$
- Simplify each term.
  $S = 96 + 144 + 48$
- Add.
  $S = 288$

Felix needs _____ 288 in² _____ of balsa wood for his jewelry box.

REFLECT

2. Adapt the formula for the surface area of a rectangular prism for a cube. What is the
formula for the surface area of a cube?

   $S = 6\ell w$

Questioning Strategies

- What shape is the house? What shape is the chimney? **Both are rectangular prisms.**

- What part of the surface area of the house will not be painted? **back right corner of the top of the house**

- What part of the surface area of the chimney will not be painted? **the bottom of the chimney**

Avoid Common Errors

Students might subtract the overlap once when calculating the surface area of one shape, but forget to subtract it again when calculating the surface area of the other shape. Have students build a model so that they can see why it is subtracted twice. The overlap area is not part of the surface area of either of the prisms that meet.

MATHEMATICAL PRACTICE **Highlighting the Standards**

This example is an opportunity to address Standard 4 (Make sense of problems and persevere in solving them). Students may choose to divide the shape in a way that makes sense to them. There are many correct methods of solution in this type of problem, but most solutions are multi-step. Students will need to persevere to find the surface area.

CLOSE

Essential Question

How do you find the surface area of a figure made of prisms? **Possible answer: Add the areas of each face on the surface of the prism.**

Summarize

Have students draw the net of a prism. Have them find the area of each face. Then, have them relate each face to a part of the formula for surface area of a prism.

Have students add formulas to the chart they started in the beginning of the unit.

Shape	2D or 3D	Measurement	Formula
Circle	2D	Circumference	$C = \pi d$ or $C = 2\pi r$
Circle	2D	Area	$A = \pi r^2$
Prism	3D	Surface Area	$S = 2(\ell w + \ell h + hw)$

PRACTICE

Where skills are taught	Where skills are practiced
1 EXPLORE	EXS. 1–2
2 EXAMPLE	EXS. 3–5
3 EXAMPLE	EXS. 6–7

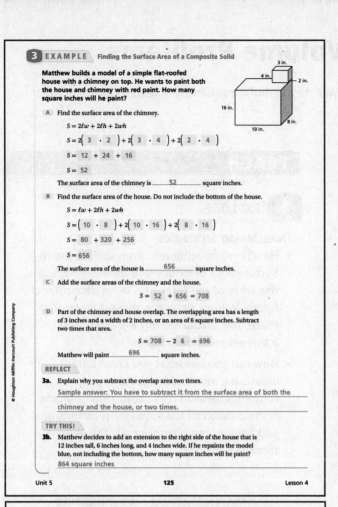

3 EXAMPLE Finding the Surface Area of a Composite Solid

Matthew builds a model of a simple flat-roofed house with a chimney on top. He wants to paint both the house and chimney with red paint. How many square inches will he paint?

A Find the surface area of the chimney.

$S = 2\ell w + 2\ell h + 2wh$

$S = 2\left(\boxed{3} \cdot \boxed{2}\right) + 2\left(\boxed{3} \cdot \boxed{4}\right) + 2\left(\boxed{2} \cdot \boxed{4}\right)$

$S = \boxed{12} + \boxed{24} + \boxed{16}$

$S = \boxed{52}$

The surface area of the chimney is ___52___ square inches.

B Find the surface area of the house. Do not include the bottom of the house.

$S = \ell w + 2\ell h + 2wh$

$S = \left(\boxed{10} \cdot \boxed{8}\right) + 2\left(\boxed{10} \cdot \boxed{16}\right) + 2\left(\boxed{8} \cdot \boxed{16}\right)$

$S = \boxed{80} + 320 + 256$

$S = 656$

The surface area of the house is ___656___ square inches.

C Add the surface areas of the chimney and the house.

$S = \boxed{52} + 656 = 708$

D Part of the chimney and house overlap. The overlapping area has a length of 3 inches and a width of 2 inches, or an area of 6 square inches. Subtract two times that area.

$S = 708 - 2\boxed{6} = 696$

Matthew will paint ___696___ square inches.

REFLECT

3a. Explain why you subtract the overlap area two times.

Sample answer: You have to subtract it from the surface area of both the

chimney and the house, or two times.

TRY THIS!

3b. Matthew decides to add an extension to the right side of the house that is 12 inches tall, 6 inches long, and 4 inches wide. If he repaints the model blue, not including the bottom, how many square inches will he paint?

864 square inches

PRACTICE

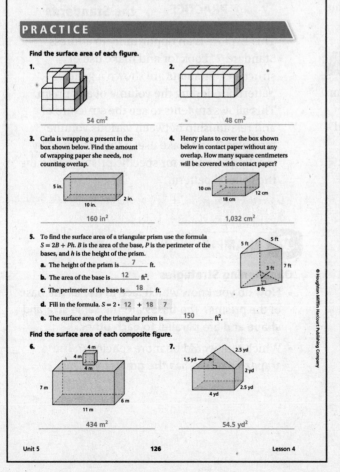

Find the surface area of each figure.

1.

54 cm²

2.

48 cm²

3. Carla is wrapping a present in the box shown below. Find the amount of wrapping paper she needs, not counting overlap.

5 in.
10 in.
2 in.

160 in²

4. Henry plans to cover the box shown below in contact paper without any overlap. How many square centimeters will be covered with contact paper?

10 cm
18 cm
12 cm

1,032 cm²

5. To find the surface area of a triangular prism use the formula $S = 2B + Ph$. B is the area of the base, P is the perimeter of the base, and h is the height of the prism.

a. The height of the prism is ___7___ ft.

b. The area of the base is ___12___ ft².

c. The perimeter of the base is ___18___ ft.

d. Fill in the formula. $S = 2 \cdot \boxed{12} + \boxed{18} \cdot \boxed{7}$

e. The surface area of the triangular prism is ___150___ ft².

5 ft   5 ft
3 ft   7 ft
8 ft

Find the surface area of each composite figure.

6.

4 m
4 m
4 m
7 m
11 m
6 m

434 m²

7.

2.5 yd
1.5 yd
2 yd
4 yd
2.5 yd

54.5 yd²

© Houghton Mifflin Harcourt Publishing Company

Solving Volume Problems

Essential question: *How do you find the volume of a figure made up of cubes and prisms?*

© Houghton Mifflin Harcourt Publishing Company

COMMON CORE Standards for Mathematical Content

CC.7.G.6 Solve real-world and mathematical problems involving area, volume, and surface area of two- and three-dimensional objects composed of triangles, quadrilaterals, polygons, cubes, and right prisms.

Prerequisites
Volume of prisms

Math Background
Volume is the capacity of a three-dimensional figure. It is measured in cubic units, so the volume expresses how many non-overlapping unit cubes will exactly fill the figure. The formula for volume is a rule for calculating the volume of a figure. The formula is adjusted as needed for different shapes, but it is essentially the same concept for all prisms: to find the product of the area of the base and the height. This lesson also includes finding the volume of composite three-dimensional figures.

INTRODUCE
Show students a box and a number cube. Ask them how many number cubes they think it would take to fill the box. Ask if they can think of a way to find the number of number cubes it would take to fill the box without actually filling it up and counting cubes. Students should already know the formula for volume of a prism. Tell students that in this lesson they will use the formula to find volumes of shapes that are composed of prisms.

TEACH

1 EXPLORE

Questioning Strategies
- How is volume different from surface area? Surface area describes two-dimensional space, the areas of the faces of a three-dimensional figure. Volume describes three-dimensional space, the space that fills the interior of a three-dimensional figure.

- How can you use what you know about measuring area and height to explain why volume is measured in cubic units? Volume is the product of base area (two-dimensional) and height (one-dimensional). The volume is three-dimensional.

MATHEMATICAL PRACTICE **Highlighting the Standards**

This Explore is an opportunity to address Standard 7 (Look for and make use of structure). Students are shown a general pattern for finding the volume of any prism. This allows students to see the structure of and relationship between various volume formulas. They make use of this structure by creating formulas for specific prisms based on the general pattern.

2 EXAMPLE

Questioning Strategies
- How do you know which face to use as the base of the prisms? The bases are the same size and shape and are parallel to each other.

- Which tent would be more spacious? The trapezoidal tent has the greater volume.

Name_____ Class_____ Date_____

5-5

COMMON
CORE

CC.7.G.6

Solving Volume Problems

Essential question: *How do you find the volume of a figure made up of cubes and prisms?*

1 EXPLORE   Finding the Volume of a Prism

A   Use centimeter cubes to build a prism like the one shown. Each cube represents a unit of measure called a cubic unit, so centimeter cubes represent cubic centimeters.

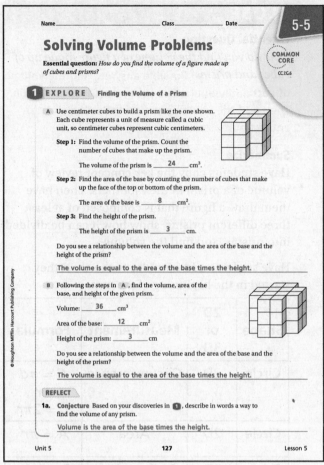

Step 1: Find the volume of the prism. Count the number of cubes that make up the prism.

The volume of the prism is ____24____ cm³.

Step 2: Find the area of the base by counting the number of cubes that make up the face of the top or bottom of the prism.

The area of the base is ____8____ cm².

Step 3: Find the height of the prism.

The height of the prism is ____3____ cm.

Do you see a relationship between the volume and the area of the base and the height of the prism?

The volume is equal to the area of the base times the height.

B   Following the steps in A , find the volume, area of the base, and height of the given prism.

Volume: ____36____ cm³

Area of the base: ____12____ cm²

Height of the prism: ____3____ cm

Do you see a relationship between the volume and the area of the base and the height of the prism?

The volume is equal to the area of the base times the height.

REFLECT

1a.   Conjecture Based on your discoveries in ❶, describe in words a way to find the volume of any prism.

Volume is the area of the base times the height.

Unit 5   127   Lesson 5

© Houghton Mifflin Harcourt Publishing Company

You can find the volume of any prism by multiplying the area of the base *B* by the height of the prism *h*.

> **Volume of a Prism**
> The volume *V* of a prism is the area of its base *B* times its height *h*.
> $$V = Bh$$

2 EXAMPLE   Finding the Volume of Prisms

Bradley is setting up two tents. One is the shape of a triangular prism and the other is the shape of a trapezoidal prism. How many cubic feet of space are in each tent?

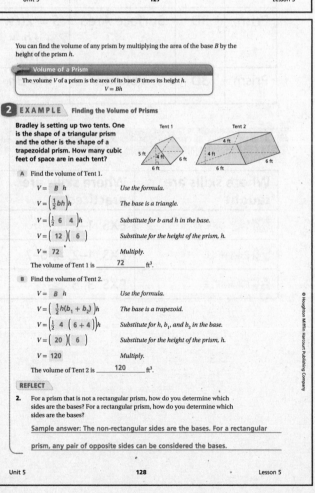

A   Find the volume of Tent 1.

$V = $ ☐ *B* ☐ *h*   *Use the formula.*

$V = \left(\frac{1}{2}bh\right)h$ *The base is a triangle.*

$V = \left(\frac{1}{2}\boxed{6}\ \boxed{4}\right)h$ *Substitute for b and h in the base.*

$V = \left(\boxed{12}\right)\left(\boxed{6}\right)$ *Substitute for the height of the prism, h.*

$V = \boxed{72}$ *Multiply.*

The volume of Tent 1 is ____72____ ft³.

B   Find the volume of Tent 2.

$V = $ ☐ *B* ☐ *h*   *Use the formula.*

$V = \left(\frac{1}{2}h(b_1 + b_2)\right)h$ *The base is a trapezoid.*

$V = \left(\frac{1}{2}\ \boxed{4}\ \left(\boxed{6+4}\right)\right)h$ *Substitute for h, b_1, and b_2 in the base.*

$V = \left(\boxed{20}\right)\left(\boxed{6}\right)$ *Substitute for the height of the prism, h.*

$V = \boxed{120}$ *Multiply.*

The volume of Tent 2 is ____120____ ft³.

REFLECT

2.   For a prism that is not a rectangular prism, how do you determine which sides are the bases? For a rectangular prism, how do you determine which sides are the bases?

Sample answer: The non-rectangular sides are the bases. For a rectangular

prism, any pair of opposite sides can be considered the bases.

Unit 5   128   Lesson 5

© Houghton Mifflin Harcourt Publishing Company

Questioning Strategies

• Which three three-dimensional figures compose this figure? three rectangular prisms

• Why do you only have to find two volumes to find the total volume? The two large prisms are the same size, so you can double that volume and add the volume of the small prism.

REFLECT

In Reflect **3a**, students are asked to compare the volume of the original aquarium with one that is twice its size. The main idea for this comparison is for students to recognize that when all 3 dimensions are doubled, the volume will be doubled 3 times, or multiplied by $2^3 = 8$.

CLOSE

Essential Question

How do you find the volume of a figure made up of cubes and prisms? Possible answer: Find the volume of each individual prism using the formula $V = Bh$. Then add the volumes to find the volume of the entire figure.

Summarize

Have students copy the key concept review of volume of a prism in their journals. Then have them draw a figure that is composed of at least three different prisms, show how it can be divided into prisms, and find the volume.

Have students add formulas to the chart they started in the beginning of the unit.

Shape	2D or 3D	Measurement	Formula
Circle	2D	Circumference	$C = \pi d$ or $C = 2\pi r$
Circle	2D	Area	$A = \pi r^2$
Prism	3D	Surface Area	$S = 2(\ell w + \ell h + hw)$
Prism	3D	Volume	$V = Bh$

PRACTICE

Where skills are taught	Where skills are practiced
1 EXPLORE	EXS. 1–2
2 EXAMPLE	EXS. 1–2, 4, 6–7
3 EXAMPLE	EXS. 3, 5

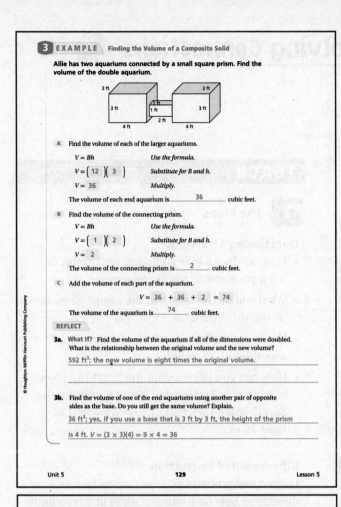

3 EXAMPLE Finding the Volume of a Composite Solid

Allie has two aquariums connected by a small square prism. Find the volume of the double aquarium.

A Find the volume of each of the larger aquariums.

$V = Bh$ *Use the formula.*

$V = (12)(3)$ *Substitute for B and h.*

$V = 36$ *Multiply.*

The volume of each end aquarium is ____36____ cubic feet.

B Find the volume of the connecting prism.

$V = Bh$ *Use the formula.*

$V = (1)(2)$ *Substitute for B and h.*

$V = 2$ *Multiply.*

The volume of the connecting prism is ____2____ cubic feet.

C Add the volume of each part of the aquarium.

$$V = 36 + 36 + 2 = 74$$

The volume of the aquarium is ____74____ cubic feet.

REFLECT

3a. **What If?** Find the volume of the aquarium if all of the dimensions were doubled. What is the relationship between the original volume and the new volume?

592 ft³; the new volume is eight times the original volume.

3b. Find the volume of one of the end aquariums using another pair of opposite sides as the base. Do you still get the same volume? Explain.

36 ft³; yes, if you use a base that is 3 ft by 3 ft, the height of the prism

is 4 ft. V = (3 × 3)(4) = 9 × 4 = 36

Unit 5   129   Lesson 5

PRACTICE

Find the volume of each figure.

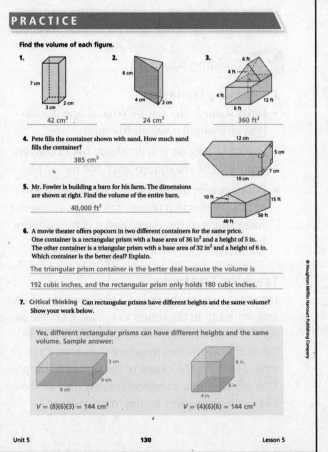

1. ____42 cm³____

2. ____24 cm³____

3. ____360 ft³____

4. Pete fills the container shown with sand. How much sand fills the container?

____385 cm³____

5. Mr. Fowler is building a barn for his farm. The dimensions are shown at right. Find the volume of the entire barn.

____40,000 ft³____

6. A movie theater offers popcorn in two different containers for the same price. One container is a rectangular prism with a base area of 36 in² and a height of 5 in. The other container is a triangular prism with a base area of 32 in² and a height of 6 in. Which container is the better deal? Explain.

The triangular prism container is the better deal because the volume is

192 cubic inches, and the rectangular prism only holds 180 cubic inches.

7. **Critical Thinking** Can rectangular prisms have different heights and the same volume? Show your work below.

Yes, different rectangular prisms can have different heights and the same volume. Sample answer:

V = (8)(6)(3) = 144 cm³   V = (4)(6)(6) = 144 cm³

Unit 5   130   Lesson 5

UNIT 5

Problem Solving Connections
Ramp Up!

CC.7.G.4 Know the formulas for the area and circumference of a circle and use them to solve problems; give an informal derivation of the relationship between the circumference and area of a circle.

CC.7.G.6 Solve real-world and mathematical problems involving area, volume, and surface area of two- and three-dimensional objects composed of triangles, quadrilaterals, polygons, cubes, and right prisms.

Materials
Calculator

INTRODUCE

Show students a bicycle tire and ask students to think of all the measurements that could be taken from that tire. List their answers, and make sure that circumference gets on the list. Then ask students to identify which measure on the list would be used to determine how far the bike travels in one revolution of the bike wheel. Explain that this project involves building a bike ramp.

TEACH

1 The Plans

Questioning Strategies
- How far does a bike go in one tire revolution? a length equal to the circumference
- What will be the length of the ramp? same length as the circumference, 75 inches
- How can you find the width of the ramp? Find one-third of 75 inches.
- How can you tell whether the 2,000-in.^{2} piece of wood that Jackie's dad has will work for the ramp? Make sure that one dimension is at least 75 in.

Differentiated Instruction
Use a circular object to demonstrate how to determine how far a wheel goes in one revolution. Dip its edge in paint. Mark the beginning point, and roll the object one time on a piece of paper.

2 Building Ramp 1

Questioning Strategies
- What shape is the ramp? What shape are the bases? triangular prism; triangles
- In Part D, why do you divide by 144 to convert square inches to square feet? 144 in.^{2} = 1 ft^2
- What parts of the ramp do B and h represent in this problem? B is the area of the triangular faces (sides of the ramp) and h is the distance between them (width of the ramp).

Teaching Strategies
Draw a square on the board. Label each side 1 foot, and write 1 ft^2 in the center as the area. On the same square, cross through 1 foot and write 12 inches. Remind students that these are the same. Then, write 144 in.^{2} in the center of the square as the area. This will help them understand why they divide by 144 to convert square inches to square feet.

Name_____ Class_____ Date_____

UNIT 5

COMMON
CORE

CC.7.G.4,
CC.7.G.6

Problem Solving Connections

Ramp Up! Carl and Jackie plan to build two different bike ramps. They have two plans and have researched the cost of materials. They want to calculate how much the materials for both ramps will cost.

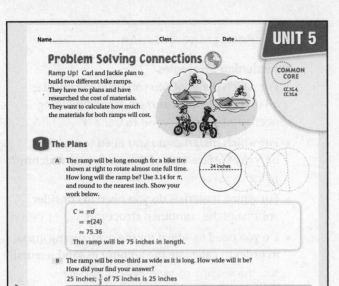

1 The Plans

A The ramp will be long enough for a bike tire shown at right to rotate almost one full time. How long will the ramp be? Use 3.14 for π, and round to the nearest inch. Show your work below.

24 inches

$$C = \pi d$$
$$= \pi(24)$$
$$\approx 75.36$$
The ramp will be 75 inches in length.

B The ramp will be one-third as wide as it is long. How wide will it be? How did your find your answer?

25 inches; $\frac{1}{3}$ of 75 inches is 25 inches

C Jackie's dad has a piece of wood that is 2,000 square inches. Is this enough wood to make the flat surface of the ramp they are planning? How much wood will they need just to make the flat surface of the ramp? What is one reason the piece of wood might not work?

They need 1,875 square inches for the flat surface of the ramp. This would be

enough square inches but the piece of wood might not be the right dimensions. If

the wood were 100 inches by 20 inches, it would not be wide enough for the ramp.

D On the ramp, they plan to place a circular logo that has the same size as the bike tire. How much of the ramp will the logo cover? Use 3.14 for π. Show your work below.

$$A = \pi r^2$$
$$= \pi(12)^2$$
$$= \pi(144)$$
$$\approx 452.16$$
The logo will cover about 452.16 square inches of the ramp.

Unit 5   **131**   Problem Solving Connections

2 Building Ramp 1

75 in.

21 in.

25 in.

72 in.

In the design, the ramp is a triangular prism. The height of the ramp is 21 inches, and the base measures 72 inches.

A Label the dimensions you found in ❶ on the design.

B What formula could you use to calculate the amount of wood needed to build the entire ramp?

Sample answer: $S = 2B + Ph$, where B is the area of the base, P is the perimeter

of the base, and h is the height of the prism.

C How much wood is needed to build the entire ramp? Show your work below.

Sample answer: $S = 2B + Ph$
$$= 2\left(\frac{1}{2} \times 21 \times 72\right) + (168 \times 25)$$
$$= 2(756) + 4,200$$
$$= 1,512 + 4,200$$
$$= 5,712$$
The ramp will need 5,712 square inches of wood.

D Find the surface area of the ramp to the nearest square foot. *Hint:* Divide the number of square inches by 144.

40 square feet

E To provide support for the ramp, Carl and Jackie fill the ramp with sand. Find the volume of sand in cubic inches that they used. Show your work below.

$$V = Bh$$
$$= \left(\frac{1}{2} \times 21 \times 72\right)(25)$$
$$= (756)(25)$$
$$= 18,900 \text{ cubic inches}$$
They used 18,900 cubic inches of sand to fill the ramp.

F What formula did you use to calculate the volume?

$V = Bh$, where B is the area of the base and h is the height of the prism.

G What is the volume of the ramp to the nearest cubic foot? *Hint:* Divide the number of cubic inches by 1,728.

11 cubic feet

Unit 5   **132**   Problem Solving Connections

3 Building Ramp 2

Questioning Strategies

- How many areas are overlapping? two overlapping areas, on both sides of the center platform where the two ramps meet it
- Do you count the overlapping areas when you are finding the amount of wood needed to build the ramp? Yes, those are structurally important pieces even if they are not on the surface.

Avoid Common Errors

Students may only subtract the overlapping areas one time each when finding the surface area. Using blocks as models, explain that the overlapping areas must each be subtracted twice from the sum of all individual surface areas because they are on the surface of both pieces meeting together, but not on the surface of the composite structure.

4 Answer the Question

Questioning Strategies

- For which materials do you need to consider all of the individual surface areas, including overlapping faces? wood to build it
- For which materials do you need to consider only the surface area of the combined structure? paint to cover it
- For which materials do you need to consider volume of the combined structure? sand to fill it
- Do you need to adjust for the overlapping areas in order to calculate the amount of sand needed? No, the volume of sand needed for the combined structure is the same as the volume needed for all three individual pieces.

CLOSE

Journal

Have students design their own bike ramp, and find the amount of wood, paint, and sand needed for it. Have them include diagrams to show all the combined pieces and their measures.

© Houghton Mifflin Harcourt Publishing Company

Notes

3 Building Ramp 2

For the second ramp, Carl and Jackie will need to duplicate the first ramp two times and build a rectangular prism to connect the ramps together. They sketch a side view with the dimensions.

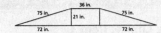

A What shape do these three figures form when combined?

trapezoidal prism

B How much wood is needed to build the entire ramp if they build each complete piece separately? Show your work below.

Triangular prisms	Rectangular prism
$S = 2B + Ph$	$S = 2B + Ph$
$= 2(\frac{1}{2} \times 21 \times 72) + (168 \times 25)$	$= 2(36 \times 21) + (114 \times 25)$
$= 2(756) + 4,200$	$= 2(756) + 2,850$
$= 1,512 + 4,200 = 5,712$	$= 1,512 + 2,850$
$2S = 5,712 \times 2$	$= 4,362$
$ = 11,424$	

$11,424 + 4,362 = 15,786$

They will need 15,786 square inches of wood.

C What is the surface area to the nearest square foot? *Hint:* Divide the number of square inches by 144.

110 square feet

D Once put together, what part of the pieces overlap, and therefore, can be subtracted from the surface area when Carl and Jackie paint it?

The vertical sides of each triangular prism meet the vertical sides of the

rectangular prism.

E What is the surface area of the ramp that will be painted?

13,686 square inches or 95 square feet

F Describe two ways to find the volume of this new ramp.

Find the volume of each piece or find the volume of the trapezoidal prism.

G How much sand, to the nearest cubic foot, would be needed to fill this ramp?

33 cubic feet

© Houghton Mifflin Harcourt Publishing Company

4 Answer the Question

A Complete the tables below to calculate the cost for each ramp.

Ramp 1			
Item	**Quantity Needed**	**Price**	**Total**
Wood	40 square feet	$1.15 per square foot	$46.00
Sand	11 cubic feet	$0.89 per cubic foot	$9.79
Paint (1 can = 300 square feet)	40 square ft	$22.00 per can	$22.00

Ramp 2			
Item	**Quantity Needed**	**Price**	**Total**
Wood	110 square feet	$1.15 per square foot	$126.50
Sand	33 cubic feet	$0.89 per cubic foot	$29.37
Paint (1 can = 300 square feet)	95 square feet	$22.00 per can	$22.00

B What is the total cost for wood for the two ramps? $172.50

C What is the total cost for sand for the two ramps? $39.16

D What is the total cost paint for the two ramps? Explain your answer.

$22.00; the total number of square feet for both ramps is only 135 square feet

and since one can of paint will cover 300 square feet only one can is needed.

E How much will the materials cost Carl and Jackie to build both ramps?

$233.66

F Design your own ramp and research prices online or at your neighborhood hardware store. Using the cost of the materials, calculate how much it would cost to make your ramp design.

> Check students' work.

© Houghton Mifflin Harcourt Publishing Company

© Houghton Mifflin Harcourt Publishing Company

© Houghton Mifflin Harcourt Publishing Company

COMMON CORE CORRELATION

Standard	Items
CC.7.G.4	6–9, 12
CC.7.G.6	1–5, 10–11, 13

TEST PREP DOCTOR ✚

Multiple Choice: Item 3
- Students who answered **A** may have found the surface area but only included the three visible sides.
- Students who answered **B** may have found the volume rather than the surface area.
- Students who answered **C** may have omitted the bottom face when finding the surface area.

Multiple Choice: Item 6
- Students who answered **F** may have taken half the radius rather than doubling the radius to find the circumference.
- Students who answered **G** may have used the radius rather than diameter to find circumference.
- Students who answered **J** may have found the area of the circle.

Multiple Choice: Item 9
- Students who answered **A** may have found the radius but did not continue to find the circumference.
- Students who answered **B** may have found the diameter but did not continue to find the circumference.
- Students who answered **C** may have found the circumference using the radius rather than the diameter.

Free Response: Item 11
- Students who answered **234 mm^2** correctly found the total surface area, but did not subtract the overlapping area.
- Students who answered **224 mm^2** correctly found the total surface area, but only subtracted the overlapping area once. They did not account for the area on both prisms.
- Students who answered **130 mm^2** found the volume of the figure rather than the surface area.

Name _____ Class _____ Date _____

MULTIPLE CHOICE

1. Flora is drawing a pattern for a mosaic. What is the area of the pattern?

8 mm
20 mm

- **A.** 28 square millimeters
- **B.** 140 square millimeters
- Ⓒ 160 square millimeters
- **D.** 200 square millimeters

2. Ned forms a larger cube from centimeter cubes. What is the surface area of the larger cube?

- **F.** 90 square centimeters
- Ⓖ 96 square centimeters
- **H.** 108 square centimeters
- **J.** 216 square centimeters

3. Maria is wrapping a present for her best friend. How much wrapping paper will she use, not counting overlap?

3 in.
2 in.
9 in.

- **A.** 51 square inches
- **B.** 54 square inches
- **C.** 84 square inches
- Ⓓ 102 square inches

4. Roberto purchases a small toy chest for his children. What is the volume of the toy chest?

8 in.
7 in.
20 in.
14 in.

- **F.** 1,120 cubic inches
- Ⓖ 1,540 cubic inches
- **H.** 1,960 cubic inches
- **J.** 3,080 cubic inches

5. Carol wants to tile her utility room. Each tile is 1 square foot. She draws the shape of her room on a grid. Each square unit on the grid represents 1 square foot. How many tiles will she need?

- **A.** 30
- **C.** 38
- Ⓑ 34
- **D.** 42

6. A circular mirror has a radius of 6 inches. What is the circumference of the mirror?

- **F.** 3π inches
- **G.** 6π inches
- Ⓗ 12π inches
- **J.** 36π inches

Unit 5   135   Test Prep

---

7. Michael plants a circular garden with a diameter of 10 feet. What is the area of his garden? Use 3.14 for π.

- **A.** 31.4 square feet
- **B.** 62.8 square feet
- Ⓒ 78.5 square feet
- **D.** 314 square feet

8. Lyle measures around his bike wheel. Then he measures its diameter. He divides the circumference by the diameter. What was the quotient?

- **F.** 1
- **H.** 3
- **G.** 2
- Ⓙ π

9. A circular quilt is made from 113.04 square feet of fabric. How much trim is needed to go around its edge? Use 3.14 for π.

- **A.** 6 feet
- **B.** 12 feet
- **C.** 18.84 feet
- Ⓓ 37.68 feet

10. An outdoor shed is a composite figure that has a floor and no windows. What is the surface area of the shed?

3.5 yd
3 yd
4 yd
4 yd

- **F.** 24 square yards
- **G.** 48 square yards
- **H.** 76 square yards
- Ⓙ 92 square yards

FREE RESPONSE

11. Patrick made a plastic model of his office building. He plans to paint the entire model. Use the model to find the surface area that Patrick will paint. Explain how you found this area.

2 mm
10 mm
5 mm
2 mm
2 mm   9 mm   2 mm

214 mm²; find the surface areas of
both buildings then subtract twice
the small area where the horizontal
building is attached to the vertical
building.

12. Paul's circular table has a circumference of 50.24 feet. He wants to know if he should buy tablecloth that says it will cover a circular table that is 200 square feet. Should he buy the tablecloth? Explain. Use 3.14 for π.

The area of the table is 200.96 square
feet, which is greater than 200
square feet, so he should not buy the
tablecloth.

13. Mary is filling a jar shaped like a square prism with a bag of confetti that is labeled as containing 100 cubic inches. The base of her prism is 3 inches by 3 inches and the height is 10 inches. Will all the confetti fit in the jar? Explain.

The jar can hold 3 × 3 × 10 = 90, or
90 cubic inches. It will not be able to
hold the whole bag of confetti.

Unit 5   136   Test Prep

UNIT 6

Statistics and Probability: Populations and Sampling

Unit Vocabulary

biased sample	(6-1)
population	(6-1)
random sample	(6-1)
sample	(6-1)

UNIT 6

Statistics and Probability: Populations and Sampling

Unit Focus

You have previously worked with populations. You found measures of center and measures of variation. When a population is large, you may only have a sample to observe and use to obtain data. You will learn how to be sure that your sample is random, not biased. You will also learn how to make sure that your data represents the entire population. You will also expand upon your understanding of population summaries by using dot plots, mean, and mean absolute deviations to compare populations.

Unit at a Glance

COMMON CORE

Lesson	Standards for Mathematical Content
6-1 Populations and Samples	CC.7.SP.1, CC.7.SP.2
6-2 Generating Multiple Samples	CC.7.SP.2
6-3 Comparing Populations	CC.7.SP.3, CC.7.SP.4
Problem Solving Connections	
Test Prep	

UNIT 6

© Houghton Mifflin Harcourt Publishing Company

Unpacking the Common Core State Standards

Use the table to help you understand the Standards for Mathematical Content that are taught in this unit. Refer to the lessons listed after each standard for exploration and practice.

COMMON CORE Standards for Mathematical Content	What It Means For You
CC.7.SP.1 Understand that statistics can be used to gain information about a population by examining a sample of the population; generalizations about a population from a sample are valid only if the sample is representative of that population. Understand that random sampling tends to produce representative samples and support valid inferences. Lesson 6-1	You will learn that sampling can be misleading, particularly after a biased survey. You will determine how to complete a random survey so that your results more accurately reflect the entire population.
CC.7.SP.2 Use data from a random sample to draw inferences about a population with an unknown characteristic of interest. Generate multiple samples (or simulated samples) of the same size to gauge the variation in estimates or predictions. Lessons 6-1, 6-2	You will use the data you collect from random samples to analyze a population. You'll use a variety of techniques, including graphing calculators, to ensure randomness. You will also use multiple samples to determine how samples vary.
CC.7.SP.3 Informally assess the degree of visual overlap of two numerical data distributions with similar variabilities, measuring the difference between the centers by expressing it as a multiple of a measure of variability. Lesson 6-3	You will use the mean absolute deviation and a measure of center to compare two data sets and note their separation. You will use dot plots to visually represent this.
CC.7.SP.4 Use measures of center and measures of variability for numerical data from random samples to draw informal comparative inferences about two populations. Lesson 6-3	You will use measures of center and variability to help describe different populations. You can also make comparisons between two populations using these measures.

UNIT 6

Unpacking the Common Core State Standards

This page lists and explains the Standards for Mathematical Content that are addressed in this unit. For information about the Standards for Mathematical Practice, which are integrated throughout the text, see Teacher Edition pages vii–xiii.

UNIT 6

Notes

Populations and Samples

Essential question: *How can you use a sample to gain information about a population?*

COMMON **Standards for**
CORE **Mathematical Content**

CC.7.SP.1 Understand that statistics can be used to gain information about a population by examining a sample of the population; generalizations about a population from a sample are valid only if the sample is representative of that population. Understand that random sampling tends to produce representative samples and support valid inferences.

CC.7.SP.2 Use data from a random sample to draw inferences about a population with an unknown characteristic of interest.

Vocabulary
population
sample
random sample
biased sample

Prerequisites
Solving proportions

Math Background
A sample must be representative of the population in order for predictions based on the sample to be valid. One way to select a representative sample is to select it randomly. A sample is random if each member of the population has an equally likely chance of being selected to be in the sample. You can use the findings from a random sample to make predictions about the population using proportional reasoning.

INTRODUCE

Suppose you want to find out the favorite TV shows among 7th graders. It may not be reasonable to ask every 7th grader. Have students suggest ways to select a sample of students that would *best* represent all 7th graders. Tell students that they will learn more about sampling methods in this lesson.

TEACH

1 EXPLORE

Questioning Strategies
- How is the number of tomatoes on each plant in the garden represented? **10 × 10 grid, where each square contains the number of tomatoes on one plant**
- What is another way to choose 10 plants at random? **Draw the numbers out of a bag.**

Teaching Strategies
Explain to students that the garden of tomato plants is the population in this situation. The sample is the set of 10 plants that are selected for calculations. Discuss circumstances that might affect a sample selected by dropping objects, like dried beans, to be NOT random, such as if the floor is not level or a fan is blowing them in one area of the grid.

2 EXAMPLE

Questioning Strategies
- How do you determine whether a sample is random? **If each member of the population has an equally-likely chance of being selected in the sample, then the sample is random.**
- What is the benefit of having a random sample? **It will fairly represent its population.**
- In part A, how can Roberto get a random sample? **He can survey adults at a place that all adults go regardless of their sports preference, such as a gas station.**

Teaching Strategies
Have students choose a population. Then, have them describe ways to gather a random sample and a biased sample. Discuss each example as a class.

© Houghton Mifflin Harcourt Publishing Company

Name _____ Class _____ Date _____

6-1

COMMON CORE
CC.7.SP.1
CC.7.SP.2

Populations and Samples

Essential question: *How can you use a sample to gain information about a population?*

1 EXPLORE Random and Non-Random Sampling

A vegetable garden has 100 tomato plants arranged in a 10-by-10 array. The gardener wants to know the average number of tomatoes on the plants. Each cell in the table below represents a plant. The number in the cell tells how many tomatoes are on that particular plant.

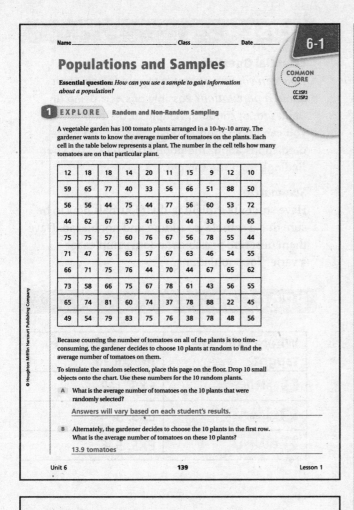

12	18	18	14	20	11	15	9	12	10
59	65	77	40	33	56	66	51	88	50
56	56	44	75	44	77	56	60	53	72
44	62	67	57	41	63	44	33	64	65
75	75	57	60	76	67	56	78	55	44
71	47	76	63	57	67	63	46	54	55
66	71	75	76	44	70	44	67	65	62
73	58	66	75	67	78	61	43	56	55
65	74	81	60	74	37	78	88	22	45
49	54	79	83	75	76	38	78	48	56

Because counting the number of tomatoes on all of the plants is too time-consuming, the gardener decides to choose 10 plants at random to find the average number of tomatoes on them.

To simulate the random selection, place this page on the floor. Drop 10 small objects onto the chart. Use these numbers for the 10 random plants.

A What is the average number of tomatoes on the 10 plants that were randomly selected?

Answers will vary based on each student's results.

B Alternately, the gardener decides to choose the 10 plants in the first row. What is the average number of tomatoes on these 10 plants?

13.9 tomatoes

REFLECT

1a. How do the averages you got with each sampling method compare?

The random sample average is greater than the average of the first row.

1b. How do the averages you got with each sampling method compare to the average for the entire population, which is 56.3?

Sample answer: The random sample is closer to the actual average.

The first row average is much lower.

1c. Why do you think the first method gave a closer average than the second method?

The first row had particularly small amounts of tomatoes on each plant which

were not representative of the amount of tomatoes on other plants.

When information is being gathered about a group, the entire group of objects, individuals, or events is called the **population**. A **sample** is part of the population chosen to represent the entire group.

A sample in which every person, object, or event has an equal chance at being selected is called a **random sample**. A random sample is more likely to be representative of the entire population than other sampling methods.

When a sample does not accurately represent the population, it is called a **biased sample**.

Use 1 to answer the following questions.

What is the population?   What is the sample?

the farmer or the tomato plants   10 tomato plants or 100 tomato plants

Which method of sampling is a random sampling?

Dropping small objects to determine the plants from which to count the tomatoes.

Which method of sampling could be a biased sampling?

Picking the first row of tomato plants could be a biased sampling.

2 EXAMPLE Identifying Samples

Determine whether each sample is a random sample or a biased sample. Explain your reasoning.

A Roberto wants to know the favorite sport of adults in his hometown. He surveys 50 adults at a baseball game.

The sample is biased because people at a baseball game are more

likely to say baseball is their favorite sport.

Questioning Strategies

- How could you estimate the answer to this problem? Possible answer: Use 5 out of 50 from the sample to overestimate 10% of 3,500, or 350.

- How can you use proportional reasoning to make predictions about a population from a random sample? Use the data from the random sample to set up a proportion with the information known about the population.

- What are the two solution methods shown? Convert the sample ratio to a percent and find that percent of the population, or solve a proportion.

MATHEMATICAL PRACTICE — Highlighting the Standards

This example is an opportunity to address Standard 2 (Reason abstractly and quantitatively). Students use quantitative data from a sample and reason proportionally to make predictions about a larger population. Students must understand that even random samples may vary, and the projection is merely an educated guess based on an assumption that the sample is representative of the population.

CLOSE

Essential Question

How can you use a sample to gain information about a population? Possible answer: Using an unbiased, or random, sample of the population, you can apply proportional reasoning to make predictions about the population based on your findings from the sample.

Summarize

Have students explain in their journals how to be sure that a sample is random and not biased. Have them describe possible random samples for a variety of populations.

PRACTICE

Where skills are taught	Where skills are practiced
1 EXPLORE	EXS. 1–2
2 EXAMPLE	EXS. 3–4
3 EXAMPLE	EXS. 5–6

B Paula wants to know the favorite type of music for students at her school. She surveys the first 60 people who enter the school doors in the morning.

The sample is random because arriving early to school has nothing to do

with a person's musical preference.

REFLECT

2. You want to know which radio station people in your neighborhood listen to the most. How would you get a random sample?

Sample answer: You could stand at a central location in your

neighborhood and ask people as they come by.

When you have a random sample, it is representative of the population. You can use the data about the sample and proportional reasoning to make inferences or predictions about the population.

3 EXAMPLE Making Predictions

A shipment to a warehouse consists of 3,500 MP3 players. The manager chooses a random sample of 50 MP3 players and finds that 3 are defective. How many MP3 players in the shipment are likely to be defective?

A It is reasonable to make a prediction about the population because this sample is _____random_____.

B Determine what percentage of the sample is damaged.

$\frac{3}{50} = \frac{6}{100}$, so _____6_____ % of the MP3s are damaged.

C Find 6% of the population, which is 6% of _____3,500_____.

0.06 × 3,500 = 210

D You could also set up a proportion to make a prediction.

$\frac{\text{defective MP3s in sample}}{\text{size of sample}} = \frac{\text{defective MP3s in population}}{\text{size of population}}$

$\frac{3}{50} = \frac{210}{3,500}$

Based on the sample, you can predict that _____210_____ MP3s in the shipment would be defective.

TRY THIS!

3a. **What If?** How many damaged MP3 players in the shipment would you predict to be damaged if 6 MP3s in the sample had been damaged?

420 damaged MP3s

REFLECT

3b. How could you use estimation as a way to see if your answer is reasonable?

Sample answer: 6 is a little more than 10% of 50. 10% of 3,500 is 350, and 420

is a little more than that.

PRACTICE

1. Paul and his friends average their test grades and find that the average is 95. The teacher announces that the average grade of all of her classes is 83. Why are the averages so different?

Sample answer: Paul's sample was

biased. Maybe his friends studied

more than other students.

2. Nancy hears a report that the average price of gasoline is $2.82. She averages the prices of stations near her home. She finds the average price of gas to be $3.03. Why are the averages different?

Sample answer: Nancy did not average

as many stations, and the report could

include stations nationwide.

Determine whether each sample is a random sample or a biased sample. Explain your reasoning.

3. Carol wants to find out the favorite foods of students at her middle school. She asks the boys' basketball team about their favorite foods.

It is a biased sample because it does

not include girls.

4. Dallas wants to know what elective subjects the students at his school like best. He surveys students who are leaving band class.

It is biased because it only includes

students that picked band as their

elective class.

5. A manager samples the receipts of every fifth person who goes through the line. Out of 50 people, 4 had a mispriced item. If 600 people go to this store each day, how many people would you expect to have a mispriced item?

48 people

6. Jerry randomly selects 20 boxes of crayons from the shelf and finds 2 boxes with at least one broken crayon. If the shelf holds 130 boxes, how many would you expect to have at least one broken crayon?

13 boxes

6-2 Generating Multiple Samples

Essential question: *How can you use samples to make and compare predictions about a population?*

COMMON CORE **Standards for Mathematical Content**

CC.7.SP.2 Use data from a random sample to draw inferences about a population with an unknown characteristic of interest. Generate multiple samples (or simulated samples) of the same size to gauge the variation in estimates or predictions.

Prerequisites
Populations and random samples

Materials
Graphing calculator

Math Background
In this lesson, students examine how the size of a sample can affect the prediction. Small samples are likely to have greater variation leading to less reliable predictions about the population. Larger samples are likely to have less variation leading to more consistent and accurate predictions about the population.

INTRODUCE

Suppose that you want to know how many of the 150 students in 7th grade got an A on their last test. Using a random sampling method, you sample 4 students and make a prediction about the 7th grade students. Discuss why the prediction may not be very accurate, and have students brainstorm how to make it more accurate.

TEACH

 EXPLORE

Questioning Strategies
• If 80% are working light bulbs, is it likely for a random sample of 4 to be all working? All defective? yes; no

• How can you improve the sample to become more representative of the population? Increase the size.

Technology
Allow students to practice using a graphing calculator to generate random numbers.

 EXPLORE

Questioning Strategies
• How is the second experiment different from the first experiment? The sample size is larger.

• Is it likely for all bulbs chosen to be working in this sample? Explain. No, it is much less likely because the sample is larger.

MATHEMATICAL PRACTICE **Highlighting the Standards**

This Explore is an opportunity to address Standard 5 (Use appropriate tools strategically). Students use graphing calculators to generate random integers that represent light bulbs. They compare the variation in results for samples of different sizes to learn that a larger sample size better represents the population.

CLOSE

Essential Question
How can you use samples to make and compare predictions about a population? Possible answer: Take random samples of different sizes. Larger samples are more likely to result in more accurate predictions.

Summarize
Have students write in their journals how to use the graphing calculator to generate random integers.

© Houghton Mifflin Harcourt Publishing Company

Name_____ Class_____ Date_____

6-2

COMMON CORE

CC.7.SP.2

Generating Multiple Samples

Essential question: *How can you use samples to make and compare predictions about a population?*

A store gets a shipment of 1,000 light bulbs, 200 of which are defective upon arrival. The store's manager does not know this. She wants to predict the number of defective light bulbs by testing a sample of the shipment.

1 EXPLORE Generating a Small Sample

A   The manager will want to use a random sample to represent the entire shipment. One way to simulate a random sample is to use a graphing calculator to generate random integers.

To simulate picking out random light bulbs between 1 and 1,000:

- Press [____], scroll right and select **PRB**, then select **5: randInt(**.
- Enter the smallest value, comma, largest possible value.
- Hit [____] to generate random numbers.

randInt(1,1000)
441
876
298
678

In this specific case, you will enter **randInt(** 1 , 1,000) because there are ___1,000___ light bulbs in the shipment.

The numbers that are generated will each represent bulbs in the shipment.

Let numbers 1 to 200 represent bulbs that are _____defective_____.

Numbers 201 to 1,000 will represent bulbs that are _____working_____.

Generate four numbers and record your results in the table below.
Sample answers:

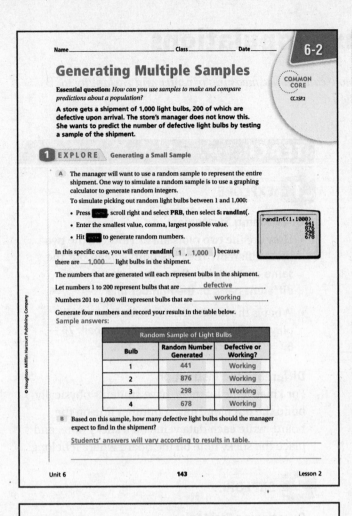

Random Sample of Light Bulbs		
Bulb	**Random Number Generated**	**Defective or Working?**
1	441	Working
2	876	Working
3	298	Working
4	678	Working

B   Based on this sample, how many defective light bulbs should the manager expect to find in the shipment?

___Students' answers will vary according to results in table.___

REFLECT

1.   You and your classmates have generated multiple samples. Compare your results to those of your classmates. How do your predictions compare?

___Sample answer: There is a lot of variation in the predictions.___

2 EXPLORE Generating a Larger Sample

A   Repeat the process. This time, collect a sample of 20 light bulbs.

On a separate sheet of paper copy the table from **1** and record your results in the table.   Check students' answers.

B   Based on this sample, how many defective light bulbs should the manager expect to find in the shipment?

___Answers will vary based on the random numbers generated.___

REFLECT

2a.   You and your classmates have generated multiple samples. Compare your results to those of your classmates. How do your predictions compare?

___Sample answer: With the larger sample, there is less variation in the predictions.___

2b.   The _____larger_____ the sample size, the _____smaller_____ the variability. Thus larger samples give _____better_____ results.

TRY THIS!

2c.   Estimate the average number of pets per household for your schoolmates. Explain your sampling process and estimate.

___Sample answer: I surveyed every fifth person leaving the cafeteria. I based my___

___estimate on the average of the 20 people surveyed.___

2d.   Compare your estimate of the average number of pets per household with those of your classmates.

___Sample answer: My estimate was about the same as those of my classmates.___

Comparing Populations

Essential question: How can you use measures of center and variability to compare two populations?

Standards for Mathematical Content

CC.7.SP.3 Informally assess the degree of visual overlap of two numerical data distributions with similar variabilities, measuring the difference between the centers by expressing it as a multiple of a measure of variability.

CC.7.SP.4 Use measures of center and measures of variability for numerical data from random samples to draw informal comparative inferences about two populations.

Prerequisites
Displaying numerical data
Measures of center and variability

Math Background
Measures of center express the typical value of a data set. Three common measures of center are mean, median, and mode. Measures of variability express the spread of a data set. Two common measures of variability are range and mean absolute deviation (MAD). The MAD is found by dividing the sum of each data value's difference from the mean by the number of data values. It describes the average number of units that the data values stray from the mean. A larger MAD value indicates a greater spread in the data.

INTRODUCE

Have students work in groups to find five numbers with a mean of 50. Give the groups different "spreads." For example, tell one group that all of their data points must be between 49 and 51. Tell another group that they must include 20 in their data points, and another that 100 is one of their points. After the groups accomplish this task, compare the spreads of the data set. Tell students they will compare data sets in terms of variation, or spread.

TEACH

1 EXPLORE

Questioning Strategies
- How are the two plots alike? How are the two plots different? **They are both spread out the same amount, but they are centered over different parts of the number line.**
- What is the range of heights for basketball players? For soccer players? **Basketball: 76 — 69 = 7 in. Soccer: 72 — 65 = 7 in.**

Differentiated Instruction
For kinesthetic learners, have students physically build the dot plot. Draw a number line on the board, write each data value on a sticky note, and place the sticky note on the board where it belongs.

2 EXPLORE

Questioning Strategies
- What does the mean value represent? What does the MAD represent? **Mean represents the center; the MAD measures how closely the values are clustered around the center.**
- Between the first and second Explores in the lesson, which measures are alike and which measures are different? **The MAD measures are alike, but the means are different.**

MATHEMATICAL PRACTICE · Highlighting the Standards

This Explore is an opportunity to address Standard 6 (Attend to precision). Students must be very precise in their calculations with data values. They must be especially careful to include every value in the multiple-step process of finding the MAD.

© Houghton Mifflin Harcourt Publishing Company

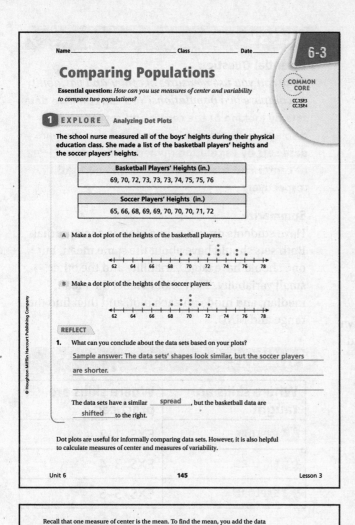

Name_____ Class_____ Date_____

Comparing Populations

Essential question: *How can you use measures of center and variability to compare two populations?*

COMMON CORE
CC.7.SP.3
CC.7.SP.4

1 EXPLORE   Analyzing Dot Plots

The school nurse measured all of the boys' heights during their physical education class. She made a list of the basketball players' heights and the soccer players' heights.

Basketball Players' Heights (in.)
69, 70, 72, 73, 73, 73, 74, 75, 75, 76

Soccer Players' Heights (in.)
65, 66, 68, 69, 69, 70, 70, 70, 71, 72

A   Make a dot plot of the heights of the basketball players.

B   Make a dot plot of the heights of the soccer players.

REFLECT

1.   What can you conclude about the data sets based on your plots?

Sample answer: The data sets' shapes look similar, but the soccer players
are shorter.
_____

The data sets have a similar _____spread_____, but the basketball data are
_____shifted_____ to the right.

Dot plots are useful for informally comparing data sets. However, it is also helpful to calculate measures of center and measures of variability.

Unit 6   145   Lesson 3

Recall that one measure of center is the mean. To find the mean, you add the data points and then divide the sum by the number of data points in the set.

To find the mean absolute deviation (MAD):

- Find the mean of the data.
- Take the absolute value of the difference between the mean and each data point.
- Then find the mean of those absolute values.

2 EXPLORE   Calculating Measures of Center and Variability

Use the data sets from **1**.

A   Calculate the mean height for the basketball players.

$69 + 70 + 72 + 73 + 73 + 73 + 74 + 75 + 75 + 76 =$ **730**

$730 \div 10 =$ **73**   The mean is _____73_____.

B   Calculate the MAD for the basketball players.

$\|69 - 73\| =$ **4**		$\|73 - 73\| =$ **0**
$\|70 - 73\| =$ **3**		$\|74 - 73\| =$ **1**
$\|72 - 73\| =$ **1**		$\|75 - 73\| =$ **2**
$\|73 - 73\| =$ **0**		$\|75 - 73\| =$ **2**
$\|73 - 73\| =$ **0**		$\|76 - 73\| =$ **3**

Find the mean of the absolute values.

$4 + 3 + 1 + 0 + 0 + 0 + 1 + 2 + 2 + 3 = 16$

$16 \div 10 =$ **1.6**   The MAD is _____1.6_____.

C   Calculate the mean height for the soccer players.

$65 + 66 + 68 + 69 + 69 + 70 + 70 + 70 + 71 + 72 =$ **690**

$690 \div 10 =$ **69**   The mean is _____69_____.

D   Calculate the MAD for the soccer players.

$\|65 - 69\| =$ **4**		$\|70 - 69\| =$ **1**
$\|66 - 69\| =$ **3**		$\|70 - 69\| =$ **1**
$\|68 - 69\| =$ **1**		$\|70 - 69\| =$ **1**
$\|69 - 69\| =$ **0**		$\|71 - 69\| =$ **2**
$\|69 - 69\| =$ **0**		$\|72 - 69\| =$ **3**

Find the mean of the absolute values.

$4 + 3 + 1 + 0 + 0 + 1 + 1 + 1 + 2 + 3 = 16$

$16 \div 10 =$ **1.6**   The MAD is _____1.6_____.

Unit 6   146   Lesson 3

Questioning Strategies

- **What is the population in this situation? What is the sample?** The population consists of all the words in the book. The sample consists of 12 randomly chosen words in the book.

- **What does the MAD represent in this situation?** The MAD describes the average difference between each word length and the mean word length of 4 letters.

- **How could you get a more accurate and representative sample of all the words in the book?** Take a sample that is larger than 12 words.

Differentiated Instruction

Have students work in groups to generate their own data from words in a book. Have each student find the length of 12 words, the mean, and the MAD. Then have the students in a group compare the results with each other.

Essential Question

How can you use measures of center and variability to compare two populations? You can compare data sets by looking at the center and spread of data displays, such as box plots. You can also compare data sets by calculating numerical measures of center and spread, such as mean and MAD, respectively.

Summarize

Have students draw two line plots in their journal. Both sets should have about the same mean, but one should have large variability and the other small variability. They should label the mean, median, and mode on each plot, and then find the range and MAD.

PRACTICE

Where skills are taught	Where skills are practiced
1 EXPLORE	EXS. 1–2
2 EXPLORE	EXS. 3–4
3 EXPLORE	EXS. 5–6

E How are the mean and the MAD reflected in the dot plots?

The mean centers the location of the dot plot on the number line.

The MAD reflects in the spread.

F Find the difference in the means.

$73 - 69 =$ 4

G Write the difference of means as a multiple of the MAD.

$4 = 1.6 \times$ 2.5

The means of the two data sets differ by _____2.5_____ times the amount that an individual height varies.

REFLECT

2. If two data sets have the same mean but different MADs, how would that reflect in the dot plot?

The sets would be centered at the same point on the number line,

but the dots would be more spread out in one of them.

In ❶ and ❷, we had the data for an entire population. Sometimes, it is only possible to get a sample of a population, but you can still use similar ideas to make comparisons about the populations using these samples.

3 EXPLORE Comparing Large Populations

Paula and Dean wanted to determine the average word length in two books. They took a random sample of 12 words each and counted the length of each word from each book.

Book 1 Word Count
3, 7, 5, 2, 4, 3, 1, 6, 4, 8, 2, 3

Book 2 Word Count
5, 4, 3, 6, 4, 5, 5, 2, 3, 4, 2, 5

A Calculate the mean for Book 1. Show your work below.

$$\frac{3+7+5+2+4+3+1+6+4+8+2+3}{12} = \frac{48}{12} = 4$$

The mean for Book 1 is 4 letters.

B Calculate the MAD for Book 1. _____1.67 letters_____

C Calculate the mean for Book 2. Show your work below.

$$\frac{5+4+3+6+4+5+5+2+3+4+2+5}{12} = \frac{48}{12} = 4$$

The mean for Book 2 is 4 letters.

D Calculate the MAD for Book 2. _____1 letter_____

E What can you infer about each population?

The length of the words in the first population varies more than the second,

but overall the average length is the same.

PRACTICE

Carol wants to know how many people live in each household in her town. She conducts two random surveys of 10 people each and asks how many people live in their home. Her results are listed below. Use the data for 1–6.

Sample A: 1, 6, 2, 4, 4, 3, 5, 5, 2, 8   Sample B: 3, 4, 5, 4, 3, 2, 4, 5, 4, 4

1. Make a dot plot for Sample A.

2. Make a dot plot for Sample B.

3. Find the mean and MAD for Sample A.

Mean: _____4_____

MAD: _____1.6_____

4. Find the mean and MAD for Sample B.

Mean: _____3.8_____

MAD: _____0.68_____

5. What can you infer about the population based on Sample A? Explain.

Sample answer: The average is 4,

but the number of people varies

greatly. You might infer that the

population lives in many different

sizes of homes.

6. What can you infer about the population based on Sample B? Explain.

Sample answer: The average is

3.8, and the MAD is small. These

people might all live in the same

neighborhood.

Problem Solving Connections
Happy Birthday!

© Houghton Mifflin Harcourt Publishing Company

 COMMON CORE Standards for Mathematical Content

CC.7.SP.1 Understand that statistics can be used to gain information about a population by examining a sample of the population; generalizations about a population from a sample are valid only if the sample is representative of that population. Understand that random sampling tends to produce representative samples and support valid inferences.

CC.7.SP.2 Use data from a random sample to draw inferences about a population with an unknown characteristic of interest. Generate multiple samples (or simulated samples) of the same size to gauge the variation in estimates or predictions.

CC.7.SP.3 Informally assess the degree of visual overlap of two numerical data distributions with similar variabilities, measuring the difference between the centers by expressing it as a multiple of a measure of variability.

CC.7.SP.4 Use measures of center and measures of variability for numerical data from random samples to draw informal comparative inferences about two populations.

INTRODUCE

Tell the students that the student council is putting on a dance for the entire 7th grade. They have asked you to poll the 7th graders to see how many people will be attending. Ask students how you might poll the 7th graders and how the student council could use this data to predict the student attendance at the dance.

TEACH

1 Using a Sample to Make a Prediction

Questioning Strategies
- Does Abby's sample represent the population well? No, she sampled close friends, which is not a representative sample of the entire grade.
- How could Abby have chosen a random sample? She could have asked students in various places at lunchtime.
- What sample might have given her a prediction that was too low? She could have only asked students whom she doesn't know at all.

Teaching Strategies
Remind students to use the survey results to find a percent equivalent to the ratio in the survey or to set up a proportion.

2 Using a Random Sample to Make a Prediction

Questioning Strategies
- How do you use the graphing calculator to generate 20 random numbers? Use randInt(1,80,20).
- How would it affect Abby's prediction if she emailed more people? Her prediction would likely be more accurate.

Technology
Consider various "What if...?" situations in order to give students the opportunity to practice generating random numbers for a variety of sample sizes.

Name_____ Class_____ Date_____

Problem Solving Connections 🌐

Happy Birthday! Abby is planning a big birthday party. She has invited everyone in her grade and has sent 80 invitations. Unfortunately, she forgot to include an RSVP on the invitation, and she wants to know how many people are coming to the party. On the invitation, Abby requested no gifts. Instead, she is asking everyone to make a donation to her favorite charity.

How much money can Abby make for her charity at her birthday party?

COMMON CORE
CC.7.SP.1,
CC.7.SP.2,
CC.7.SP.3,
CC.7.SP.4

HAPPY BIRTHDAY!

1 Using a Sample to Make a Prediction

A Abby asks 10 of her closest friends, and 9 of them will be attending the party. Based on this survey, how many people should Abby expect to come to the party? Show your work below.

> Sample answer: $\frac{9}{10} = \frac{90}{100}$, so 90% of Abby's close friends will attend.
> 90% of 80 is $0.90 \times 80 = 72$
>
> Based on her survey, 72 people will attend the party.

B Who is the population in this event?

Abby's entire class

C Who is the sample in Abby's survey?

Abby's closest friends.

D Is the sample random? Explain.

Sample answer: No, the sample is not random, Abby only asked

her closest friends.

E Explain why Abby's sample could be biased.

Sample answer: Abby only asked her best friends, who are most

likely to attend her party.

F Do you think that Abby's results are too high or too low? Explain.

Sample answer: The results are too high because Abby did not ask people

who are not her close friends or may not want to come to the party.

Unit 6   **149**   Problem Solving Connections

2 Using a Random Sample to Make a Prediction

A Why is it important for a sample to be random in order to make an accurate prediction?

Random samples more accurately reflect the entire population.

B How might Abby obtain a random sample?

Sample answer: Abby could put the names of everyone who was invited in

a hat and draw ten names. Abby could then ask those people if they will be

attending the party.

C What can Abby do to increase the accuracy of her random sample?

Increase the number of people in the sample or use multiple samples.

D Abby has a list of everyone in her class. She numbers all the names on the list from 1 to 80. Then, Abby uses her graphing calculator to generate 20 random numbers. She e-mails each of the people who correspond to the randomly generated numbers and asks whether or not he or she plans to attend the party. Of the 20 people surveyed, 6 are not able to come to the party. Based on this sample, predict the total number of people who will attend the party. Show your work below.

> Sample work: $\frac{6}{20} = \frac{30}{100}$, so 30% of the people Abby invited will not attend.
> 30% of 80 is $0.30 \times 80 = 24$
>
> $80 - 24 = 56$
>
> Based on this survey, 56 people will attend the party.

E How does this random sample provide a more accurate count of who might not attend the party than the first sample?

Sample answer: This second sample is better because it surveys a random

selection of people that Abby invited, not just her close friends.

F Why might this still not be an accurate prediction?

Sample answer: Things can happen at the last minute causing people that

intended to come to the party not be able to.

Unit 6   **150**   Problem Solving Connections

3 Comparing Populations

Questioning Strategies

- In part A, how are the plots alike and how are they different? They both appear to be centered near 12.5, but the plot of girl donations is more widespread than the plot of boy donations.

- Can you find the mean and MAD just by looking at a dot plot? You can estimate and compare the mean and MAD at a glance, but to find the actual values, you would still have to calculate using each data value.

- What does the MAD represent in this situation? The average amount that each donation varies from the mean donation.

- If someone brings a $100 donation, how would that affect the mean and MAD? They would both increase.

```
⋰ MATHEMATICAL   Highlighting
   PRACTICE       the Standards
```

This real-world problem addresses Standard 3 (Construct viable arguments and critique the reasoning of others). Students use statistics and proportional reasoning to support their arguments about the predicted attendance at a birthday party. They also use their statistical knowledge to critique the predictions resulting from other methods.

4 Answer the Question

Questioning Strategies

- Is the mean the only possible way to find the measure of center for the donations? No, the median or mode could also be used.

- Why is the mean a good choice? There are no extreme outliers, so the mean is a good choice.

Differentiated Instruction

Have students work in groups to check each other's final calculations and discuss their solutions. Then, after the discussion, students can modify their answers as needed. This will give each student a chance to develop his or her thoughts before having to present it.

CLOSE

Journal

Have students write in their journal a summary of their project. They should include a description of how statistics are used to plan a party and predict the amount of money raised.

Research Options

Do research to find an organization for which you could hold a fundraising party. Write a plan for the party, including a prediction for attendance and how much money you estimate can be raised. Use data from surveys to support your predictions.

© Houghton Mifflin Harcourt Publishing Company

3 **Comparing Populations**

The first 10 monetary donations from boys and the first 10 monetary donations from girls were recorded.

Donation Amounts from Boys ($)
15, 10, 10, 5, 12, 20, 15, 5, 10, 10

Donation Amounts from Girls ($)
10, 20, 5, 1, 20, 25, 15, 15, 10, 5

A Make a dot plot for each set of data.

B What can you infer about the donations of each of the populations?

Answers will vary. Sample answer: The girls gave a variety of different

amounts, while most of the boys donated between $10 and $15.

C Find the mean and mean absolute deviation for the boys' donations. Show your work below.

Mean: $\frac{15 + 10 + 10 + 5 + 12 + 20 + 15 + 5 + 10 + 10}{10} = \frac{112}{10} = 11.2$ Mean: $11.20

MAD:
$|15 - 11.2| = 3.8$ $|20 - 11.2| = 8.8$
$|10 - 11.2| = 1.2$ $|15 - 11.2| = 3.8$
$|10 - 11.2| = 1.2$ $|5 - 11.2| = 6.2$
$|5 - 11.2| = 6.2$ $|10 - 11.2| = 1.2$
$|12 - 11.2| = 0.8$ $|10 - 11.2| = 1.2$

$\frac{3.8 + 1.2 + 1.2 + 6.2 + 0.8 + 8.8 + 3.8 + 6.2 + 1.2 + 1.2}{10} = \frac{34.4}{10} = 3.44$

MAD: 3.44

D Based on the data set and the line plots, how would you expect the mean and the mean absolute deviation for the girls' donations to compare?

The mean may be close to or a bit higher than the boys' mean donation,

and the MAD should be greater.

E Find the mean and the mean absolute deviation for the girls' donations. Show your work below.

Mean: $\frac{10 + 20 + 5 + 1 + 20 + 25 + 15 + 15 + 10 + 5}{10} = \frac{126}{10} = 12.6$ Mean: $12.60

MAD:
$|10 - 12.6| = 2.6$ $|25 - 12.6| = 12.4$
$|20 - 12.6| = 7.4$ $|15 - 12.6| = 2.4$
$|5 - 12.6| = 7.6$ $|15 - 12.6| = 2.4$
$|1 - 12.6| = 11.6$ $|10 - 12.6| = 2.6$
$|20 - 12.6| = 7.4$ $|5 - 12.6| = 7.6$

$\frac{2.6 + 7.4 + 7.6 + 11.6 + 7.4 + 12.4 + 2.4 + 2.4 + 2.6 + 7.6}{10} = \frac{64}{10} = 6.4$

MAD: 6.4

4 **Answer the Question**

A To find the average student donation, average the girls' mean donation and the boys' mean donation. Show your work below.

Mean: $\frac{11.20 + 12.60}{2} = \frac{23.8}{2} = 11.9$

The mean donation is $11.90.

B Based on the mean student donation, and Abby's prediction from **2** of how many people will come to her party, how much money could be raised in donations?

$11.90 \times 56 = 666.4$

It is possible that $666.40 could be raised in donations.

C Since people generally make donations in whole dollar amounts, find the amount of money that could be raised in donations based on all the information given. Explain your reasoning and show your work below.

Sample answer: $12 \times 50 = 600$; I rounded the average donation to $12 and also rounded to the nearest ten for the number of people attending since it is possible some people would not come to the party or make a donation. It is possible that about $600 could be raised in donations.

Notes

COMMON CORE CORRELATION

Standard	Items
CC.7.SP.1	2, 3, 12
CC.7.SP.2	4–6, 9, 13
CC.7.SP.3	7, 10, 15
CC.7.SP.4	1, 8, 11, 14, 16

TEST PREP DOCTOR ✚

Multiple Choice: Item 2

- Students who answered **F** may not understand that choosing a sports team will bias a survey about sports.
- Students who answered **G** may not realize that asking only the band is not representative of the student population.
- Students who answered **J** may not understand that choosing spectators of a sport will bias a survey about sports.

Multiple Choice: Item 6

- Students who answered **G** may not understand that the prediction ratio and the polled ratio must be equivalent fractions.
- Students who answered **H** may have simplified the ratio 40:200 incorrectly, dividing the numerator by 4 and the denominator by 8.
- Students who answered **J** may have simplified the ratio 40:200 incorrectly, dividing the numerator by 20 and the denominator by 4.

Multiple Choice: Item 7

- Students who answered **A** may think that having no dots in the middle of the plot makes a low MAD.
- Students who answered **B** may have confused the mean and MAD.
- Students who answered **D** may have confused the MAD with an outlier.

Free Response: Item 15

- Students who answered that **the dot plots would look the same because the mean is the same** may not understand that the MAD reflects the spread.
- Students who answered that **the dot plots would have different centers** may have confused the mean with the MAD.
- Students who answered that **Jack's dot plot would have a greater spread than Jane's dot plot** may have confused the MAD with the minimum value of the data.

UNIT 6 TEST PREP

Name _____ Class _____ Date _____

MULTIPLE CHOICE

1. Which is a measure of center?

   A. distance

   B. mean absolute deviation

   C. mean

   D. sample

2. You want to know the favorite sport of middle school students. Which group would provide a random sample?

   F. the girls' soccer team

   G. the band

   H. every fifth person who leaves the school building at the end of the school day

   J. every tenth person who enters the stadium before a football game

3. How can you make a random sample more accurately reflect the population it represents?

   A. carefully select the data pieces

   B. increase the number of pieces of random data

   C. use a graphing calculator to provide random integers

   D. survey a biased group

4. A department store receives a shipment of 1,000 glasses. Out of a random sample of 10 glasses, 2 are broken. How many glasses would you expect to be broken in the entire shipment?

   F. 2

   G. 50

   H. 200

   J. 250

5. A random sample of a shipment of furniture shows that 2 out of 50 boxes do not contain all of the correct parts. Which proportion could help you find the number of boxes that will not contain the correct parts out of a shipment of 500?

   A. $\frac{2}{50} = \frac{500}{x}$ C. $\frac{50}{500} = \frac{x}{2}$

   B. $\frac{x}{50} = \frac{500}{2}$ D. $\frac{2}{50} = \frac{x}{500}$

6. A restaurant manager predicts that out of the 200 people that will come to the restaurant in one day, 40 people will order dessert. He based this on a random sample of people he polled yesterday. What ratio could his prediction be based on?

   F. $\frac{1}{5}$ H. $\frac{10}{25}$

   G. $\frac{7}{10}$ J. $\frac{2}{50}$

7. Maria collects data about the scores on a math test. She finds that the test has a low mean absolute deviation. Which dot plot could represent this data?

   A.

   B.

   C.

   D.

8. What does the mean absolute deviation tell you?

   F. the average of the data

   G. where the data is centered on a number line

   H. how many dots are above each value on a dot plot

   J. how far the data is spread out from the mean

9. A teacher randomly reads 10 one-page reports written by her students. She finds that 3 of the reports have misspellings. How many reports would she expect to have misspellings if she reads 150 reports?

   A. 10   B. 45

   C. 50   D. 100

FREE RESPONSE

Peter records the monthly high temperatures, in degrees Fahrenheit at his house for a year. He calculates the mean to be 63 and the mean absolute deviation to be 4.67.

Jorge records the monthly high temperatures, in degrees Fahrenheit at his house for a year. He calculates the mean to be 63 and the mean absolute deviation to be 21.67.

Use this information for 10–11.

10. How would the dot plots of the data differ for Peter and Jorge?

    They would both center around

    63, but Jorge's would be spread

    much farther.

11. What can you infer from the data about the areas where Peter and Jorge live?

    Sample answer: Peter lives in a temperate

    zone, and Jorge lives where there is

    greater variation in the temperature.

12. Explain why surveying 100 different people from the phone book might not be a random sample.

    Sample answer: People that have no

    phone or unlisted phone numbers

    cannot be surveyed.

13. A factory produces 500,000 nails per day. The manager of the factory estimates that there are less than 1,500 misshapen nails made per day. A random survey of 500 nails finds 4 misshapen ones. Is the manager correct in his estimate? Explain.

    No, the manager is not correct. Based

    on the survey, there will be about

    4,000 misshapen nails out of the

    500,000 that are made each day.

Jane reports the number of years she has known each person in her close group of friends: 5, 8, 4, 2, 9, 10, 3, 11

Jack reports the same information for his group of friends: 4, 2, 3, 1, 4, 3, 5, 2

Use the data for 14–16.

14. Find the mean and mean absolute value for both Jane's data and Jack's data.

    Jane's data: Mean: 6.5; MAD: 3

    Jack's data: Mean: 3; MAD: 1

15. How would you expect the data sets' dot plots to compare to each other?

    Jane's data would be farther right on

    the number line and more spread out

    than Jack's data.

16. What can you infer about both groups of friends?

    Both Jack and Jane continue to make

    new friends yearly. Jane's friendships

    have lasted longer.

UNIT 7

Probability and Simulations

Unit Vocabulary

complement	(7-1)
compound event	(7-4)
event	(7-1)
experiment	(7-1)
experimental probability	(7-3)
outcome	(7-1)
probability	(7-1)
sample space	(7-4)
theoretical probability	(7-2)
trial	(7-1)

UNIT 7

UNIT 7

Probability and Simulations

Unit Focus

In this unit, you will learn about probability. You will learn how to express the likelihood of something occurring. You will learn the definitions of an experiment, a trial, an outcome, and an event. You will calculate the experimental probability of an event and compare that number to its theoretical probability. You will make predictions based on probability. You will also learn about compound probability and different ways to find its value. Additionally, you will conduct simulations using a random number generator on a graphing calculator.

Unit at a Glance

COMMON CORE

Lesson		Standards for Mathematical Content
7-1	Understanding Probability	CC.7.SP.5
7-2	Theoretical Probability	CC.7.SP.6, CC.7.SP.7a
7-3	Experimental Probability	CC.7.SP.6, CC.7.SP.7a, CC.7.SP.7b
7-4	Compound Events	CC.7.SP.8a, CC.7.SP.8b
7-5	Conducting a Simulation	CC.7.SP.8c
	Problem Solving Connections	
	Test Prep	

UNIT 7

© Houghton Mifflin Harcourt Publishing Company

© Houghton Mifflin Harcourt Publishing Company

Unpacking the Common Core
State Standards

This page lists and explains the Standards for Mathematical Content that are addressed in this unit. For information about the Standards for Mathematical Practice, which are integrated throughout the text, see Teacher Edition pages vii–xiii.

Unpacking the Common Core State Standards

Use the table to help you understand the Standards for Mathematical Content that are taught in this unit. Refer to the lessons listed after each standard for exploration and practice.

COMMON CORE Standards for Mathematical Content	What It Means For You
CC.7.SP.5 Understand that the probability of a chance event is a number between 0 and 1 that expresses the likelihood of the event occurring. Larger numbers indicate greater likelihood. A probability near 0 indicates an unlikely event, a probability around 1/2 indicates an event that is neither unlikely nor likely, and a probability near 1 indicates a likely event. Lesson 7-1	You will describe the likelihood of an event using words and numbers from 0 to 1. You will find the probability of an event and its complement.
CC.7.SP.6 Approximate the probability of a chance event by collecting data on the chance process that produces it and observing its long-run relative frequency, and predict the approximate relative frequency given the probability. Lessons 7-2, 7-3	You will calculate theoretical and experimental probabilities and compare the experimental probability to the theoretical probability.
CC.7.SP.7a Develop a uniform probability model by assigning equal probability to all outcomes, and use the model to determine probabilities of events. Lessons 7-2, 7-3	You will work with ratios that represent the theoretical probabilities of events.
CC.7.SP.7b Develop a probability model (which may not be uniform) by observing frequencies in data generated from a chance process. Lesson 7-3	You will use real-life observations to find the experimental probability of an event.
CC.7.SP.8a Understand that, just as with simple events, the probability of a compound event is the fraction of outcomes in the sample space for which the compound event occurs. Lesson 7-4	You will find all the outcomes in the sample space of a compound event. Then using that sample space you will find the probability of the compound event.
CC.7.SP.8b Represent sample spaces for compound events using methods such as organized lists, tables and tree diagrams. For an event described in everyday language (e.g., "rolling double sixes"), identify the outcomes in the sample space which compose the event. Lesson 7-4	You will find all possible outcomes for a sample space and you will find those outcomes that make up a compound event.
CC.7.SP.8c Design and use a simulation to generate frequencies for compound events. Lesson 7-5	You will conduct trials of an experiment using a random number generator.

156

Probability and Simulations

© Houghton Mifflin Harcourt Publishing Company

Notes

_____

_____

_____

_____

_____

_____

_____

_____

_____

© Houghton Mifflin Harcourt Publishing Company

Unit 7   156   Probability and Simulations

7-1 Understanding Probability

Essential question: *How can you describe the likelihood of an event?*

COMMON CORE Standards for Mathematical Content

CC.7.SP.5 Understand that the probability of a chance event is a number between 0 and 1 that expresses the likelihood of the event occurring. Larger numbers indicate greater likelihood. A probability near 0 indicates an unlikely event, a probability around 1/2 indicates an event that is neither unlikely nor likely, and a probability near 1 indicates a likely event.

Vocabulary

experiment

trial

outcome

event

probability

complement

Prerequisites

Percents, fractions, and decimals

Materials

number cube

Math Background

An *experiment* is an activity in which results are observed. Each round of an experiment is called a *trial*, and the result of a trial is called an *outcome*. A set of one or more outcomes is an *event*. The probability of an event, denoted *P*(event), measures the likelihood that the event will occur. *Probability* is a measure ranging from 0 to 1 and can be written as a fraction, a decimal, or a percent.

INTRODUCE

Discuss the meaning of the words/phrases: *impossible, unlikely, as likely as not, likely*, and *certain*. Ask students to use each word to describe the occurrence of a real event. For example, it is unlikely to snow in North America in the summer months. Tell students that in this lesson they will learn numerical measures to express likelihood.

TEACH

1 EXPLORE

Questioning Strategies

- What are the possible outcomes of rolling a number cube? **1, 2, 3, 4, 5, 6**

- What is an example of an impossible outcome? **Possible answer: rolling an 8**

- What is an example of a certain outcome? **Possible answer: rolling less than 7**

Teaching Strategies

To help students begin ordering the events, first have them write, for each event, all the ways the event can occur. Then have them count up all the ways. Explain that if an event is impossible, they write 0. Students then order the number of ways for the events. The order of likelihood is the same as the order of the number of ways the events can occur.

2 EXAMPLE

Questioning Strategies

- How do you determine if an event is as likely as not? **If there are as many ways for an event to occur as not to occur, then the event is as likely as not.**

- How do you determine if an event is likely? **If there are a greater number of ways for an event to occur than not to occur, then the event is likely.**

Teaching Strategies

Encourage students to first list all of the possible outcomes in an experiment. Then to determine the likelihood of an event, they can count the number of ways that the event can occur and compare it with the number of possible outcomes.

© Houghton Mifflin Harcourt Publishing Company

7-1

COMMON
CORE

CC.7.SP.5

Name_____ Class_____ Date_____

Understanding Probability

Essential question: *How can you describe the likelihood of an event?*

1 EXPLORE Likelihood of an Event

When a number cube is rolled once, the possible
numbers that could show face up are __1, 2, 3, 4, 5, or 6__.

Each time you roll the cube, a number lands face up. This is called an *event*.
Below is a list of 9 different events.

Work with a partner to order the events from those least likely to happen to the
ones that are most likely to happen when you roll the number cube one time.

Use the space next to each event to write any notes that might help you
order them.

Rolling a number less than 7 _____

Rolling an 8 _____

Rolling a 1, 2, or 3 _____

Rolling a 5 _____

Rolling a number other than 6 _____

Rolling an even number _____

Rolling a number greater than 5 _____

Rolling an odd number _____

Rolling a prime number _____

The order I wrote the events in is:

Sample answer: Rolling an 8, rolling a 5, rolling a number greater than 5, rolling a

prime number, rolling an odd number, rolling an even number, rolling a 1, 2, or 3,

rolling a number other than 6, rolling a number less than 7

REFLECT

1a. How did you sort the events?

Sample answer: I started with those that had no numbers or one

number which, were least likely to happen. Next, I listed those with more

numbers which were more likely to happen.

Unit 7   157   Lesson 1

1b. Are any of the events impossible?

Sample answer: Rolling an 8 is impossible because there is no 8 on the

number cube.

An **experiment** is an activity involving chance in which results are observed. Each
observation of an experiment is a **trial**, and each result is an **outcome**. A set of one
or more outcomes is an **event**.

The **probability** of an event, written *P*(event), measures the likelihood that the
event will occur. Probability is a measure between 0 and 1 as shown on the
number line and can be written as a fraction, a decimal, or percent.

If the event is not likely to occur very many times, the probability of the event
is close to 0. Likewise, if an event is likely to occur many times, the event's
probability is closer to 1.

Impossible		As likely as not		Certain
	Unlikely		Likely	
0	$\frac{1}{4}$	$\frac{1}{2}$	$\frac{3}{4}$	1
0	0.25	0.5	0.75	1.0
0%	25%	50%	75%	100%

2 EXAMPLE Describing Events

Determine whether each event is impossible, unlikely, as likely as not, likely,
or certain. Then, tell whether the probability is 0, close to 0, $\frac{1}{2}$, close to 1, or 1.

A You flip a coin. The coin lands heads up.

This event is as likely as not. The probability is $\frac{1}{2}$.

B You roll two number cubes and the sum of the numbers is 10.

This event is unlikely to happen. Its probability is close to 0.

C A bowl contains 14 red marbles and 3 green marbles. You pick a red marble.

This event is likely to happen. Its probability is close to 1.

D A spinner has 10 equal sections marked 1 through 10. You spin and land on a number
greater than 0.

This event is certain to happen. Its probability is 1.

TRY THIS!

Describe each event as impossible, unlikely, as likely as not, likely, or
certain. Tell whether the probability is 0, close to 0, $\frac{1}{2}$, close to 1, or 1.

2a. A hat contains pieces of paper marked
with the numbers 1 through 16. You pick
an even number.

as likely as not; $\frac{1}{2}$

2b. A spinner has 6 equal sections marked
1 through 6. You spin and land on 0.

impossible; 0

Unit 7   158   Lesson 1

Questioning Strategies

- Can you explain why the sum of probabilities of an event and its complement is equal to 1? **The sum of probabilities of all possible outcomes is 1. An event and its complement comprise all possible outcomes.**

- The relationship between the probabilities of an event and its complement can be described by this addition statement:

$$P(\text{Event}) + P(\text{Complement}) = 1$$

How can you express this relationship with a subtraction statement?

$$1 - P(\text{Event}) = P(\text{Complement}) \text{ or}$$
$$1 - P(\text{Complement}) = P(\text{Event})$$

MATHEMATICAL PRACTICE **Highlighting the Standards**

This example is an opportunity to address Standard 2 (Reason abstractly and quantitatively). Students find the probability of the complement of an event by reasoning abstractly to identify the complement of the event. Students then reason quantitatively by subtracting the probability of one outcome from the probability of all possible outcomes.

CLOSE

Essential Question

How can you describe the likelihood of an event?
Describe the likelihood of an event using a scale from 0 (impossible) to 1 (certain) using fractions, decimals, or percents.

Summarize

Have students write an example of each type of event in their journals.

- An impossible event
- An event with probability close to 1 but not 1
- An event that is as likely as not
- A certain event
- An event with probability close to 0 but not 0.

PRACTICE

Where skills are taught	Where skills are practiced
1 EXPLORE	EX. 1, 10
2 EXAMPLE	EXS. 2–7
3 EXAMPLE	EXS. 8–9

REFLECT

2c. The probability of event A is $\frac{1}{3}$. The probability of event B is $\frac{1}{4}$. What can you conclude about the two events?

Sample answer: Neither is very likely, but event A is more likely to happen

than event B.

The **complement** of an event is the set of all outcomes *not* included in the event. For example, consider the event that you roll a number cube and get a 3. The complement is the event that you do not roll a 3. The complement is rolling a 1, 2, 4, 5, or 6.

🔑 The sum of the probabilities of an event and its complement equals 1.

$$P(\text{event}) + P(\text{complement}) = 1$$

3 **EXAMPLE** Using the Complement of an Event

In a standard deck of cards, the probability of choosing a card at random and getting an ace is $\frac{1}{13}$. What is the probability of not getting an ace?

$$P(\text{event}) + P(\text{complement}) = \underline{\quad 1 \quad}$$

$$P(\text{ace}) + P(\underline{\quad \text{not getting an ace} \quad}) = 1$$

$$\frac{1}{13} + P(\underline{\quad \text{not getting an ace} \quad}) = 1$$

$$P(\text{not getting an ace}) = 1 - \frac{1}{13}$$

$$= \frac{12}{13}$$

TRY THIS!

3a. A jar contains balls marked with the numbers 1 through 8. The probability that you pick a number at random and get a 5 is $\frac{1}{8}$. What is the probability of not picking a 5?

$$\frac{7}{8}$$

3b. You roll a number cube. The probability that you roll an even number is $\frac{1}{2}$. What is the probability you will roll an odd number?

$$\frac{1}{2}$$

REFLECT

3c. Why do the probability of an event and the probability of its complement add up to 1?

The complement is made up of all outcomes not in the event. When you

put the outcomes of an event and its complement together, you get all

possible outcomes of an event. The probability of getting all the possible

outcomes equals 1.

3d. Give an example of a real-world event and its complement.

Sample answers: getting homework or not getting homework; in a bag

of blue and white marbles, pulling out a blue marble or pulling out a

white marble

PRACTICE

1. In a hat, you have index cards with the numbers 1 through 10 written on them. You pick one card at random. Order the events from least likely to happen to most likely to happen.

You pick a number greater than 0.   You pick a number that is at least 2.
You pick an even number.   You pick a number that is at most 0.

You pick a number that is at most 0. You pick an even number. You pick a

number that is at least 2. You pick a number that is greater than 0.

Determine whether each event is impossible, unlikely, as likely as not, likely, or certain. Then, tell whether the probability is 0, close to 0, $\frac{1}{2}$, close to 1, or 1.

2. randomly picking a green card from a standard deck of playing cards

impossible; 0

3. randomly picking a red card from a standard deck of playing cards

as likely as not: $\frac{1}{2}$

4. picking a number less than 15 from a jar with papers labeled 1 to 12

certain; 1

5. picking a number that is divisible by 5 from a jar with papers labeled 1 to 12

unlikely; close to 0

6. The probability of rolling a 5 on a number cube is $\frac{1}{6}$. What is the probability of not rolling a 5? $\frac{5}{6}$

7. The probability that a coin will land heads when flipping a coin is $\frac{1}{2}$. What is the probability of getting tails? $\frac{1}{2}$

8. The probability of spinning a 4 on a spinner with 5 equal sections marked 1 through 5 is $\frac{1}{5}$. What is the probability of not landing on 4? $\frac{4}{5}$

9. The probability of picking a queen from a standard deck of cards is $\frac{1}{13}$. What is the probability of not picking a queen? $\frac{12}{13}$

10. Describe an event that has a probability of 0% and an event that has a probability of 100%.

Sample answer: pulling a red marble out of a bag that contains blue marbles;

pulling a white marble out of a bag of that contains only white marbles.

Theoretical Probability

Essential question: *How can you find the theoretical probability of an event?*

© Houghton Mifflin Harcourt Publishing Company

COMMON CORE Standards for Mathematical Content

CC.7.SP.6 Approximate the probability of a chance event by collecting data on the chance process that produces it and observing its long-run relative frequency, and predict the approximate relative frequency given the probability.

CC.7.SP.7a Develop a uniform probability model by assigning equal probability to all outcomes, and use the model to determine probabilities of events.

Vocabulary
theoretical probability

Prerequisites
Understanding probability
Percents, fractions, and decimals

Math Background
Theoretical probability is the probability of an event when all of the outcomes of the experiment are equally likely. The probability of such an event is found by the ratio:

$$P(\text{event}) = \frac{\text{number of ways the event can occur}}{\text{total number of equally likely outcomes}}$$

You can use theoretical probability to predict the likelihood that a certain event will occur.

INTRODUCE

Draw 3 circles, 3 triangles, and 6 squares. Ask students to count the number of shapes that are circles, triangles, squares, and *not* circles. Explain to students that they will find probability in a similar way. They will count the number of items that satisfy a given condition. Then they will find the theoretical probability of that event by finding the ratio of the number of counted items to the total number of items.

TEACH

1 EXPLORE

Questioning Strategies
- How can you tell which spinner gives you a better chance of winning? For each spinner, you make a ratio of the number of stars to the total number of sections. The spinner with the greater ratio gives you a better chance of winning.
- Will you win if you pick the spinner with a better chance of winning? It is not certain, only more likely.

Teaching Strategies
Students may count the ratio of starred sections to unstarred sections. If so, they are finding the *odds* of the spinner landing on a star, not probability. Make sure that students understand that the ratio for probability is the number of starred sections to the number of all sections.

2 EXAMPLE

Questioning Strategies
- In part A, how do you find the number of possible outcomes? Find the total number of marbles in the bag: 8 red + 12 green = 20 total.
- In part B, how do you find the number of outcomes in the event? The event is rolling a 3 or 4, so 2 out of all the possible outcomes are in the event.

Avoid Common Errors
Students sometimes get confused while counting because they try to do counting and calculations all mentally. Encourage students to write out all the possible outcomes, count them, and record the number in the denominator. Then have them count the number of those possible outcomes that meet the conditions of the event described and record that number in the numerator. Then simplify.

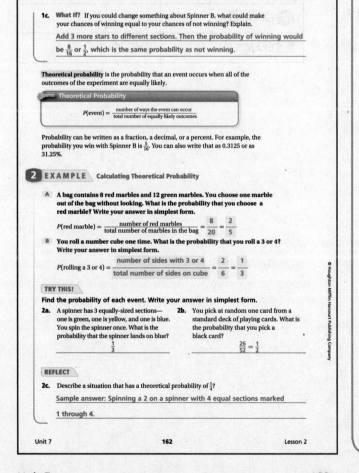

Name_____ Class_____ Date_____

7-2

COMMON CORE
CC.7.SP.6
CC.7.SP.7a

Theoretical Probability

Essential question: *How can you find the theoretical probability of an event?*

1 EXPLORE Finding Theoretical Probability

At a school fair, you have a choice of spinning Spinner A or Spinner B. You win a MP3 player if the spinner lands on a section with a star in it. Which spinner should you choose if you want the best chance of winning?

Complete the table.

Spinner A

Spinner B

	Spinner A	Spinner B
Total Number of Outcomes	8	16
Number of Sections with Stars	3	5
P(winning MP3) = number of sections with stars / Total number of outcomes	$\frac{3}{8}$	$\frac{5}{16}$

Compare the ratios for Spinner A and Spinner B.

The ratio for Spinner ___A___ is greater than the ratio for Spinner ___B___.

I should choose ___Spinner A___ for the best chance of winning.

REFLECT

1a. *Theoretical probability* is a way to describe how you found the chance of winning a MP3 player in the scenario above. Using the spinner example to help you, explain in your own words how to find the theoretical probability of an event.

Sample answer: The theoretical probability of an event is a ratio comparing

the number of ways the event can occur to the total number of outcomes

for the experiment.

1b. Suppose you choose Spinner A. What is the probability that you will not win? Show your work below.

$1 - \frac{3}{8} = \frac{5}{8}$; the probability of losing is $\frac{5}{8}$.

Unit 7   161   Lesson 2

1c. What If? If you could change something about Spinner B, what could make your chances of winning equal to your chances of not winning? Explain.

Add 3 more stars to different sections. Then the probability of winning would be $\frac{8}{16}$ or $\frac{1}{2}$, which is the same probability as not winning.

Theoretical probability is the probability that an event occurs when all of the outcomes of the experiment are equally likely.

Theoretical Probability

$$P(\text{event}) = \frac{\text{number of ways the event can occur}}{\text{total number of equally likely outcomes}}$$

Probability can be written as a fraction, a decimal, or a percent. For example, the probability you win with Spinner B is $\frac{5}{16}$. You can also write that as 0.3125 or as 31.25%.

2 EXAMPLE Calculating Theoretical Probability

A A bag contains 8 red marbles and 12 green marbles. You choose one marble out of the bag without looking. What is the probability that you choose a red marble? Write your answer in simplest form.

$P(\text{red marble}) = \frac{\text{number of red marbles}}{\text{total number of marbles in the bag}} = \frac{8}{20} = \frac{2}{5}$

B You roll a number cube one time. What is the probability that you roll a 3 or 4? Write your answer in simplest form.

$P(\text{rolling a 3 or 4}) = \frac{\text{number of sides with 3 or 4}}{\text{total number of sides on cube}} = \frac{2}{6} = \frac{1}{3}$

TRY THIS!

Find the probability of each event. Write your answer in simplest form.

2a. A spinner has 3 equally-sized sections— one is green, one is yellow, and one is blue. You spin the spinner once. What is the probability that the spinner lands on blue?

$\frac{1}{3}$

2b. You pick at random one card from a standard deck of playing cards. What is the probability that you pick a black card?

$\frac{26}{52} = \frac{1}{2}$

REFLECT

2c. Describe a situation that has a theoretical probability of $\frac{1}{4}$?

Sample answer: Spinning a 2 on a spinner with 4 equal sections marked

1 through 4.

Unit 7   162   Lesson 2

Questioning Strategies

- In part A, how can you predict the probability of the event when there are 600 rolls of the number cube? **First find the theoretical probability of the event in one roll. Then multiply the probability by the number of times the number cube is rolled.**

- In part B, what is the theoretical probability of landing on blue? **There are 2 blue sections out of 6 equally-sized sections. $P(\text{blue}) = \frac{2}{6}$, or $\frac{1}{3}$.**

Teaching Strategies

Remind students that in order to multiply a fraction by a whole number, they should write the whole number as a fraction with a denominator of 1, multiply the fractions, and then write the answer as a simplified mixed number.

MATHEMATICAL PRACTICE **Highlighting the Standards**

This example is an opportunity to address Standard 7 (Look for and make use of structure). Students use the structure of a formula to guide them through finding a probability ratio that describes the likelihood of an event. Regardless of the event, the probability ratio is the same. Students also use probability ratios to make predictions about outcomes in the same way they have used ratios to make predictions in the past.

CLOSE

Essential Question

How can you find the theoretical probability of an event? The theoretical probability of an event is found by using the following ratio:

$$\frac{\text{number of ways the event can occur}}{\text{total number of equally likely outcomes}}$$

Summarize

Have students come up with their own experiment with equally likely outcomes. Encourage students to write the experiment with four different events:

1. An event with the word *or*

2. A complement of an event

3. An event using the words *at least*

4. An event with probability near 1

Then have students exchange papers and find the probabilities of the four events.

PRACTICE

Where skills are taught	Where skills are practiced
1 EXPLORE	EXS. 1–2
2 EXAMPLE	EXS. 3–4
3 EXAMPLE	EXS. 5–8

Probability can be used to make predictions. If the theoretical probability of an event is $\frac{1}{3}$, you expect it to happen about $\frac{1}{3}$ of the time. When performing multiple trials, you can use probability to predict the number of times the outcome should theoretically occur.

3 EXAMPLE Making a Prediction

A If you roll a number cube 600 times, about how many times do you expect to roll a 3 or 6?

Step 1: Find the probability of the event. Write your answer in simplest form.

$$P(\text{rolling a 3 or 6}) = \frac{\text{number of sides with 3 or 6}}{\text{total number of sides on cube}} = \frac{2}{6} = \frac{1}{3}$$

Step 2: Predict the number of times you will roll a 3 or a 6 in 600 trials. Multiply the probability of the event by 600.

$$\frac{1}{3} \times 600 = 200$$

You can expect to roll a 3 or a 6 about __200__ times out of 600.

B A spinner has six sections of equal size. Two sections are colored blue, 3 sections are colored red, and 1 section is colored yellow. If you spin the spinner 50 times, how often do you expect to land on blue?

Step 1: Find the probability of the event. Write your answer in simplest form.

$$P(\text{blue}) = \frac{2}{6} = \frac{1}{3}$$

Step 2: Predict the number of times the spinner will land on blue in 50 trials. Multiply the probability of the event by 50.

$$\frac{1}{3} \times 50 = \frac{50}{3} = 16\frac{2}{3}$$

Since the fraction is greater than $\frac{1}{2}$, round the mixed number to the nearest whole number.

You can predict that the spinner will land on blue about __17__ times out of 50 spins.

REFLECT

3. Look back to your answer in **A** . Do you think your answer means you will definitely roll a 3 or a 6 exactly the amount given by your answer?

No, the actual outcome will not always match the results because a prediction

is what you expect to happen, not a certainty.

PRACTICE

At a school fair, you have a choice of randomly picking a ball from Basket A or Basket B. Basket A has 5 green balls, 3 red balls, and 8 yellow balls. Basket B has 7 green balls, 4 red balls, and 9 yellow balls. You can win a digital book reader if you pick a red ball.

	Basket A	Basket B
Total Number of Outcomes	16	20
Number of Red Balls	3	4
$P(\text{win}) = \frac{\text{Number of red balls}}{\text{Total number of outcomes}}$	$\frac{3}{16}$	$\frac{4}{20} = \frac{1}{5}$

1. Complete the chart. Write each answer in simplest form.

2. Which basket should you choose if you want the better chance of winning?

   Basket B has the better chance of winning.

3. Jim has 4 nickels, 6 pennies, 4 dimes and 2 quarters in his pocket. He picks a coin at random. What is the probability that he will pick a nickel or a dime? Write your answer as a fraction, as a decimal, and as a percent.

   $\frac{1}{2}$; 0.50; 50%

4. A class has 12 boys and 15 girls. The teacher randomly picks one child to lead the class in singing.

   a. What is the probability that the teacher picks a boy? __$\frac{4}{9}$__

   b. What is the probability that the teacher picks a girl? __$\frac{5}{9}$__

   c. Describe two different ways you could find the answer to part **b**.

   You could find the compliment of part a; $1 - \frac{4}{9} = \frac{5}{9}$; or you could find

   the theoretical probability $\frac{\text{number of girls}}{\text{total number of students}} = \frac{15}{27} = \frac{5}{9}$

Use the spinner for 5–8.

5. In 20 spins, about how often can you expect to land on a number evenly divisible by 2? __10__

6. In 150 spins, about how often can you expect to land on a number less than 6? __94__

7. In 200 spins, about how often can you expect to land on a 1? __25__

8. **Error Analysis** Rudolfo says there is a greater chance of landing on an even number than on an odd number. What is his error?

   The chances of landing on an even number are $\frac{1}{2}$ which is the same probability

   as landing on an odd number.

Notes

Experimental Probability

Essential question: *How do you find the experimental probability of an event?*

© Houghton Mifflin Harcourt Publishing Company

COMMON CORE Standards for Mathematical Content

CC.7.SP.6 Approximate the probability of a chance event by collecting data on the chance process that produces it and observing its long-run relative frequency, and predict the approximate relative frequency given the probability.

CC.7.SP.7a Develop a uniform probability model by assigning equal probability to all outcomes, and use the model to determine probabilities of events.

CC.7.SP.7b Develop a probability model (which may not be uniform) by observing frequencies in data generated from a chance process.

Vocabulary

experimental probability

Prerequisites

Understanding probability

Percents, fractions, and decimals

Math Background

When it is impossible or inconvenient to calculate theoretical probabilities, experimental probability can be used to estimate the probability of an event. Experimental probability is found by conducting trials of an experiment and comparing the number of times an event occurs to the total number of trials.

INTRODUCE

Connect to previous learning by reviewing the definition of theoretical probability. Explain that experimental probability is also found by making a ratio, but that ratio is based on the actual number of times the event occurs, instead of a number of possible outcomes that are possible in an event.

TEACH

1 EXPLORE

Questioning Strategies

- If students work in groups, will all the groups have the same results? No, the probabilities may be different.

- Do all group results show the same conclusion for the *most likely* outcome? Answers may vary. Most groups will probably say that the cup is most likely to land on its side.

Teaching Strategies

Be sure that students toss the cup randomly for each trial, meaning that they do not try to toss the cup in a deliberate way so that it lands a certain way. Explain that tossing the cup randomly ensures that the calculated experimental probabilities are not influenced by the actions of the people tossing the cups.

2 EXAMPLE

Questioning Strategies

- Why is the total number of marbles in the bag not needed when finding the experimental probability? The denominator of the experimental probability ratio is the total number of trials for the experiment instead of the number of marbles in the bag.

- Will the total of all experimental probability ratios have a sum of 1? Explain. Yes; each outcome (draw from the bag) is used in the numerator of one of the experimental probability ratios, and the total number of trials is the same in each ratio. The sum of the numerators is equal to the total number of trials in the denominator, so the sum of the ratios is 1.

Name_____ Class_____ Date_____

7-3

Experimental Probability

Essential question: *How do you find the experimental probability of an event?*

COMMON CORE
CC.7.SP.6
CC.7.SP.7a
CC.7.SP.7b

1 EXPLORE Finding Experimental Probability

You can toss a paper cup to demonstrate *experimental probability.*

Consider tossing a paper cup. What are the three different ways the cup could land?

It could land with the open end facing up, open-end facing down, or on its side.

Toss a paper cup twenty times. Record your observations in the table.
Check students' answers.

Outcome	Number of Times
Open-end up	
Open-end down	
On its side	

REFLECT

1a. Which outcome do you think is most likely?

Sample answer: The cup will most likely land on its side.

1b. Describe the three outcomes using the words *likely* and *unlikely*.

Sample answer: The cup is most likely to land on its side. It is somewhat likely

to land open-end down. It is unlikely to land open-end up.

Check students' answers.

1c. Use the number of times each event occurred to calculate the probability of each event.

1d. What do you think would happen if you performed more trials?

Sample answer: The probability of the cup landing on its side would increase.

Outcome	Experimental Probability
Open-end up	$\dfrac{\text{open-end up}}{20} = \dfrac{}{20}$
Open-end down	$\dfrac{\text{open-end down}}{20} = \dfrac{}{20}$
On its side	$\dfrac{\text{on its side}}{20} = \dfrac{}{20}$

1e. What is the sum of the three probabilities in 1c?

The sum equals 1.

It is sometimes impossible or inconvenient to calculate theoretical probabilities. You can use *experimental probability* to estimate the probability of an event. The **experimental probability** of the event is found by comparing the number of times the event occurs to the total number of trials.

Experimental Probability

$$\text{probability} \approx \frac{\text{number of times the event occurs}}{\text{total number of trials}}$$

2 EXAMPLE Calculating Experimental Probability

Martin has a bag of marbles. He removed one marble, recorded the color and then placed it back in the bag. He repeated this process several times and recorded his results in the table.

Color	Frequency
Red	12
Blue	10
Green	15
Yellow	13

A Number of trials = ___50___

B Complete the table of experimental probabilities. Write each answer in simplest form.

Color	Experimental Probability
Red	$\dfrac{\text{frequency of the event}}{\text{total number of trials}} = \dfrac{12}{50} = \dfrac{6}{25}$
Blue	$\dfrac{\text{frequency of the event}}{\text{total number of trials}} = \dfrac{10}{50} = \dfrac{1}{5}$
Green	$\dfrac{\text{frequency of the event}}{\text{total number of trials}} = \dfrac{15}{50} = \dfrac{3}{10}$
Yellow	$\dfrac{\text{frequency of the event}}{\text{total number of trials}} = \dfrac{13}{50}$

REFLECT

2. What are two different ways you could find the experimental probability of the event that you do not draw a red marble?

Sample answer: You could add the frequencies for blue, green, and yellow and

then find the ratio of those frequencies to the total number. Another way is

to you could use the complement and subtract the probability of red from 1.

Questioning Strategies

- Why are the experimental probabilities and theoretical probabilities not necessarily equal? Theoretical probability is based on the conditions of the experiment; theoretical probability only changes if those conditions change. Experimental probability is based on the results of an experiment; the results may change with each trial of the experiment.

- Do you think the experimental probabilities would begin to get closer to theoretical probabilities with more trials? Explain. Yes; by performing many more trials of the experiment, the variations in the experiments should balance out better and the experimental probability ratios would get closer to the theoretical probability ratios.

Teaching Strategies

If you lack enough time to allow each student group to perform enough experiments to see the experimental probabilities approach the theoretical probabilities, combine the trials of all the student groups into one large experiment.

MATHEMATICAL PRACTICE   **Highlighting the Standards**

This Explore is an opportunity to address Standard 4 (Model with mathematics). Students conduct repeated trials of an experiment to find experimental probabilities. As the number of trials in the experiment increases, students see that the experimental probability ratios begin to get closer to the theoretical probabilities that they model.

CLOSE

Essential Question

How do you find the experimental probability of an event? The experimental probability of an event is found by using the following ratio:

$$\frac{\text{number of times the event occurs}}{\text{total number of trials}}$$

Summarize

Have students compare and contrast experimental and theoretical probabilities. Tell students to consider the methods of calculating probabilities and using probabilities. Have them also include the nature of experimental probabilities as the number of trials in the experiment increases.

PRACTICE

Where skills are taught	Where skills are practiced
1 EXPLORE	EXS. 1, 5
2 EXAMPLE	EXS. 1, 3
3 EXPLORE	EXS. 2, 4–7

3 EXPLORE — Comparing Theoretical and Experimental Probability

A You roll a number cube once. Complete the table of theoretical probabilities for the different outcomes. Remember that theoretical probability is the ratio of the number of ways an event can occur to the total number of equally likely outcomes.

Number	1	2	3	4	5	6
Theoretical Probability	$\frac{1}{6}$	$\frac{1}{6}$	$\frac{1}{6}$	$\frac{1}{6}$	$\frac{1}{6}$	$\frac{1}{6}$

B Using your knowledge of theoretical probability, predict the number of times each number will be rolled out of 30 total rolls.

1: 5 times   3: 5 times   5: 5 times

2: 5 times   4: 5 times   6: 5 times

C Roll a number cube 30 times. Complete the table for the frequency of each number and then find its experimental probability. Check students' tables.

Number	1	2	3	4	5	6
Frequency						
Experimental Probability						

D Look at the tables you completed. How do the experimental probabilities compare with the theoretical probabilities?

Sample answer: The experimental probabilities are not close to the theoretical probabilities.

E **Conjecture** By performing more trials, you tend to get experimental results that are closer to the theoretical probabilities. Combine your table from **C** with those of your classmates to make one table for the class. How do the class experimental probabilities compare with the theoretical probabilities?

Sample answer: The experimental probabilities are closer to the theoretical probabilities.

REFLECT

3. Could the experimental probabilities ever be exactly equal to the theoretical probability? Why or why not?

Sample answer: Yes, the experimental probabilities could eventually come out to be equal to the theoretical probabilities, but it is very unlikely.

© Houghton Mifflin Harcourt Publishing Company

PRACTICE

1. Toss a coin at least 20 times. Record the outcomes in the table. Check students' tables.

2. What do you think would happen if you performed more trials?

The probability would be close to the theoretical probability of $\frac{1}{2}$.

Tossing of Coin	Number of Times	Experimental Probability
Heads		
Tails		

3. Sonja has a bag of ping pong balls. She removed one ball, recorded the marking and then placed it back in the bag. She repeated this process several times and recorded her results in the table. Find the experimental probability of each marked ping pong ball. Write your answers in simplest form.

Type	Frequency
Stripes	12
Polka dots	13
Stars	18
Solid color	17
Squares	10

Stripes: $\frac{6}{35}$ Polka dots: $\frac{13}{70}$

Stars: $\frac{9}{35}$ Solid color: $\frac{17}{70}$ Squares: $\frac{1}{7}$

Use a spinner with six equal sections for 4–6.

4. What is the theoretical probability of landing on a specific section of your spinner?

$\frac{1}{6}$

5. Spin the spinner 30 times. Complete the table. Check students' tables.

Color or Numbered Section						
Frequency						
Experimental Probability						

6. Look at the tables you completed. How do the experimental probabilities compare with the theoretical probabilities?

Sample answer: The experimental probabilities are fairly close to the theoretical probabilities.

7. **Critical Thinking** Patricia finds that the experimental probability of her dog wanting to go outside between 4 P.M. and 5 P.M. is $\frac{7}{12}$. About what percent of the time does her dog not want to go out between 4 P.M. and 5 P.M.?

$\frac{5}{12}$ or about 41.7% of the time the dog does not want to go out between

4 P.M. and 5 P.M.

© Houghton Mifflin Harcourt Publishing Company

Compound Events

Essential question: *How do you find the probability of a compound event?*

COMMON CORE Standards for Mathematical Content

CC.7.SP.8a Understand that, just as with simple events, the probability of a compound event is the fraction of outcomes in the sample space for which the compound event occurs.

CC.7.SP.8b Represent sample spaces for compound events using methods such as organized lists, tables and tree diagrams. For an event described in everyday language (e.g., "rolling double sixes"), identify the outcomes in the sample space which compose the event.

Vocabulary
compound event

sample space

Prerequisites
Theoretical probability

Math Background
A compound event consists of two or more single events, sometimes described with a conjunction, such as *and* or *or*. The sample space of an experiment is the set of all possible outcomes. A table, tree diagram, or organized list of the sample space can be used to help you find all the outcomes that are described by a given compound event.

INTRODUCE

Discuss the meaning of the word *compound*. Explain that the word is used to describe anything with two or more parts. Some examples of common usage of the word are **compound word** and **compound sentence**. Explain that a compound event is made up of two or more single events, sometimes joined by a *conjunction*, such as *and* or *or*.

TEACH

1 EXPLORE

Questioning Strategies

- How does the table represent the sample space for rolling two number cubes? **The possible outcomes for one number cube are listed in the left column, and the possible outcomes for the other number cube are listed in the top row.**

- How can you tell from the table which sum is least likely to be rolled? Most likely? **The sum of 2 and the sum of 12 can only occur in one way, so they are least likely. The sum of 7 can occur in the greatest number of ways, so it is most likely.**

MATHEMATICAL PRACTICE

Highlighting the Standards

This Explore is an opportunity to address Standard 1 (Make sense of problems and persevere in solving them). Students will find the sums of the numbers rolled on the cubes and then find the number of outcomes that belong to the given compound event. They will solve the problem in two steps—first filling in the chart and then circling the correct outcomes.

---

2 EXAMPLE

Questioning Strategies

- How does a tree diagram represent the sample space for a randomly selected sandwich? **The tree diagram lists all possible combinations of bread-meat-cheese for the sample space.**

- How many different sandwiches are possible? How many sandwiches on white bread are possible? **12; 6**

Name_____ Class_____ Date_____

7-4

Compound Events

Essential question: *How do you find the probability of a compound event?*

COMMON CORE

CC.7.SP.8a
CC.7.SP.8b

A **compound event** consists of two or more single events. To find the probability of a compound event, write a ratio of the number of ways the compound event can happen to the total number of possible outcomes. The **sample space** of an experiment is the set of all possible outcomes. To find the sample space for an experiment, you can use tables, lists, and tree diagrams.

1 EXPLORE Using a Table with Compound Events

Jacob rolls two fair number cubes. Find the probability that the sum of the numbers he rolls is 8.

A Use the table to find the sample space for rolling a particular sum on two number cubes. Each cell is the sum of the first number in that row and column.

	1	2	3	4	5	6
1	2	3	4	5	6	7
2	3	4	5	6	7	⑧
3	4	5	6	7	⑧	9
4	5	6	7	⑧	9	10
5	6	7	⑧	9	10	11
6	7	⑧	9	10	11	12

B How many possible outcomes are in the sample space?

_____36_____

C Circle the outcomes that give the sum of 8.

D How many ways are there to roll a sum of 8? ____5____

E What is the probability of rolling a sum of 8? ____$\frac{5}{36}$____

TRY THIS!

Find the probability of each event.

1a. Rolling a sum less than 5 $\frac{6}{36} = \frac{1}{6}$

1b. Rolling a sum of 7 or a sum of 9 $\frac{10}{36} = \frac{5}{18}$

REFLECT

1c. Give an example of an event that is more likely than rolling a sum of 8.
Sample answer: Rolling a sum of 7

1d. Give an example of an event that is less likely than rolling a sum of 8.
Sample answer: Rolling a sum of 1 or a sum of 12

Unit 7   169   Lesson 4

2 EXAMPLE Using a Tree Diagram with Compound Events

A deli prepares a selection of grab-and-go sandwiches with one type of bread (white or wheat), one type of meat (ham, turkey, or chicken), and one type of cheese (cheddar or Swiss). Each combination is equally likely. Find the probability of choosing a sandwich at random and getting turkey and Swiss on wheat bread.

A Complete the tree diagram to find the sample space for the compound event.

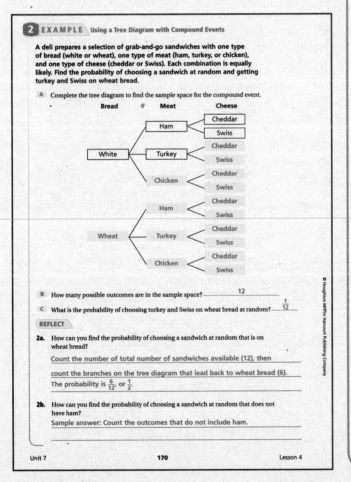

| Bread | Meat | Cheese |

B How many possible outcomes are in the sample space? ____12____

C What is the probability of choosing turkey and Swiss on wheat bread at random? ____$\frac{1}{12}$____

REFLECT

2a. How can you find the probability of choosing a sandwich at random that is on wheat bread?

Count the number of total number of sandwiches available (12), then

count the branches on the tree diagram that lead back to wheat bread (6).

The probability is $\frac{6}{12}$, or $\frac{1}{2}$.

2b. How can you find the probability of choosing a sandwich at random that does not have ham?

Sample answer: Count the outcomes that do not include ham.

Unit 7   170   Lesson 4

Questioning Strategies

- How is a list similar to a chart and a tree diagram? A list contains all possible outcomes.

- How is a list different from a chart and a tree diagram? A chart and a tree diagram have a structure that helps you include all possible outcomes, but you must organize a list in such a way that gives structure to the outcomes so that all of the outcomes will be listed exactly once.

MATHEMATICAL PRACTICE

Highlighting the Standards

This Example is an opportunity to address Standard 7 (Look for and make use of structure). In this lesson students write out sample spaces for compound events in order to find probabilities. Tables and tree diagrams inherently have an organized structure so that all of the possible outcomes in the sample space are accounted for exactly one time. In this Example, students must find a way to make organized lists of the sample space in order to account for all the possible outcomes exactly one time.

CLOSE

Essential Question

How do you find the probability of compound events? Write a ratio of the number of ways the event can happen to the total number of possible outcomes. To help find the sample space, you can use tables, tree diagrams, or organized lists.

Summarize

Have students write about each of the different tools for writing out the sample space that they have learned in this lesson: tables, tree diagrams, and organized lists. Have them give an example of how to use each tool for writing the sample space to find the probability of a compound event.

PRACTICE

Where skills are taught	Where skills are practiced
1 EXPLORE	EXS. 1–3
2 EXAMPLE	EXS. 4–5
3 EXAMPLE	EXS. 6–7

3 EXAMPLE Using a List with Compound Events

When a person opens a new account at Joe's bank, he or she is randomly assigned a temporary PIN. The PIN is a 3-digit security code that uses the digits 5, 6, or 7. Any of these numbers may be repeated. Find the probability that Joe's temporary PIN is 777.

Make an organized list to find the sample space.

A   First list all the PINs that start with 5 and have 5 as the second digit.
Fill in the third digit with all the possibilities.

5	5	5
5	5	6
5	5	7

B   Next, list the PINs that start with 5 and have 6 as the second digit.
Fill in the third digit with all the possibilities.

5	6	5
5	6	6
5	6	7

C   Next, list the PINs that start with 5 and have 7 as the second digit.
Fill in the third digit with all the possibilities.

5	7	5
5	7	6
5	7	7

D   You have now listed all the PINs that start with 5.
Repeat A through C for PINs that start with 6.

6	5	5		6	6	5		6	7	5
6	5	6		6	6	6		6	7	6
6	5	7		6	6	7		6	7	7

E   Repeat A through C for PINs that start with 7.

7	5	5		7	6	5		7	7	5
7	5	6		7	6	6		7	7	6
7	5	7		7	6	7		7	7	7

F   How many possible outcomes are in the sample space? __27__

G   What is the probability that Joe's temporary PIN is 777? __$\frac{1}{27}$__

REFLECT

3a. What is the probability that Joe's PIN includes at least one 5? __$\frac{19}{27}$__

3b. What is the probability that Joe's PIN includes exactly two 6s? __$\frac{6}{27} = \frac{2}{9}$__

Unit 7   171   Lesson 4

PRACTICE

Drake rolls two fair number cubes.

1. Complete the table to find the sample space for rolling a particular product on two number cubes.

	1	2	3	4	5	6
1	1	2	3	4	5	6
2	2	4	6	8	10	12
3	3	6	9	12	15	18
4	4	8	12	16	20	24
5	5	10	15	20	25	30
6	6	12	18	24	30	36

2. What is the probability that the product of the two numbers Drake rolls is a multiple of 4? __$\frac{15}{36}$__

3. What is the probability that the product of the two numbers Drake rolls is less than 13? __$\frac{23}{36}$__

Mattias gets dressed in the dark one morning and chooses his clothes at random. He chooses a shirt (green, red, or yellow), a pair of pants (black or blue), and a pair of shoes (checkered or red).

Shirt	Pants	Shoes
Green	Blue	Checkered / Red
	Black	Checkered / Red
Red	Blue	Checkered / Red
	Black	Checkered / Red
Yellow	Blue	Checkered / Red
	Black	Checkered / Red

4. Use the space at right to make a tree diagram to find the sample space.

5. What is the probability that Mattias picks an outfit at random that includes red shoes? __$\frac{1}{2}$__

Lockers at Erin's gym have a lock with a randomly assigned three-digit code. The code uses the digits 2, 3, or 8. Any of these numbers may be repeated.

222, 223, 228, 232, 233, 238,
282, 283, 288, 322, 323, 328,
332, 333, 338, 382, 383, 388,
822, 823, 828, 832, 833, 838,
882, 883, 888

6. Use the space at right to make an organized list to find the sample space.

7. What is the probability that Erin's locker has a code with at least one 8? __$\frac{19}{27}$__

Unit 7   172   Lesson 4

Unit 7   172   Lesson 4

© Houghton Mifflin Harcourt Publishing Company

COMMON CORE Standards for Mathematical Content

CC.7.SP.8c Design and use a simulation to generate frequencies for compound events.

Prerequisites
Theoretical and experimental probability

Materials
Graphing calculator

Math Background
A simulation is a process used to model random events in an experiment. A simulation is designed so that its outcomes reflect the ways that outcomes can occur in the real-world. You can use random number generators to simulate the outcomes in a simulation.

INTRODUCE

Discuss the definition of *simulation* and its use in probability. Discuss why it may be easier to do a simulation than to carry out an experiment with real-world outcomes, such as when finding probabilities about flights. Tell students they will use the random number generator of a graphing calculator to conduct simulations.

TEACH

1 EXPLORE

Questioning Strategies
- Could you use another set of three numbers to represent the winning boxes of cereal? **Yes, because any number from 1 to 10 has an equal chance of being generated, any 3 numbers can represent the 30% of winning boxes.**
- In this experiment, what does a trial represent? **buying cereal boxes until getting a winning box**
- Does a simulation result in theoretical or experimental probabilities? **experimental**

> **MATHEMATICAL PRACTICE** **Highlighting the Standards**
>
> This Explore is an opportunity to address Standard 5 (Use appropriate tools strategically). Students use a random number generator of a graphing calculator to help them perform a simulation. The random number generator allows students to find experimental probabilities of events that would otherwise be difficult to find.

2 EXPLORE

Questioning Strategies
- How is Erik's 25% success rate represented? **In random numbers from 1 to 4, the number 1 represents Erik making a basket.**
- What does each trial represent? **Each trial represents Erik's 20 attempts.**
- Which results do you count? **Count the results that represent Erik making 6 or more baskets.**

CLOSE

Essential Question
How can you use simulations to estimate probabilities? **You can design a simulation to model a real-world experiment. Use a random number generator to represent possible outcomes. Then estimate using the experimental probabilities.**

Summarize
Have students design a simulation to represent a real-world experiment. Tell students to describe the simulation in terms of what it represents and justify the design of the simulation. Students should perform the experiments and give results of estimated probabilities.

Name_____ Class_____ Date_____

7-5

COMMON CORE
CC.7.SP.8c

Conducting a Simulation

Essential question: *How can you use simulations to estimate probabilities?*

1 EXPLORE — Designing and Conducting a Simulation

There are winning prize codes in 30% of a cereal company's cereal boxes. What is the probability that you have to buy at least 3 boxes of cereal to find a winning prize code?

A Design a simulation to model the situation.

Represent each box by a random number from 1 to 10. Since 30% of the boxes have a winning prize code, the numbers 1 to 3 will represent the boxes containing a winning code. The numbers 4 to 10 represent the boxes not containing a winning code.

B Conduct trials and record the results in the second column of the table.

For each trial, use a random number generator on a graphing calculator to generate a random integer from 1 to 10. Continue generating random numbers until you get a number from 1 to 3 (representing a winning code). Conduct 10 trials. **Sample answer shown.**

C In the third column of the table, record how many boxes were needed to find a winning code. Circle the trials that required 3 or more boxes.

D Calculate the experimental probability of needing to buy at least 3 boxes of cereal in order to find a winning code.

Sample answer: $\frac{4}{10} = \frac{2}{5}$

Trial	Random Numbers	Boxes Bought
1	6 5 8 1	(4)
2	4 10 3	(3)
3	8 10 3	(3)
4	4 1	2
5	10 2	2
6	1	1
7	6 9 10 3	(4)
8	3	1
9	2	1
10	1	1

REFLECT

1. Combine your results with your classmates and calculate the experimental probability. Do you think this value is a better approximation of the theoretical probability than your result from only 10 trials?

Sample answer: I think the experimental probability from the combined

trials is closer to the theoretical probability.

Unit 7   173   Lesson 5

2 EXPLORE — Conducting Another Simulation

When Erik plays basketball, he usually makes 25% of the baskets that he attempts. Suppose Erik attempts 20 baskets. What is the probability that he makes at least 6 baskets?

A Design a simulation to model the situation.

Represent each attempt by a random number from 1 to 4. Since Erik usually makes 25% of his attempted baskets, the number 1 represents making a basket. The numbers 2 to 4 represent not making a basket.

B Conduct trials and record the results in the second column of the table.

For each trial, use a random number generator to generate a random integer from 1 to 4. Generate 20 numbers for each trial to represent 20 attempted baskets. Conduct 10 trials. **Sample answer shown.**

Trial	Random Numbers	Baskets
1	2 3 1 4 2 3 4 1 2 3 3 1 2 2 4 1 4 3 1 4	5
2	1 3 4 3 2 2 1 3 2 1 3 2 1 4 4 1 2 3 4 3	5
3	4 1 3 1 2 4 3 1 1 3 2 1 4 1 2 1 1 4 2 3	(8)
4	2 1 4 3 2 1 3 1 4 3 3 1 1 1 3 3 4 2 1 2	(7)
5	1 4 1 3 2 4 2 1 1 4 3 3 3 4 3 4 3 2 1	5
6	3 2 4 2 3 1 4 1 2 4 3 4 1 2 2 2 4 4 2 2	3
7	3 2 1 4 2 3 1 1 3 4 1 3 3 4 4 2 4 3 2 2	4
8	4 2 3 2 2 4 3 4 2 1 4 4 2 3 2 2 1 1 2 3	3
9	1 1 3 4 2 2 3 2 3 4 1 3 1 3 2 1 4 4 2 3	5
10	2 4 3 4 1 4 3 2 1 3 1 1 3 1 3 4 4 2 1 2	(6)

C In the third column of the table, record how many baskets Erik made (count the 1s). Circle the trials that show Erik made 6 or more baskets.

D Calculate the experimental probability that Erik makes at least 6 baskets.

Sample answer: $\frac{3}{10}$

TRY THIS!

2. At a local restaurant, about 50% of the customers order an appetizer. Design a simulation to estimate the probability that 4 of the next 10 customers order an appetizer. Explain your methods.

Check students' work.

Unit 7   174   Lesson 5

© Houghton Mifflin Harcourt Publishing Company

COMMON CORE Standards for Mathematical Content

CC.7.SP.5 Understand that the probability of a chance event is a number between 0 and 1 that expresses the likelihood of the event occurring. Larger numbers indicate greater likelihood. A probability near 0 indicates an unlikely event, a probability around 1/2 indicates an event that is neither unlikely nor likely, and a probability near 1 indicates a likely event.

CC.7.SP.6 Approximate the probability of a chance event by collecting data on the chance process that produces it and observing its long-run relative frequency, and predict the approximate relative frequency given the probability.

CC.7.SP.7a Develop a uniform probability model by assigning equal probability to all outcomes, and use the model to determine probabilities of events.

CC.7.SP.7b Develop a probability model (which may not be uniform) by observing frequencies in data generated from a chance process.

CC.7.SP.8a Understand that, just as with simple events, the probability of a compound event is the fraction of outcomes if the event occurs.

CC.7.SP.8b Represent sample spaces for compound events using methods such as organized lists, tables, and tree diagrams. For an event described in everyday language (e.g., "rolling double sixes"), identify the outcomes in the sample space which compose the event.

CC.7.SP.8c Design and use a simulation to generate frequencies for compound events.

INTRODUCE

Discuss with students different types of fundraisers. For example, sometimes groups sell raffle tickets to raise money. In order to make a profit while giving away prizes, the group has to determine that they will be keeping more money than they will be giving away. Tell students that they will use probabilities to determine how to have a *profitable* fundraiser while giving away prizes.

TEACH

1 Describing Events

Materials
Materials to make a spinner

Questioning Strategies
- How can you find theoretical probability of winning each game? Find the ratio of the number of ways to win to the total number of possible outcomes.

- What games, other than those identified already, might work well for the fundraiser? Explain. Games 1 and 4 both have a 50% chance of winning, so even though these games lead to a break-even scenario, and no profit would be made, the games might bring in more people if they are popular.

Avoid Common Errors
Review the probabilities that students found for each game. Check that students read the game description well enough to find the right theoretical probability. For example, in Game 3 make sure that students correctly counted outcomes *greater than* 5, and not just equal to 5. Remind students to read the events carefully and encourage them to circle key words.

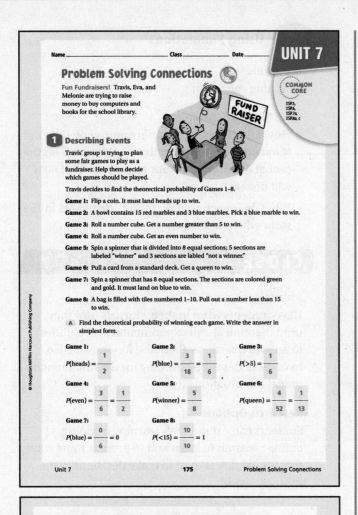

Name_____ Class_____ Date_____

Problem Solving Connections

Fun Fundraisers! Travis, Eva, and Melonie are trying to raise money to buy computers and books for the school library.

COMMON CORE
7.SP.5,
7.SP.6,
7.SP.7a,
7.SP.8a, c

1 Describing Events

Travis' group is trying to plan some fair games to play as a fundraiser. Help them decide which games should be played.

Travis decides to find the theorectical probability of Games 1–8.

Game 1: Flip a coin. It must land heads up to win.

Game 2: A bowl contains 15 red marbles and 3 blue marbles. Pick a blue marble to win.

Game 3: Roll a number cube. Get a number greater than 5 to win.

Game 4: Roll a number cube. Get an even number to win.

Game 5: Spin a spinner that is divided into 8 equal sections; 5 sections are labeled "winner" and 3 sections are labled "not a winner."

Game 6: Pull a card from a standard deck. Get a queen to win.

Game 7: Spin a spinner that has 8 equal sections. The sections are colored green and gold. It must land on blue to win.

Game 8: A bag is filled with tiles numbered 1–10. Pull out a number less than 15 to win.

A Find the theoretical probability of winning each game. Write the answer in simplest form.

Game 1:
$P(\text{heads}) = \dfrac{1}{2}$

Game 2:
$P(\text{blue}) = \dfrac{3}{18} = \dfrac{1}{6}$

Game 3:
$P(>5) = \dfrac{1}{6}$

Game 4:
$P(\text{even}) = \dfrac{3}{6} = \dfrac{1}{2}$

Game 5:
$P(\text{winner}) = \dfrac{5}{8}$

Game 6:
$P(\text{queen}) = \dfrac{4}{52} = \dfrac{1}{13}$

Game 7:
$P(\text{blue}) = \dfrac{0}{6} = 0$

Game 8:
$P(<15) = \dfrac{10}{10} = 1$

B Based on the theoretical probability, which game(s) has the greatest probability of winning? Which game(s) has the least probability?

Greatest Probability of Winning: _____Game 8_____

Least Probability of Winning: _____Game 7_____

C Travis thinks that lots of people will like Game 5. Predict how many times people will win Game 5 if it is played 100 times. Show your work.

$P(\text{winner}) = \dfrac{5}{8}; \qquad \dfrac{5}{8} \times 100 = \dfrac{500}{8}$

$= 62\frac{1}{2} \approx 63 \text{ times}$

D In Game 5 the prize that is given to each winner costs $0.50. The cost to play the game is $0.75. Based on Travis' prediction, about how much profit will he make if 100 people play Game 5?

63 winners × 0.50 = $31.50
100 players × 0.75 = $75
$75 − $31.50 = $43.50
Travis could make $43.50 profit from the game.

E Make a spinner like the one described in Game 5. Spin it 20 times. Complete the table for the frequency of each result.

Sample answer given.

Result	Frequency
Winner	12
Not a Winner	8

Find the experimental probability of being a winner in Game 5.

Sample answer: $\dfrac{12}{20} = \dfrac{3}{5}$

F Now find the profit for Game 5 based on the experimental probability.

Sample answer: $\dfrac{3}{5} \times 100 = \dfrac{300}{5} = 60$

60 winners × 0.5 = $30;

$75 − $30 = $45

G Compare the profits calculated in **D** and part **F**.

The profits are pretty close to being about the same amount.

_____

2 Drawing a Tree Diagram

Questioning Strategies

• **How does the tree diagram help you answer the question in part B?** The tree diagram lists all the possible outcomes in the sample space, so you can count the number of ways that the event occurs.

MATHEMATICAL PRACTICE | **Highlighting the Standards**

This section is an opportunity to address Standard 1 (Make sense of problems and persevere in solving them). Students draw a large tree diagram to organize all the possible outcomes in a compound event. Students then use the diagram to find probabilities that can help them make decisions.

---

3 Using Simulations

Materials
Graphing calculator

Questioning Strategies

• **How are donating customers represented? Why?** Numbers 1–4 out of numbers 1–10; based on the probability from previous experience that 40% will donate.

• **What does each trial represent?** customers in the store within one hour

CLOSE

Journal
Have students write in their journals how they used theoretical and experimental probabilities to answer questions about the fundraiser. Also, have them describe how they used a simulation to model the situation.

Research Options
Students can extend their learning by doing online research to learn and to present some ways that probability is used to make decisions in the business world.

2 Drawing a Tree Diagram

Eva's group decides to make gift baskets to be auctioned at the fundraising dinner for the library.

Each gift basket includes one of the items from each group described below:

• A gift card to either Frannie's Department Store or Giorgio's Italian Restaurant
• A bar of fragrant soap, a set of cookie cutters, or a crystal vase
• A watch, a walkie-talkie set, or an MP3 player

A basket of each possible combination of items will be made and auctioned. Bidders will not know which basket they are bidding on.

A Draw a tree diagram in the space below to find all the possible baskets.

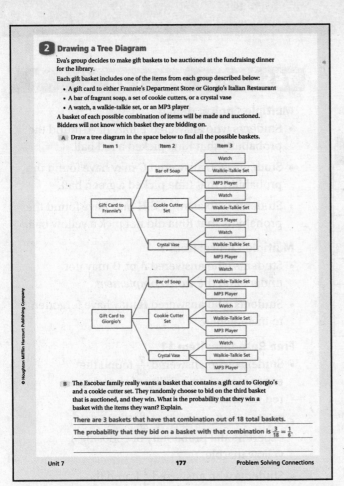

B The Escobar family really wants a basket that contains a gift card to Giorgio's and a cookie cutter set. They randomly choose to bid on the third basket that is auctioned, and they win. What is the probability that they win a basket with the items they want? Explain.

There are 3 baskets that have that combination out of 18 total baskets.

The probability that they bid on a basket with that combination is $\frac{3}{18} = \frac{1}{6}$.

3 Using Simulations

Melonie's group sets up a booth in front of a local grocery store to collect donations. Based on previous experience, they know that about 40% of the store's customers will donate money. What is the probability that there will be at least 4 customers in an hour in order to collect a donation?

A The committee wants to develop a simulation to estimate the probability that there must be at least 4 customers in an hour in order to collect a donation in that hour. Design a simulation to model the situation.

Represent each customer with a number from 1 to 10. Numbers 1–4 represent

customers who give a donation. Each trial represents 1 hour. For each trial,

use a random number generator to generate a number from 1 to 10. Continue

generating numbers until you get a number from 1 to 4. Count the number of

customers needed each hour in order to get a donation (a number from 1 to 4).

Circle the trials that require at least 4 customers.

B Conduct ten trials and record the results in the table. For each trial use a random number generator on a graphing calculator. **Sample answers shown.**

Trial Number (Hour)	Random Numbers					Customers
1	7	8	5	10	4	(5)
2	8	5	3			3
3	10	9	1			3
4	1					1
5	8	4				2
6	7	9	10	6	2	(5)
7	8	6	3			3
8	8	3				2
9	2					1
10	3					1

C Calculate the experimental probability that there must be at least 4 customers in an hour in order to collect a donation. Sample answer: $\frac{2}{10} = \frac{1}{5}$

CORRELATION

Standard	Items
CC.7.SP.5	8–9
CC.7.SP.6	5, 15
CC.7.SP.7a	1–2, 4–7, 12–14, 16–17
CC.7.SP.7b	11
CC.7.SP.8a	3
CC.7.SP.8b	10

TEST PREP DOCTOR ✚

Multiple Choice: Item 4

- Students who answered **F** may have found the probability that Rina picked a red ball.
- Students who answered **G** may have found the probability that Rina picked a green ball.
- Students who answered **H** may have found the probability that Rina did not pick a yellow ball.

Multiple Choice: Item 7

- Students who answered **A** or **D** may not understand the word *complement*.
- Students who answered **B** may have forgotten to include blue.

Free Response: Item 11

- Students who answered $\frac{7}{40}$ found the experimental probability of choosing a red marble.
- Students who answered $\frac{9}{40}$ found the experimental probability of choosing a yellow marble.
- Students who answered $\frac{1}{4}$ found the experimental probability of choosing a purple marble.

Free Response: Item 14

- Students who answered $\frac{1}{13}$ may not have known how to find the complement of the event.
- Students who answered $\frac{9}{13}$ found the complement of the event of getting an ace or a picture card.
- Students who answered $\frac{1}{2}$ found the complement of the event of getting a red card or the complement of the event of getting a black card.

Name _____ Class _____ Date _____

MULTIPLE CHOICE

1. You roll a standard number cube once. Which of the following gives all of the outcomes of the sample space for this experiment?

   A. 1, 2, 3

   B. A, B, C, D

   C. 1, 2, 3, 4, 5, 6

   D. 2, 4, 6, 8, 10

A hat contains 5 red balls, 8 green balls, and 9 yellow balls. Rina chooses one ball at random from the hat. Use this information for 2–5.

2. What is the probability that Rina chooses a green ball?

   F. $\frac{1}{11}$ H. $\frac{9}{22}$

   G. $\frac{4}{11}$ J. $\frac{5}{11}$

3. What is the probability that Rina chooses a red ball or a green ball?

   A. $\frac{13}{22}$ C. $\frac{17}{22}$

   B. $\frac{7}{11}$ D. $\frac{40}{22}$

4. What is the probability that Rina does **not** choose a red ball?

   F. $\frac{5}{11}$ H. $\frac{13}{22}$

   G. $\frac{4}{11}$ J. $\frac{17}{22}$

5. What is the probability that Rina chooses a yellow ball?

   A. $\frac{7}{22}$ C. $\frac{13}{22}$

   B. $\frac{9}{22}$ D. $\frac{17}{22}$

6. A standard number cube is rolled once. What is the probability that a number less than 3 is rolled?

   F. $\frac{1}{6}$ H. $\frac{1}{2}$

   G. $\frac{1}{3}$ J. $\frac{2}{3}$

7. A spinner has white, green, violet, indigo, and blue sections. Which of the following is the complement of the event that the spinner lands on violet?

   A. The spinner lands on green.

   B. The spinner lands on white, green, or indigo.

   C. The spinner lands on white, green, indigo, or blue.

   D. The spinner does not land on blue.

8. The probability that a new car at a local dealership has a bad headlight is 0.003. Which statement best describes the probability of this event?

   F. It is likely that a new car at a local dealership has a bad headlight.

   G. It is unlikely that a new car at a local dealership has a bad headlight.

   H. It is neither unlikely nor likely that a new car at a local dealership has a bad headlight.

   J. It is impossible that a new car at a local dealership has a bad headlight.

9. Which event is impossible?

   A. A bowl has 10 red marbles and 12 green marbles. You choose a red marble from the bowl.

   B. A bag has pieces of paper numbered from 1 to 100. You choose a number divisible by 3.

   C. A spinner has sections lettered A through H. The spinner lands on the 10th letter of the alphabet.

   D. You roll two standard number cubes and the sum of the numbers rolled is 12.

© Houghton Mifflin Harcourt Publishing Company

10. At A-1 Truck Dealership, a customer can order a red, turquoise, or green truck. The truck can have leather or cloth seats. A customer can also choose a black, tan, or grey interior color. From how many possible trucks can a customer choose?

    F. 8   H. 27

    G. 18   J. 36

FREE RESPONSE

11. Yvonne draws a marble from a basket. She records the color and puts the marble back into the basket. The experiment is repeated several times. She records the frequency of each color in the table.

Color	Frequency
Red	7
Yellow	9
Green	14
Purple	10

What is the experimental probability of choosing a green marble?

$\frac{14}{40} = \frac{7}{20}$

12. A hockey team has 12 girls and 9 boys. Each week the coach chooses one player at random to play goalie for the next game. What is the probability that the coach chooses a girl to be the goalie for the next game?

$\frac{12 \text{ girls}}{21 \text{ players}} = \frac{4}{7}$

The probability of choosing a 6 at random from a standard deck of playing cards is $\frac{1}{13}$. Use this information for 13 and 14.

13. What is the complement of the event of choosing a 6?

The complement of the event is the event of not choosing a 6.

14. What is the probability of the complement of the event of choosing a 6?

The probability is $1 - \frac{1}{13} = \frac{12}{13}$.

15. You roll a standard number cube 1,000 times. Predict the number of times you will roll a 2 or a 5.

The probability of rolling a 2 or a 5 is $\frac{1}{3}$; $\frac{1}{3} \times 1,000 = 333.3$, or about 333 times.

Use the spinner for 16 and 17. Tell whether each student is correct and explain.

16. Ashley said, "There are four numbers on this spinner. One of these numbers is 2. Therefore, the probability that this spinner lands on 2 is $\frac{1}{4}$."

No; the outcomes 1, 2, 3, and 4 are not equally likely. The spinner has 8 equal outcomes, one of which is 2, so the probability that the spinner lands on 2 is $\frac{1}{8}$.

17. Suzanne said, "There are two colors on this spinner. One of these colors is blue. Therefore, the probability that this spinner lands on blue is $\frac{1}{2}$."

Yes; the outcomes blue and gray are equally likely.

© Houghton Mifflin Harcourt Publishing Company

Correlation of *On Core Mathematics Grade 7* to the Common Core State Standards

Ratios and Proportional Relationships	Citations
CC.7.RP.1 Compute unit rates associated with ratios of fractions, including ratios of lengths, areas and other quantities measured in like or different units.	pp. 35–38, 51–54
CC.7.RP.2 Recognize and represent proportional relationships between quantities. a. Decide whether two quantities are in a proportional relationship, e.g., by testing for equivalent ratios in a table or graphing on a coordinate plane and observing whether the graph is a straight line through the origin. b. Identify the constant of proportionality (unit rate) in tables, graphs, equations, diagrams, and verbal descriptions of proportional relationships. c. Represent proportional relationships by equations. d. Explain what a point (x, y) on the graph of a proportional relationship means in terms of the situation, with special attention to the points $(0, 0)$ and $(1, r)$ where r is the unit rate.	pp. 39–42, 43–46, 51–54
CC.7.RP.3 Use proportional relationships to solve multistep ratio and percent problems.	pp. 39–42, 43–46, 47–50, 51–54, 63–64, 81–84

The Number System	Citations
CC.7.NS.1 Apply and extend previous understandings of addition and subtraction to add and subtract rational numbers; represent addition and subtraction on a horizontal or vertical number line diagram. a. Describe situations in which opposite quantities combine to make 0. b. Understand $p + q$ as the number located a distance $|q|$ from p, in the positive or negative direction depending on whether q is positive or negative. Show that a number and its opposite have a sum of 0 (are additive inverses). Interpret sums of rational numbers by describing real-world contexts. c. Understand subtraction of rational numbers as adding the additive inverse, $p - q = p + (-q)$. Show that the distance between two rational numbers on the number line is the absolute value of their difference, and apply this principle in real-world contexts. d. Apply properties of operations as strategies to add and subtract rational numbers.	pp. 7–9, 11–14, 27–30
CC.7.NS.2 Apply and extend previous understandings of multiplication and division and of fractions to multiply and divide rational numbers. a. Understand that multiplication is extended from fractions to rational numbers by requiring that operations continue to satisfy the properties of operations, particularly the distributive property, leading to products such as $(-1)(-1) = 1$ and the rules for multiplying signed numbers. Interpret products of rational numbers by describing real-world contexts. b. Understand that integers can be divided, provided that the divisor is not zero, and every quotient of integers (with non-zero divisor) is a rational number. If p and q are integers, then $-(p/q) = (-p)/q = p/(-q)$. Interpret quotients of rational numbers by describing real-world contexts. c. Apply properties of operations as strategies to multiply and divide rational numbers. d. Convert a rational number to a decimal using long division; know that the decimal form of a rational number terminates in 0s or eventually repeats.	pp. 3–6, 15–18, 19–22, 27–30

CC.7.NS.3 Solve real-world and mathematical problems involving the four operations with rational numbers	pp. 23–26, 27–30, 35–38
Expressions and Equations	**Citations**
CC.7.EE.1 Apply properties of operations as strategies to add, subtract, factor, and expand linear expressions with rational coefficients.	pp. 59–62, 81–84
CC.7.EE.2 Understand that rewriting an expression in different forms in a problem context can shed light on the problem and how the quantities in it are related.	pp. 63–64, 81–84
CC.7.EE.3 Solve multi-step real-life and mathematical problems posed with positive and negative rational numbers in any form (whole numbers, fractions, and decimals), using tools strategically. Apply properties of operations to calculate with numbers in any form; convert between forms as appropriate; and assess the reasonableness of answers using mental computation and estimation strategies.	pp. 77–80, 81–84
CC.7.EE.4 Use variables to represent quantities in a real-world or mathematical problem, and construct simple equations and inequalities to solve problems by reasoning about the quantities. a. Solve word problems leading to equations of the form $px + q = r$ and $p(x + q) = r$, where p, q, and r are specific rational numbers. Solve equations of these forms fluently. Compare an algebraic solution to an arithmetic solution, identifying the sequence of the operations used in each approach. b. Solve word problems leading to inequalities of the form $px + q > r$ or $px + q < r$, where p, q, and r are specific rational numbers. Graph the solution set of the inequality and interpret it in the context of the problem.	pp. 65–68, 69–72, 73–76, 81–84
Geometry	**Citations**
CC.7.G.1 Solve problems involving scale drawings of geometric figures, including computing actual lengths and areas from a scale drawing and reproducing a scale drawing at a different scale.	pp. 89–92, 103–106
CC.7.G.2 Draw (freehand, with ruler and protractor, and with technology) geometric shapes with given conditions. Focus on constructing triangles from three measures of angles or sides, noticing when the conditions determine a unique triangle, more than one triangle, or no triangle.	pp. 93–96, 103–106
CC.7.G.3 Describe the two-dimensional figures that result from slicing three-dimensional figures, as in plane sections of right rectangular prisms and right rectangular pyramids.	pp. 97–98, 103–106
CC.7.G.4 Know the formulas for the area and circumference of a circle and use them to solve problems; give an informal derivation of the relationship between the circumference and area of a circle.	pp. 111–114, 115–118, 131–134
CC.7.G.5 Use facts about supplementary, complementary, vertical, and adjacent angles in a multi-step problem to write and solve simple equations for an unknown angle in a figure.	pp. 99–102, 103–106
CC.7.G.6 Solve real-world and mathematical problems involving area, volume and surface area of two- and three-dimensional objects composed of triangles, quadrilaterals, polygons, cubes, and right prisms.	pp. 119–122, 123–126, 127–130, 131–134

© Houghton Mifflin Harcourt Publishing Company

Statistics and Probability	Citations
CC.7.SP.1 Understand that statistics can be used to gain information about a population by examining a sample of the population; generalizations about a population from a sample are valid only if the sample is representative of that population. Understand that random sampling tends to produce representative samples and support valid inferences.	pp. 139–142, 149–152
CC.7.SP.2 Use data from a random sample to draw inferences about a population with an unknown characteristic of interest. Generate multiple samples (or simulated samples) of the same size to gauge the variation in estimates or predictions.	pp. 139–142, 143–144, 149–152
CC.7.SP.3 Informally assess the degree of visual overlap of two numerical data distributions with similar variabilities, measuring the difference between the centers by expressing it as a multiple of a measure of variability.	pp. 145–148, 149–152
CC.7.SP.4 Use measures of center and measures of variability for numerical data from random samples to draw informal comparative inferences about two populations.	pp. 145–148, 149–152
CC.7.SP.5 Understand that the probability of a chance event is a number between 0 and 1 that expresses the likelihood of the event occurring. Larger numbers indicate greater likelihood. A probability near 0 indicates an unlikely event, a probability around 1/2 indicates an event that is neither unlikely nor likely, and a probability near 1 indicates a likely event.	pp. 157–160, 175–178
CC.7.SP.6 Approximate the probability of a chance event by collecting data on the chance process that produces it and observing its long-run relative frequency, and predict the approximate relative frequency given the probability.	pp. 161–164, 165–168, 175–178
CC.7.SP.7 Develop a probability model and use it to find probabilities of events. Compare probabilities from a model to observed frequencies; if the agreement is not good, explain possible sources of the discrepancy. **a.** Develop a uniform probability model by assigning equal probability to all outcomes, and use the model to determine probabilities of events. **b.** Develop a probability model (which may not be uniform) by observing frequencies in data generated from a chance process.	pp. 161–164, 165–168, 175–178
CC.7.SP.8 Find probabilities of compound events using organized lists, tables, tree diagrams, and simulation. **a.** Understand that, just as with simple events, the probability of a compound event is the fraction of outcomes in the sample space for which the compound event occurs. **b.** Represent sample spaces for compound events using methods such as organized lists, tables and tree diagrams. For an event described in everyday language (e.g., "rolling double sixes"), identify the outcomes in the sample space which compose the event. **c.** Design and use a simulation to generate frequencies for compound events.	pp. 169–172, 173–174, 175–178